Harmonic Farming: a love style

Werner M. Gysi

Gooly Mooly Publishing

1995

Canadian Cataloguing in Publication Data

Gysi, Werner M., 1949-
    Harmonic Farming

    ISBN 1-896424-00-7

    1. Farming. 2. Gardening. I. McAvity, Margaret, 1939-
II. Love, John, 1934- III. Title.

S493.G97 1995   631.5   C95-910439-9

Published by: Gooly Mooly Publishing

Inquiries: Gooly Mooly Publishing
                    Box 978
                    Enderby, British Columbia
                    Canada V0E 1V0
                    (604) 838-0350

PRINTED IN CANADA by Canadian Photoscene

Acknowledgement

Starting out in Europe, with a limited land resource in the little country of Switzerland, and all the enthusiasm ever possible, we lived on a hobby farm the size of half an acre. One of our main sources of information and inspiration, besides books from Rudolf Steiner and many others, was my uncle, Röbi, who was a road sign we could not miss. Who would have thought that years later and after some detours to India, where our two oldest sons were born, and visiting various countries in South America, we would end up across the water to find a marvelous peaceful corner in Canada. With the birth of our youngest son Pascal in the pop-up trailer while traveling through Mexico in 1993, we now are a family of 8, living on and off this corner. By conducting workshops on the farm we have shared our knowledge and this work has taken shape. Many thanks to all the participants in the workshops for their valuable input and all the people who dedicated their time, foremost Margaret McAvity and John Love to whom I could trust my "unpolished English" to be transferred to reveal a marvel, this book. I give the highest appreciation to Brigitte, for being more than a wife, for her contribution and unsurpassed ability to make us stick together as a family.

People & Nature

With responsibility given away

to politicians and others to say

reverence and respect follow

this almighty power

and things can turn sour.

Once dignity is restored

and nature's first points scored

reverence and respect follow

as we will spread it thorough

for all to know tomorrow.

W. M. Gysi, Jan./ 94

Gooly Mooly Art Farm

The name Gooly Mooly came to life at the very beginning of our adventure on the land while clearing a spot for the garden. Roots were being dug out and rocks picked when our work was abruptly halted for one small root that did not want to give way. A large hole had been dug around it and with every human force on site we could not pull that root. This made me call out "Gooly Mooly" using the Swiss dialect. We all had a good laugh. "Guli" means a hole or worse a manure pit, "Muuli" means to argue, to talk back, and in context it meant "arguing out of the stinky hole". In order to pronounce the words properly in English we decided to write it as Gooly Mooly. We later met a person who taught some of our family how to sculpt marble and thus became an Art Farm.

It is indeed an art to be in harmony with all the Gooly Moolies encountered while working the land and therefore I think the name to be appropriate, sculpting or not. The root however acquiesced and has been kept as an attraction for all of us. I have since told our kids many stories about Gooly Mooly, while holding the root in my hand for inspiration to create ever new stories.

Table of Contents

Table of Contents

Table of Contents

Introduction

We have to face it, the purchase of a first aid kit is not going to heal the wounds nature is showing us with an increasing intensity. There are not necessarily more disasters or changes in nature's pattern, but the occurrences are more extreme. We must reconnect with nature and regain ecological balance. We can prepare ourselves for good times to come when our existing destructive society will have faded to be replaced by a nature loving one. If we continue with today's farming techniques our society is doomed to kill itself slowly. With the ever more turbulent times ahead, future generations will have increasing difficulties in feeding themselves, for lack of skills and understanding. No longer can we live just from what nature provides. We have domesticated ourselves to eat cultivated food, vegetarians and non-vegetarians alike. Our little dust-ball earth may take us for a spin with the same reverence towards us as we have to the ants crawling along the top of the soil. If we want to become true living beings, we have to be independent of a non-fulfilling system and to face the adventures that follow.

In life, not time but timing is of importance and the same applies to the process of growing food. The material in this book is structured in sequence with the seasons, starting with the dormancy of winter and guiding the reader through each phase of activity, eventually ending up with a composition of satisfaction, independence, self development, food and harmony with nature. It will explain how to look at nature as being composed of living bodies, having spirits which can sense actions and make the person part of the process of growth. You will explore the ways to sense intuitive signals. But more so the book will bring forward all the practical skills and tools required to do the job effectively and efficiently. Methods and materials have been used that have proven simple and effective in order to supply a wide selection of food with the least amount of time involved. Some things mentioned, such as the composting toilet or the use of hemp, may not be of any help at this time. It is, however, important to anticipate change and to think of alternative ways to reduce negative impacts on nature.

For 8 years, starting in 1983 I ran a computer store to provide the financial requirements to settle on a 5 acre parcel. At the same time, as a family with two small children, we started out to integrate with the land and to set up with two milking goats, a billy goat, chickens, bees, rabbits, a fruit orchard, berries and a large vegetable garden. Such an environment properly managed still left us enough time to do other things, like running a business and now writing this book. Life on the land can provide an excellent balance to any activity, creative or not. What you need to look for, is what really is in you. Self-esteem, confidence and consciousness will be developed while going along in harmony with the natural world. You grow inside to become a member of your "self" rather then having a membership or a title, framed with the ideology of an organization that is accepted only by a fading society. The latest signs of such a society may be summarized as follows.

- Risk of skin cancer when
  exposed to the sun because of
  the ozone depletion.

- The outlook of a global change in weather patterns.
- A warming trend world wide due to the greenhouse effect causing, for example, grain to become under attack by insects while stored (rust beetle).
- Bacteria resistant to antibiotics.
- Destruction of entire fish stocks and forests, water pollution and acid rain, caused by humans at a scale impossible in the past and no common ground to halt it by the world's leading nations.

Economic reasons have shut out our inner feelings and the sense to recognize the warning signs. However on the positive side, many individuals have come to their senses and changed their life style to a **love style**. It is encouraging to see fully booked workshops at the Gooly Mooly Art Farm and a trend towards holistic life styles.

We need not turn our backs on technology, but we must build and use it with a new approach, using nature as a measuring stick. This book has been prepared with a computer, laser printer and a video camera. The illustrations are intended to inform rather than to present the latest in technology. Because we self published this book and had sympathetic support from a local print shop, we were able to use non-bleached, 100% recycled paper and vegetable based ink. On the other hand, in order to impress today's consumer and to make you grab this book, the cover had to be done to attract. We were however able to select materials that generated the least amount of impact on our environment and still produced a durable product.

As I had a great craving for apples, we enjoyed settling in a region where apple trees grew. Such a decision needed to be made right at the start. This usually brings with it the need to settle in a more populated area as the more moderate climate will attract people. The land we found was not an agriculture marvel of soil nor was it flat land, but it was far enough away from mechanized hi-tech agribusiness in order to keep bees. Over time the rocks have given way to a wholesome, rich in organic materials, sandy soil. Today, with a family of 8 we can live completely independently of the income of the land; selling food, renting out a cabin, provide tourists with a tour through our farm, having a room for Bed & Breakfast and as mentors for workshops in **Harmonic Farming**. These workshops have provided the basic blocks to bring this book to life. It is my sincere effort to bring across the many practical skills we have come to think of as routine, and that the reader will generate the same **enthusiasm and endurance** as we did when coming to Canada in 1981. We have never stayed such a long time in any one place but here. A place which gives us the possibility to be.

Dedicated To All Those Who Like To Travel With Nature.

1

Building an Understanding

Plants, animals and me

1. General

When the human species became part of this world, plants and animals were here to provide food for each other. It was a matter of gathering the necessary foods from the wild to stay alive. As time went on, humans demanded more comfort. More people asked for more material goods. The development of wealth with material goods or reputation neglected other directions in the development of the human species, and still today **travels** on that success. This success is achieved with the high cost of depleting non-renewable resources and damaging plant and animal life beyond repair, but more importantly, with the loss of values for a spiritual development of dignity, reverence, respect and responsibility. Such values will ultimately lead to one's peace and complete harmony with the plant and animal world. Unfortunately, the materialistic society that has evolved, has created **individuals of spiritual emptiness**. Once every effort goes into learning from nature and tuning ourselves in to its voice through intuition and other sensory inputs (sometimes in support of the ear- eye- nose- taste- or feel- message), can we then experience a new way of perceiving and with it understanding the values of nature. It is important to recognize that plants easily live without animals, that animals can easily live without humans, but that humans can not live without plants. We should actually give the highest respect to plant life, without it we could not exist. Without plants, we would not have enough oxygen to breathe. In contrast to today's meat-eating habits, hunting in the olden days was a necessity and people did so to survive or to balance their diet. We should at least consider having reverence for nature no matter what our eating habits are.

Whatever we do to our surrounding, it will affect a cycle and return to burden or nurture us.

2. Cycles

Many cycles, structured like a web, influence our behavior and that of plants and animals. Some are obvious, others have been researched, and still others have not been accepted by science. We have to recognize the web of cycles that **influence each other**. In fig. 1-1, the cycles that need to be recognized are shown. These cycles repeat over and over again and can be called **vibrations**. They are, by nature, in tune with each other and as such, are in **harmony**. Looking outwards from the food cycle are the **Earth Cycle, Weather Cycle, Moon Cycle, Planet Cycles** and **Solar Cycle**. The food cycle is the one we influence the most with the new ways of food production. Some obvious signs that we alter this cycle are reflected in the destruction of the soil, the extinction of plant and animal species, the manipulation of seed stock

Many cycles influence us. The earth is only one small part in the world we know as the solar system and a smaller factor yet in the universe and other galaxies.

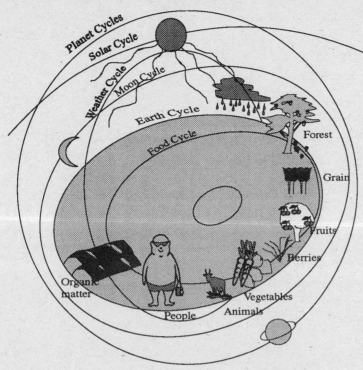

Figure 1-1, Cycles that influence our life

Bacteria and fungi in the soil are the most valuable resource.

The natural non-renewable resource, oil, should be used for producing goods that can not otherwise be produced.

towards dependency on chemical fertilizers and the failure to turn organic matter back into the soil. For the latter we have found a substance, call it fertilizers, to substitute for the process of decay. We interrupt the cycle and with it harmony diminishes. This disharmony may be compared to an orchestra where some of the players don't find the right tune anymore but still try to catch up. Substances used nowadays include oil based products such as gasoline, fertilizers, pesticides and many drugs which interrupt the cycle and therefore the harmony and web of cycles as a whole. As oil is a nonrenewable substance, the use of it should be limited to applications where there is no alternative. The **earth cycle** is characterized by the four seasons and with this the rebuilding of fresh air by plant life. The oxygen supply in the earth's atmosphere is a product of photosynthesis by green plants. The earth cycle also reflects the volcanic activities and the movement of soil, water and air, all challenged by pollution; the **weather cycle** by rain and evaporation, challenged by global warming; the **moon** and **planetary cycles** by patterns of dy-

namics, moods and growth; and the **solar cycle** as the heat and energy source.

Accepting the existence of these cycles around us, and because they are repetitive I like to call them vibrations. We might think of the existence of vibrations inside us as well, or in other life forms in general. When such vibrations cycle at a fast pace, they may become invisible to our eye, similar to a stick held in your hand and oscillated back and forth. The faster the movement the less it can be identified as being a stick. We see it as being at any place for any given time, even though our knowledge tells us that this can not be true. We could easily imagine that the stick could move so fast to be anywhere, invisible. Micro chip designers try hard to achieve ever faster switching devices like microprocessors. They control all the things (peripherals, memory, etc.) in a computer so fast that it appears to us to happen all at once. What we do not see still exists or, in other words, what exists is not just what we see. This knowledge may become even more valuable, while analyzing a half-inch-thick crumb of soil which contains millions of miniature insects and billions of bacteria, all invisible to us. These organisms, many more than the human population, account for harmony within the soil structure and, in essence, form organic matter as they decay. These lives can be compared with we humans who organize ourselves on the surface of the soil. As humans on this earth we construct many pathways and buildings and control the vastness of the forests and lands. Everybody is just too busy to follow up the tasks at hand. Some tasks may be fruitless in terms of the society or even destructive. Usually this happens when too many people are put too close together, such as in large cities. Crime rates go up and accidents are more common. A similar situation may occur in the soil and its "humans". Diversification in the structure of the soil is important and is achieved by the construction of many small communities. The fact that we are upsetting this delicate structure by applying millions of gallons of chemical rich mixtures should open our eyes to the possibility of choosing a more harmonious path.

3. Eating habits and the crops

Many of us are no longer connected to food except in the belief that it will produce the strength to tackle the world. We think of more important things in life. Packaging of food has become so important in order to sell the products (cereals, processed food, etc.), that more money goes into advertising, design and material than the content itself is worth. Items that can't be put into a package have to look nice or big. To point out what **really is important**, I will explain with a parable.

Maintenance of a house can be done with poor materials (e.g. paint), or with quality materials to make it last. The same applies to the body. Quality food maintains our health and that of future generations. We look at a house built with poor quality wood. The weakness will not show outside but it also won't give the lasting life of a properly-built house. Every new born child is like one newly built house.

When I say lasting life, I don't mean a longer life but one lived consciously or with awareness until the end of one's life on earth. Eating too much of one type of food or other is not improving our health. As well as seeking a balanced food source, we should also look for products that are free of chemicals or additives. We can also eat food that is available regionally or locally, before accepting food that has traveled thousands of miles. Over 50% of freon produced is used for cooling-houses and transportation units (trucks, train wagons, ships). This, in turn, contributes to ozone depletion. Furthermore, plastic and other additional packing materials are needed for transport. The pleasure of eating something exotic, of tasting a unique flavour, of impressing friends with a culinary whiz are alluring but do not contribute proportionately to the health of our bodies nor do they improve the environment. Local crops are readily available, and the best value in **food is that which you grow yourself.**

The aberration from nature and resulting mechanized approach to food production is reflected in so many aspects of our life such as art, music, architecture and how we relate towards the environment. It also has generated designs on food packages that address the "techno food" for "techno people" image. The picture of Granny on a round shaped label definitely has disappeared or is only used to remind us of the "old-fashioned good old times".

4. Concept of Harmonic Farming

Many years ago while living in Switzerland, I became aware that organic farming was becoming another tool for industry to cash in on. Standards and regulations had been set up to control it. It became one more way to do business. One aspect that could not be put into the standard was and will continue to be the philosophy and with it the concept of **people growing the food**, so that the people at least find a connection to where the food came from.

The consumer does not question how food gets on the table. How are animals treated? How is the land cultivated? What chemicals are put into the soil, then into our bodies? What impact do contemporary practices have on the environment and our future? The more people connect to the food they eat the more they will look for food closer to home, where they can oversee the process involved and the sooner we

Achieve harmony by eliminating the need for food distribution, large cooling houses, advertising and packaging of goods.

can change the existing industry and improve the impact on the environment.

At some point money may be the issue while joining an organization. You can market your product as registered and therefore have an edge over the competition. This may be helpful as long as issues like the animal's dignity, nature's sustainability, growing healthy food, growing your own food and living with a vision in reverence to nature, will **not be neglected**. In addition, it is very hard, if not impossible, to police, for example, organic farming and the best connection to food is **to grow it yourself**.

Harmonic Farming is not an organization. What Harmonic Farming can be is described below.

Capture nature, do it the way she does, have profound reverence for her.

– **It is homesteading with profound reverence for nature first.**

– **It is organic farming with profound reverence for nature first.**

– **It is part of, but not limited to, the larger concept of Harmonic Living as outlined below.**

5. Harmonic living

Using our brains to handle the knowledge gained by education may displace our knowledge of ourselves.

As a traveler passing through this world, it is my **consciousness** that forms the way I live. The harmonic life assembles many of the available concepts of life and combines them in practical terms. It includes:

1. Harmonic Spiritual Connecting

2. Harmonic Farming

3. Harmonic Family life

4. Harmonic Recreating

These above fields are tightly interwoven with each other but we have little knowledge of this harmony. This book will cover the first two topics listed above. Workshops given on the Gooly Mooly Art Farm (see Appendix A) are intended to develop experience in these life forms with hands-on sessions. Without knowing the above concepts, it is difficult to find harmony. Practicing these methods is what will make the change. A brief review of some of my experiences on the first topic, Harmonic Spiritual Connecting, is mentioned below as it weaves with the topic at hand and needs to be understood first, in order to grow healthy nutritious food.

5.1. Harmonic spiritual connection

Harmonic Spiritual Connection is one of the most important things to understand. Spiritual connections with all living things will nourish our physical body. Our spiritual body is similar to our physical body. In order to keep the physical body functioning, you have to eat and exercise. That there is a spiritual life (body) may be understood while listening to what Jesus said: "I'm not from this world" (John 8:23), or "Keep the commandments if you want to enter **life**." (Matthew 19:17) Nourishing the **real life,** our spiritual body, can be achieved by:

a) Meditation

b) Consciousness about a spiritual body

c) Living without fear, guilt or other depressive behaviors

d) Love

5.1.a. Meditation

Meditation is a tool to address your real "self". There are many ways to achieve it.

Prayer, sitting quietly and seeing with your inner eyes, shamanic methods, yoga, etc. It is very much related to the person doing meditation, to what works. I, myself, need to play the guitar interlaced with quietness to achieve spiritual connection or to relax within a natural setting. Don't expect to get answers or to hear voices. The result of meditation is not immediate. Visual impressions may occur. To follow the light in such appearances is my recommendation. It may come from the words that Jesus said: "I am the light of the world" (John 8:12). But again, it may be different for others. Daily meditation will be needed and time depends on your capability. Do not equate this with the capacity to be a medium, a person to speak, write, see or act while in trance. Such a connection is to another **real life** (someone else's spirit). I recommend you find yours first rather than those of other living things.

5.1.b. Consciousness of a spiritual body

Spiritual forces can be manifested within a person, while consciously emptying the brain (I often like to call it cup to illustrate how easily it can overflow) that is filled with thoughts, throughout the day. The knowledge gained day in and day out can be called the intellectual body, reflecting the knowledge of our world. Temporarily setting this body away, as well as the physical body (some may call this relaxing or recreation), will enable us to concentrate on our spiritual body. Goals set may not be achieved immediately but the new direction taken will usually lead to harmony with the environment. I like to say, don't set a goal, even if this world's reality demands this. You may have learned otherwise in a business seminar. These goals are set to gain material riches or success and are mostly based on competitiveness and rivalries. Setting a goal is a very dangerous process. The richest experience in the material world is to be, to **travel** (doing things) rather than

to have. But with setting a goal, a person works hard towards something to have or to get. The dramatic part of this is that this person may not enjoy the travel along the way towards the goal. The travel may even become a drag while trying with everything possible to hold on to the goal. It should be understood that the journey is what counts, not the destination. Once you have achieved the goal, the reward is of short duration anyway and you want to achieve some other thing. It is important to **enjoy traveling** through the world while doing things (like driving a motorbike), not by having them! This may be the second most important thing to understand.

Setting a goal is useful to integrate with the existing society, but not necessarily with your "self". Ask yourself next time around what you would like to achieve.

It may be much more useful to dream (daydream, meditate) of the **travel**, rather than to set a goal of what you would like to achieve. Our dreams will become a vision and will come true. Many of the profound experiences in my life have been thoughts and daydreams put into reality. These thoughts, first invisible, were formed into a vision (something I could see with my inner eye) and with time were transformed into my physical life. A vision does not limit itself to time or space (no goals). We are, however, intellectually analyzing it for adaptability to these limits, in order to experience it. This is the transformation process. Being able to trust our capability that we can do this, without fear of failure, and to know that thoughts will take form as described above will provide us with a map to **travel** with.

Our society tends to find happiness in having things, but the fun of a motorbike is not in having it but in riding it. The same applies to our life.

5.1.c. Living without fear, guilt or other depressive behaviors

One big step in the right direction is to apply **positive thinking**. See the good things and pick out the good parts of any situation. If fear builds up within a person, the person may have lost the spiritual connection. First of all, the person denies the possibility of help from this source. Secondly, the person's spiritual body feels locked out while the person tries to solve the problem intellectually. With the knowledge of the spirit to guide a person through the material maze of this world, fear will become irrelevant. I consciously say knowledge, not belief in the same way as I say that the reader knows about, rather than believes in, his physical existence. A person may still be scared about some situations but can also get calm faster by understanding, **knowing** the concept given here.

5.1.d. Love

Nourishing the spirit is also achieved by way of love. It is often mentioned to be the most important thing to understand. I wonder how well education has given a description of this word. Here I put my thoughts to it. When a person lives with the human race, it is sometimes hard to figure out what love is. I had to learn a way to experience love, unconditional love. It may be described most easily by looking at the plant world. A person who plants a seed, will usually see it grow into a plant, returning great joy. The person will be **touched** by that experience. This plant may return more joy when tended well but it will always try to do its best to please. Once the person is able to receive this message from the plant (to be **touched** by its response), then love has been given by the person. It is with plants that there is always that reflection. Even while mistreating a plant, it still tries to please, but in this case the person will not be **touched** anymore. This person's brain (cup) is full, filled with rejection or hate which then caused his action. The person will not have the capacity anymore to receive the reflection, love. Also, humans do not necessarily want to please each other. When such reflection **-to be touched-** is absent no love is flowing, but no war is started either; but if the other person's cup is full of destructive thoughts as well, a fight may be inevitable. Learning

to love is most easily achieved through plants.

6. Where to go from here

No matter how experienced you are, the main direction to travel is clear. These new senses have to be tried and applied within nature and what would be closer than to **produce your own food while learning**. With these few basic bits of information, the approach to gardening may change altogether. More important, I would like to repeat the message, not to set a goal but to enjoy every moment **traveling** through your life. The following chapters will cover many practical aspects to get an infrastructure established to provide you with nourishing food for **body and spirit. Keep both in mind while reading**.

Summary of activities:

Winter

- Take time for meditation.

- Envision, plan, but don't set a goal.

- Follow up on your arts and crafts skills or learn something new.

- Read.

2

Where to Start

Things to consider

1. Land

No matter what the size of your property you can always grow food. A very important thing to look for is water and the more the better. A rich sandy clay or similar soil will enable you to get started right away. First make sure the soil has not been contaminated with pesticides or chemical fertilizers. If it has been contaminated you may first have to do some soil improvement. Some insecticides and herbicides contain arsenic compounds that later find their way into the food chain. Arsenic compounds remain potent for up to 10 years and certain salts containing arsenic are possibly related to cancer of the skin and liver. One method is to plant lots of sunflowers, which over time are said to have the capacity to neutralize arsenic compounds due to the selenium stored in the seeds. But it does not matter what soil it is, provided it is not just rock. Plants will grow and with time and loving care will carry you into a paradise. More about soil will be said in chapter five. A well, producing 3½ gal/min (15.8 l/min), used in conjunction with trickle irrigation will effectively irrigate about ½ an acre (20a), leaving enough for a family household and some livestock.

To become self sufficient, an area of about ¼ acre (10a), 10892 sq. ft., or about 100 ft. x 100 ft. (1024 m^2 or 32 m x 32 m)

of average soil will support a family of four with **vegetables, berries, fruits** and about four rabbits in a **movable rabbit pen** that can be located on your lawn. With another ¼ acre (10a) in pasture, you could keep a goat and some chickens (e.g. in a mobile pen), provided you buy:

Any type of soil will be useful but water is a must. Fruit trees need a warmer climate. See what is grown in the neighborhood.

- grains (or pellets) for the chickens over the whole year.

- hay for the winter months, about 30 bales for 8 months (242 days no pasture), or a shed the minimum size of 8 ft. x 8 ft. x 7 ft. high (2.5 m x 2.5 m x 2 m) to store loose hay.

- oats, approx. 1.5 lb./day (700g/day), for the goat.

It may not be an ideal solution to have only one goat, but once you are able to become a good friend to it (and please understand this, the goat will make that decision), it will not feel too lonely. More will be written about goats in chapter six. With the above information you will be able to determine the kind of structure you will need. You also have to rotate crops, including the goats' pasture. Bees can be kept to provide honey and wax, no matter how small the farm is. Such a setting is what this book describes. With an additional one acre, you can add crops such as hard wheat, rye, oats and more beans or other legumes, applying the methods of crop rotation and other techniques described in chapter five. This can provide feed for the goats and

Sunflowers have allelopathic properties, to release toxins, and with this hinder the growth of weeds like the red sorrel, lamb's-quarter and wild mustard.

chickens. If you want to have more meat you can also keep pigs.

The way we live is reflected in the way we build.

Pigs can roam in the same run as the goats but will need to be put into their own pen during the arrival of kids (baby goats). Pigs are also **very clever** and not always easy to handle. They may grow so fat that butchering will become awkward, because of size and weight, and difficult because of their strength to run away and squeal so loud. This can make anyone nervous and one could loose heart. We have cared for pigs for a few years but we no longer eat pig meat. I do not recommend that somebody start with pigs with the intention of butchering them. Keeping goats and pigs is a slow but effective way to clear land, and should be compared with other methods, such as using a horse or a tractor. Better yet may be to have a small area in the yard to turn into the garden or, if you are lucky, you may find some already cleared land along a creek.

Integrating a cow may produce too much milk for only a short period of about 8 months in a year. Furthermore marketing the surplus may cause a problem. For example in British Columbia, Canada you are not allowed to sell your milk, unless your setup has been inspected by the Ministry of Food and Health. For other areas check with the appropriate authority. This may put a restraint on you and you may want to rethink your strategies. For a family with six children a couple of goats will provide plenty of milk throughout the year provided you breed the goats with a gap of at least two breeding cycles (approx. 42 days).

Finally you could add a team of horses to do all the field work, independent of commercial fuel. In order to work fields more easily with horses, especially land that hadn't been worked before, flat land would be much preferred over hilly land. Again, to borrow or rent a tractor could come in handy to first cultivate the land. As everybody is different, so will all the farms look different and a ½ acre (20a) will be a good start. Once mastered, there is so much more to venture out for and, the experience and the knowledge gained while constantly "traveling", will be limited by the sky only.

2. Structures and root cellars

The way we live is reflected in the way we build. Most people build nice houses, because they are nice people. It may also help to build a useful structure (a nice looking house is not necessarily a useful structure). In order to supply healthy food, it becomes most important to provide storage during the roughly six months of winter (in a climate where apple trees still grow) when no plants grow outside. In this instance it is most practical to have a root cellar within close proximity of the kitchen. Of course a large freezer would be a storage possibility too. A small one for a backup system may be a good idea, but it depends on a continuous power source and freon is used as a liquid gas in the cooling process. Freon is a gas contributing to the destruction of the ozone layer but new models are now coming on the market using a different liquid. I recommend not to become dependent on large freezers. Without the possibility to accommodate storage in the house (some crawl space may be useful too) an underground structure like the one illustrated in fig. 2-2 and discussed later in this chapter, will work as well. However, you may appreciate the convenience of going shopping to your own, close by, basement super market.

In a root cellar you can store large amounts of vegetables such as potatoes, carrots, beets, cabbages, canned products, eggs and fruits such as apples and pears. The storage of honey frames is also prac-

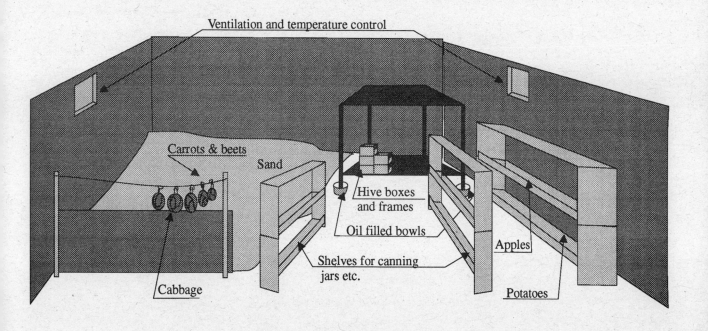

Figure 2-1, Root cellar below main floor (basement)

tical. The wax moth, a common problem, will not develop in the dark, cool environment. Furthermore, canned apple juice will stay nice and cool.

2.1. In-house root cellar

Now let us look at fig. 2-1. Potatoes can be stored very well on a wooden cradle. They also keep well in potato sacks made out of jute and set on a slab wood floor. They should be as far away from apples as possible. The closer together, the less time you can store both without signs of shrinking. I have experienced, however, that storing apples above potatoes works quite well (on another shelf at least 27" (70 cm) up), first laying out some newspaper to put the apples on. Golden delicious will keep without shrinkage until about April. At that point we eat dried apples to bridge the gap until about mid-July, at which time the early apples like Lodi or Transparent are getting ripe. Potatoes will start putting out shoots at the end of January, but will grow very slowly as long as it is dark and cool. They are still edible until about June.

The temperature is quite important. As it is impossible to keep it at a temperature just above 32° F (0° C) , we can keep it below or stable at around 42°F (7°C) until about April. Two openings, 1 ft. x 2 ft. (30 cm x 60 cm) in size, can be blocked with insulation or wood to allow temperature control. Openings need a screen with a mesh smaller than ½" (12.5 mm) to keep mice out (mosquito wire screen works just fine, mice chew through nylon). Furthermore a natural floor will allow a more stable temperature and consistent moisture content which should be at around 80%.

Store potatoes as far away from apples as you possibly can.

To store carrots or beets, a sand bed is a must. Any fine sand from the gravel pit will do. I also have used fairly sandy soil by sieving out the larger rocks and other particles with a ½" (12.5 mm) screen placed at a 60 degree angle. The construction of such a sieve is described under Equipment and Tools in this chapter. **At least 1 ft.** of sand is needed, right above the dirt base or above the high water table, depending on where you live. More sand is better and will stabilize the temperature. Carrots will

*One of the valuable things to make use of in the root cellar is the **sand bed**.*

keep well until the new crop is put into storage (October). We stored beets for two years, and still found them to taste very good. Cabbage can be stored hung up, with roots upside down. It usually keeps until the end of February and the larger heads keep well into March. It will also work with the roots cut off and placed on the sand with a newspaper or similar wrap to act as a vapour barrier. Cabbage stored like this has to be turned around once in a while, especially when confronted with an unusually high moisture content in the sand. Witloof (Chicory, Belgian Endive) is another vegetable to store in the sand. It will grow in the sand around the end of February, to provide the first fresh salad. Witloof can also be left out in the garden to provide green salad early in the new season, once the snow is gone (April).

All other goods such as eggs, canned juice, fruits, pickles, vegetables, jams and honey (in a closed container) can be stored well on a shelf. Do not keep smoked meat in the root cellar as the high moisture content will make it go moldy. To keep ants out of your stored honey frames (usually kept in hive boxes), place the legs of the shelf in a bowl. Of course this shelf is not supposed to touch any other structure. To make bowls as mentioned above, use empty one gallon plastic containers such as windshield washer containers. Cut them off at about 2" (5 cm). Then fill them with about ¼" (6 mm) of oil (old car oil) and place them so that the legs come to stand in them.

2.2. The outside root cellar

In warmer regions use a root cellar to store fresh produce.

The outdoor root cellar provides the same possibilities in storing goods as does the inside root cellar just described. To build a root cellar outside may take some time in order to dig. The easiest way may be to build it into the hillside. This is what fig. 2-2 shows. The logs used, 3.5" to 6" (9 to 15 cm) in diameter, can be easily found at clear cut logging sites (as long as practiced). Lumber companies do not bother about these trees, found pushed over on the ground. Cedar logs up to 20 ft. (6 m) long can easily be found. Check with authorities to obtain a permit to gather fire wood. This is usually issued at no cost. Information about which wood you are allowed to remove will be supplied.

Make sure that the roof logs closest to the ground rest on a rock 7" (18 cm) off the ground to avoid rotting. Arrange the joists in such a manner that they even out all across the roof line, that means the largest diameter joist goes on one side reducing to the smallest joist on the other side. It also means that you place all the butt ends to the back side of the roof. Try to eliminate any bow, by nailing the joists into the 140" (356 cm) long centre log. Mounting the sheet metal as shown in fig. 2-2, will divert the water to the side with the smaller diameter joists. It also avoids a snow slide which could obstruct the entrance. The snow on the roof will be useful as an extra insulation so the slope to the side should be minimal.

All other wood can be obtained from a sawmill. The slabs used are generated by the sawmill while cutting the trees into dimensional lumber. Slab wood is usually given away or sold very cheaply as fire wood, three bundles to a cord, with many pieces of good slabs in a bundle. All that has to be purchased is: sheet metal, nails and cement, mixed with sand 1:6 to create mortar (or use ready mixed cement), in order to seal the rocks from both sides (inside and outside). Instead of sawdust, fiberglass insulation could be used for the roof for extra insulation and in colder regions you may want to put hay or straw bales on top to further improve the insulation. Warmer regions can use this design as well to keep goods fresh. During the hot

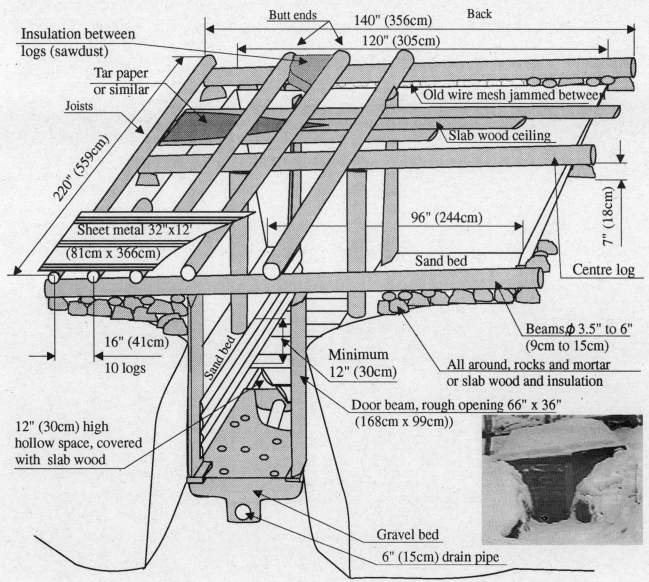

Insulation between
logs (sawdust)

Tar paper
or similar

Joists

Butt ends 140" (356cm) Back

120" (305cm)

Old wire mesh jammed between

Slab wood ceiling

220" (559cm)

Sheet metal 32"x12'
(81cm x 366cm)

96" (244cm)

7" (18cm)

Sand bed

Centre log

16" (41cm)

10 logs

Sand bed

Minimum
12" (30cm)

Beams,ϕ 3.5" to 6"
(9cm to 15cm)

All around, rocks and mortar
or slab wood and insulation

12" (30cm) high
hollow space, covered
with slab wood

Door beam, rough opening 66" x 36"
(168cm x 99cm))

Gravel bed

6" (15cm) drain pipe

Headroom: front appprox 70" (178cm), back more, depending on slope (typical 98" (249cm).

Figure 2-2, Root cellar built into a hillside

summer days at 90° F (32° C) the inside temperature is steady at about 59°F (15°C).

When digging, it may be easiest to dig a 3 foot (90 cm) trench into the hill, until you reach an overhead of about 8' (244 cm) as you dig in. Then you maintain that height until the desired depth is reached. This means your floor may go up slightly. A machine may be used to dig the trench, so that only the side pockets need to be dug out. All the soil from the trench can be used to build a terrace or a similar structure. For a sandy soil, most of the side pockets' soil (about ¾) may be sieved as described earlier and the gravel used at the entrance as shown in fig. 2-2, which will act as a drain field. After the trench is done, two 220" (559 cm) long logs are placed, the two logs acting as roof joist in the centre. Then the support posts are placed, including the ones at front also being part of the door frame. These posts act as supports for the slab wood along the trench. The slab woods and the wood floor can now be placed at the required height and, during construction,

An outside root cellar may be easily realized while building into a hillside. Locate a sandy soil to make things easier yet.

the latter covered up with plastic. Now a quarter of the larger pocket (right side shown in fig. 2-2) near the entrance can be removed. Set up the sieve in the dug out area in such a way that the gravel and particles fall into the trench in front of the wood floor (the drain pipe in place). Larger rocks can be picked out as needed and placed under the logs. Now work towards the back, piling the sand as high as possible, leaving the sieve in the front section. Once the larger pocket is sieved, the smaller pocket (left side shown in fig. 2-2) can be dug out after which the sand can be distributed evenly. The more sand you keep in the root cellar the better it will maintain the temperature. Try to keep the entrance as small as possible, but allow for a wheelbarrow to go in without difficulty. The drain pipe also acts as an air intake drawing in air at the bottom. An opening underneath the back log, that supports the roof logs, acts as an air vent and is covered with a screen, or a wire mesh is jammed between the ground and the log. For cold days the opening has to be plugged up from the inside, with a rug or some jute bags, to minimize draft. You may cover the end of the drain pipe with a screen smaller than ½" (12.5 mm) to keep mice away, although experience has shown, that they may still find a way in between the roof and the insulation. To provide more storage area it would be possible to mount shelves above the sand beds, to keep canning jars, etc.

The hollow space between the wood floor and the ground will enable run off water to flow freely below the sand bed and to be drained effectively outwards via the drain pipe. A small amount of runoff water may be a welcome feature, as it will maintain a low temperature well into early summer. Outside, a trench along the roof line will divert the water from entering the cellar. The building technique applied here, using raw logs, will provide strong structures and can also be used to build sheds

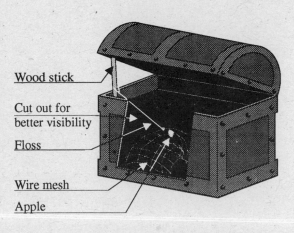

Wood stick
Cut out for better visibility
Floss
Wire mesh
Apple

Figure 2-3, Live trap for chipmunks

for the animals. For these structures bracing of the posts with the logs that hold the roof is necessary.

The best solution to keep mice under control is to have a couple of cats around. If a mouse gets into the root cellar a mouse trap may have to be used and the mice fed to the cats **on site**. Cats usually search out the area later on for more of the same and will keep the surrounding of the root cellar free of them. I once had a chipmunk that constantly fed on the apples stored in the outside root cellar. I boxed the apples up but the chipmunk kept coming back to chew between the gaps on the apple boxes until an entrance was gained. Eventually I had all the holes and gaps covered and plugged up with regular newspaper when the chipmunk finally had no other choice but to give up. I learned that chipmunks **do not like** to chew **newspaper**. Another way is to build a live trap using a hinged box similar to the one shown in fig. 2-3. The bulged up chicken wire mesh will give way as the chipmunk likes to approach a piece of apple jammed in the centre. This will pull the floss tied onto the wire mesh and with it the wood stick set at the edge of the rim. The lid of the box will close shut. This way the chipmunk can be set free in another area.

With a 6" insulated door and about 4" fiberglass insulation in the roof (and usually some snow on top), the temperature in the root cellar stays just above freezing while the outside temperature is at about 14°F (-10°C). After that a 60W light bulb will maintain the temperature until the outside temperature drops to about 5°F (-15°C) at which time a 1200W heater needs to be plugged in and run at the minimum setting. Without the availability of energy, the insulation in and on the roof has to be improved. An easy way to measure the temperature is by using small tin cans filled with water. Set them up in different places in the cellar and check for ice forming in them twice a day, usually in the morning and evening. Of course a temperature drop towards the evening will always mean that yet cooler temperatures can be expected in the early morning and appropriate actions will have to be taken. In a normal winter, temperatures usually drop below the 14°F (-10°C) mark twice, once around mid December and then mid January. A deviating pattern to, for example an earlier date, usually means an earlier spring. You have to observe these patterns in your area to be alert. You also have to recognize the temperature closer to the door to be lower than in the back of the root cellar. Cabbages and most apples do not mind a touch below freezing. The roots in the sand have also no problem with that, but you want to be alert, once the water starts freezing. Consciously monitoring nature like this will give lots of fun and you will soon be able to do what needs to be done intuitively.

2.3. Smoke chamber

The smoke chamber is mentioned in this chapter as it can conveniently be built into the construction of a new building but, of course, you may have seen the boxes connected to stove pipes leading to outside fire pits to achieve the same. It is convenient and economical to use the same smoke as

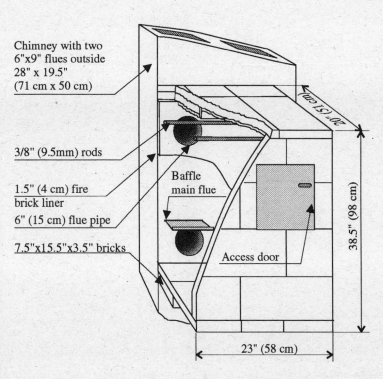

Chimney with two 6"x9" flues outside 28" x 19.5" (71 cm x 50 cm)

3/8" (9.5mm) rods

1.5" (4 cm) fire brick liner

6" (15 cm) flue pipe

7.5"x15.5"x3.5" bricks

Baffle main flue

Access door

20" (51 cm)

38.5" (98 cm)

23" (58 cm)

Figure 2-4, Smoke chamber built onto chimney

the wood stove generates. Even better is a **wood cook stove**, given that you are willing to chop the fire wood into a bit smaller-than-usual blocks. Such a stove can heat, cook, bake, dry fruits, dry the winter cloth, warm up food, heat the utility water by using a built in water jacket and, after all else, smoke the meat.

Be alert to changes in nature in order to develop a weather sense. With your consciousness to monitor these events, you become able to act intuitively.

The smoke chamber should be made as far up the chimney as possible (except if you build a 10-story house) to allow the smoke to cool off somewhat. A two-story house is an ideal layout. Depending on the wood used, a change in the taste of the meat will be noticed and you may try with several different types of wood. Many recommend hickory. I do not know of abundant hickory stands and prefer alternatives such as birch wood, which is found in far more regions and which is an excellent wood for smoking goats' meat. A birch tree will always regrow on its own from the stump left behind, which means no planting is needed for

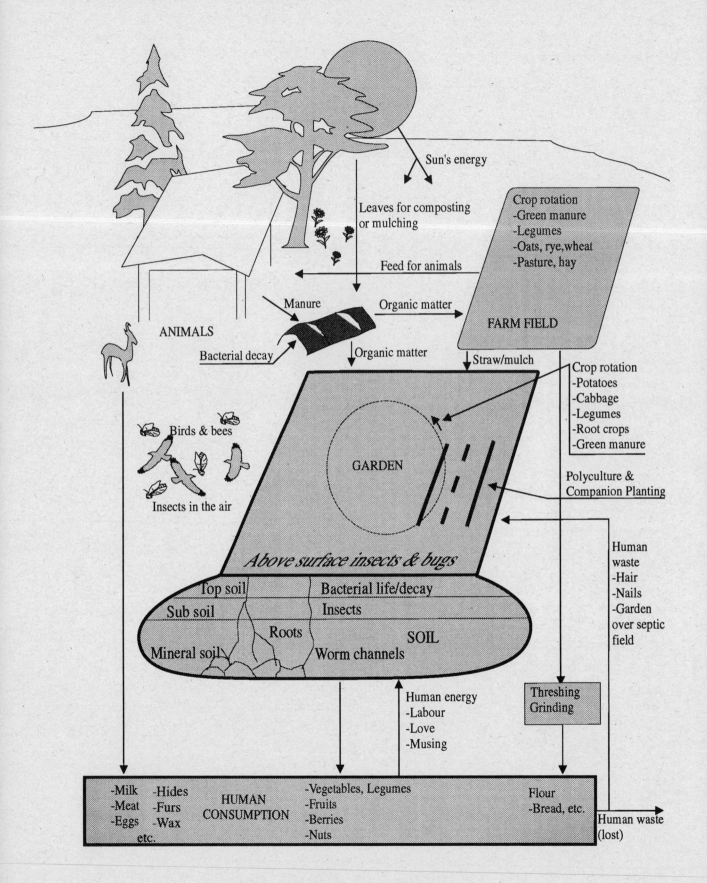

Sun's energy

Leaves for composting
or mulching

Feed for animals

Crop rotation
-Green manure
-Legumes
-Oats, rye, wheat
-Pasture, hay

Manure

Organic matter

ANIMALS

FARM FIELD

Bacterial decay

Organic matter

Straw/mulch

Crop rotation
-Potatoes
-Cabbage
-Legumes
-Root crops
-Green manure

Birds & bees

GARDEN

Polyculture &
Companion Planting

Insects in the air

Human
waste
-Hair
-Nails
-Garden
over septic
field

Above surface insects & bugs

Top soil

Bacterial life/decay

Sub soil

Insects

Roots

SOIL

Mineral soil

Worm channels

Human energy
-Labour
-Love
-Musing

Threshing
Grinding

-Milk   -Hides
-Meat   -Furs
-Eggs   -Wax
       etc.

HUMAN
CONSUMPTION

-Vegetables, Legumes
-Fruits
-Berries
-Nuts

Flour
-Bread, etc.

Human waste
(lost)

Figure 2-5, Food Cycle, soil structure

regeneration. Fig. 2-4 shows such a smoke chamber as part of a chimney with two flues. However, only one flue is required. The inside height, from the rods to the bottom, is approx. 25" (64 cm) and can hold a good-sized hind leg of a pig (ham) or about 4 to 5 pieces from a goat. Preparing meat will be described in chapter 12.

3. Animals, pens

Keeping animals is not everyone's interest. But many of us have a cat or a dog to care for. On a farm these two animals are part of the farm and many other animals are usually kept for economic reasons. The danger is that economic reasons become the major factor in keeping animals. Once chickens become machines squeezed into a wire cage and monitored on the daily production of an egg or for their meat, and after a year chopped up (sometimes for dog food only), then economic values have taken over. Quality is not even talked about. The above example applies for any animal. Once they become part of a factory machinery, it is too late.

Providing reasonable pens and plenty of ground to roam about is one of the primary needs. Fresh, wholesome food, plus steady human care are two others. But one more factor in Harmonic Farming that has to be recognized is, to close the food cycle, which means to bring back manure to the land, and the closer to home the better. In the olden days, human waste was recycled to the fields. Our hygienic standards (mainly a product of too many people living too close together) do not allow us to do that anymore. Regulations about health standards set out by government bodies, slow to change, usually hold up many new developments in the treatment of human waste. Compost toilets used in new housing projects, in Sweden however, provide such inventive technology to change human waste to compost with great success. Such a toilet

may generate 10 to 30 l of dry waste (compost) per year per person. For now, fig. 2-5 will show human waste as being lost, except for the garden area above the septic field, that profits from the extra heat generated.

Animal waste, decayed, is still one of the soil's best food. This makes it worth while to keep animals. On the other hand it will create some more work. Depending on how much time a person can spend, a wider variety of food can be made available, such as eggs, meat, milk and honey. The amount of time you will spend for these tasks will be explained in chapter five. More time spent yet, will bring with it hides, furs, bees wax and other products. Of course all these goods can be sold, and it would be advantageous to do this with not just the economic factor in mind, and to deal with local (bioregional) consumers first. Fig. 2-5 shows the food cycle as mentioned earlier (see fig. 1-1), but with the main interactions shown, including the soils' structure.

3.1. Goat pens

Goats are easy to house. A floor plan, as in fig. 2-6, will give an idea of the size of such a shed to be used by two goats. Somewhere inside the pen, a box or something similar should be mounted to the wall in which to place the salt block. A nail in the wall provides the hook to hang a water pail. These items should be arranged so that the rim is at a height just above the goat's tail to avoid any contamination. Goats are somehow picky about clean water. A little straw or similar item in it will discourage the goat from drinking the water. One window is needed, if possible to the south. You should be able to close it, to minimize draft, especially on very cold days. The wall facing the hay storage can be constructed as shown in fig. 2-7. These measurements will provide the full grown goat with enough room to maneuver its head and horns into the hay

Once chickens become machines squeezed into wire cages and monitored on the daily output of eggs or increase in weight, then economic values have taken over.

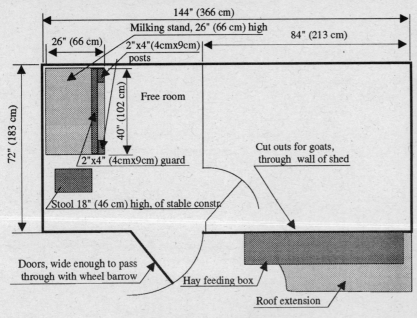

144" (366 cm)

Milking stand, 26" (66 cm) high

84" (213 cm)

26" (66 cm)

2"x4"(4cmx9cm) posts

40" (102 cm)

72" (183 cm)

Free room

2"x4" (4cmx9cm) guard

Stool 18" (46 cm) high, of stable constr.

Cut outs for goats, through wall of shed

Doors, wide enough to pass through with wheel barrow

Hay feeding box

Roof extension

Figure 2-6, Goats' pen

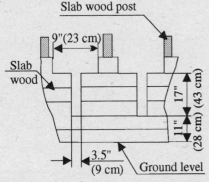

Slab wood post

9"(23 cm)

Slab wood

17" (43 cm)

11" (28 cm)

3.5" (9 cm)

Ground level

Figure 2-7, Cut outs in the wall.

Figure 2-8, Milk stand

the back legs of the goat. With some skill you are able to make milking a pleasurable task.

The shed can be built with slab wood using the same technique as described in constructing a root cellar as shown in fig. 2-2. Gaps between boards should be kept to a minimum, at least for the pen itself. As briefly mentioned earlier, there are usually many good-sized straight pieces in a bundle of slab wood. These pieces can also be used very well to build fences as shown in fig. 2-9, 52" to 60" (132 cm to 152 cm) high, depending on the kind of goats. The Toggenburg goat, with a skill to jump almost anything, does need a bit higher fence than a Saanen goat. A valuable

feeding box and to minimize spillage of hay. There may be a problem with young goats, as they will crawl through the openings. Therefore the sides of the hay feeding box should be at a height of about 3 ft. (90 cm) so that the kids can't get out of the pen. A natural floor will do very well. With wood floors, you always get mice living underneath. A plywood floor is also hard to clean.

The free room beside the milk stand allows the temporary separation of goats, if required, during kidding. With such a milk stand as drawn in fig. 2-6 and shown in fig. 2-8, you are milking the goat from the back, but it would be possible to do it from the side. When milking from the back, the back of the hands will develop a skill to control the movement (if any at all) of

Figure 2-9, Goat fencing

piece of advice: Do not use stucco wire to fence goats or cows. When exposed to the weather, this wire mesh will, over time, rust at the intersections, producing wire crosses. These can be swallowed by animals and create more problems than you want. You also need to think about where to store the oats and hay according to the requirements mentioned earlier. It would be practical to have it next to the hay feeding box, which means extending the roof enough to accommodate this.

3.2. Chicken pens

For 30 chickens a pen the size of 10 ft. by 10 ft. (3 m x 3 m) will do well. Every 3 ft. (90 cm) of 2½" x 1½" (6 cm by 4 cm) plank provides room for 4 chickens to sleep. The 2½" (6 cm) width is required for the chicken to comfortably stand on the plank and may be slightly rounded off. Planks should be spaced 12" (30 cm) or more apart to form a roost. The distance from the wall to the first plank should be 12" (30 cm). Snow clearing may not be everyone's task and an extra 10 ft. x 10 ft. (3 m x 3 m) area of roofed-over space should be provided for the chickens to roam or have a large tree right next to the chicken pen's entrance which will keep the ground more or less clear. You should plan for a deciduous tree, as it will be feeding on lots of nitrogen. Birch trees seem to do just fine but not cedar trees. This area could be the scratching pen and if it faces south-east the snow will not stay very long. For a small flock of about 6 chickens a pen as shown in fig. 2-12 will do well. In this case two laying nests will be required. Moving it around will provide for lots of greens, insects and other food sources and no further pens are needed. For more chickens, you should have two good sized grazing pens, besides the scratching pen.

The scratching pen, from which the chickens can reach one or the other grazing pen, is a small fenced area, where you throw all the unwanted garden material and kitchen scraps. Chickens will love to roam about. In spring and fall you empty the scratching pen by removing the top layer of droppings completely and put it into a proper compost heap. You need add no extra nitrogen to activate it. The grazing pens are fenced pens, with gates arranged in such a way that the hens can be admitted into one of the pens while being denied access to the other. The two pens should be sown with a grass, clover and herb mixture. You allow the hens to run in one pen until the grass is eaten right down; then you admit them to the other. Because the hens are doing most of the scratching in the scratching pen they should not tear up the grazing pens too severely. If you find that they do, you can limit their access to only a few hours a day.

Openings for air circulation and light are necessary, covered with a ½" (12.5 mm) wire mesh. It keeps the chickens in and

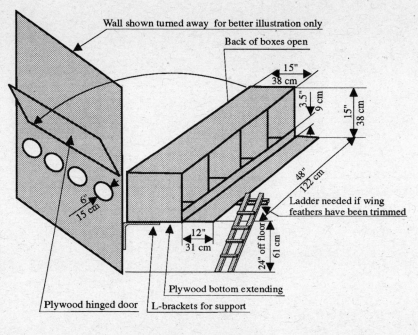

Figure 2-10, Laying nests

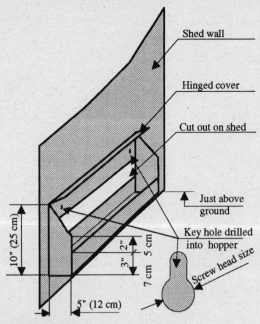

Shed wall

Hinged cover

Cut out on shed

Just above ground

10" (25 cm)

3" | 2"

7 cm | 5 cm

Key hole drilled into hopper

Screw head size

5" (12 cm)

Figure 2-11, Food hopper

in fig. 2-11, provided with a hinged cover to prevent chickens from stepping into the food, are mounted on the outside for convenient filling. Chickens can eat from both sides, provided that the pen's wall is cut out. Such a trough provides food for 2 chickens per ft. (2 chickens per 30 cm). Fresh water is required all the time. Steady running water will provide an optimal solution, but feeders available in stores will work as well if refilled twice daily.

3.3. Rabbit or chicken pen

Rabbit pens are most practical when built on wheels. Over the winter, usually only a buck and a doe are kept, unless you want to breed lots of rabbits. Products such as the meat and fur are very useful. Two practical pens are shown in fig. 2-12 and fig. 2-13. With this type of pen, the animals can eat a lot of fresh greens, while moved once or twice daily. With four rabbits in a cage as shown in fig. 2-12, you will have a wonderful lawn mower. In order to keep the lid closed, a rock can be placed on top

other animals out. Laying nests are shown in fig. 2-10. They are most easily constructed with ½" (12.5 mm) or better plywood. For 10 hens three laying nests are required. Food hoppers as shown

Above picture shows the pen using slabs to build the door and printing press sheets over the wire mesh to create an enclosure. This eliminates the use of plywood.

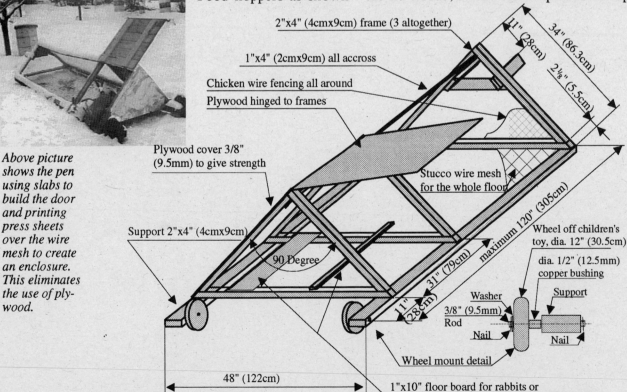

2"x4" (4cmx9cm) frame (3 altogether)

1"x4" (2cmx9cm) all accross

Chicken wire fencing all around

Plywood hinged to frames

11" (28cm)

34" (86.3cm)

2⅛" (5.5cm)

Plywood cover 3/8" (9.5mm) to give strength

Stucco wire mesh for the whole floor

maximum 120" (305cm)

Support 2"x4" (4cmx9cm)

90 Degree

31" (79cm)

11" (28cm)

Wheel off children's toy, dia. 12" (30.5cm)

dia. 1/2" (12.5mm) copper bushing

Washer

Support

3/8" (9.5mm) Rod

Nail

Nail

Wheel mount detail

48" (122cm)

1"x10" floor board for rabbits or 2.5"x1.5" (6cmx4cm) planks for chickens

Figure 2-12, Rabbit/chicken pen, up to 6 animals

of the lid or leaned against it or a hook can be screwed through a slot in the lid.

4. Equipment and tools

I have experienced many times over that buying a cheap tool does not work out in the long run. But buying an expensive tool is not necessarily the solution either. A tool has to be designed properly, and so many products are out there, that it is hard to know the answer. The first thing is to ask as many people as possible who are also gardeners. Usually they know if it worked for them or what is needed. For a small garden of ½ acre (20 a) you may get by without using a rotary tiller (rototiller), provided you have the muscle strength to work the soil, and the soil has already been worked before. Once you have worked the soil for two or three years, using the techniques of mulching, crop rotating, etc., as described in chapters 4 & 5, you may not need to turn the soil anymore. What you always need is

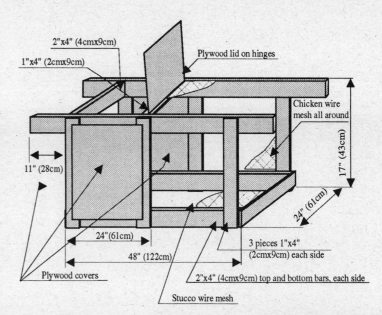

Figure 2-13, Rabbit pen, for one rabbit

shown in fig. 2-14. Tools used for beekeeping and honey extraction are mentioned in chapter seven.

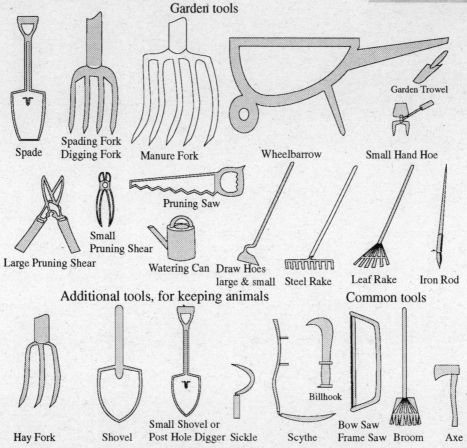

Figure 2-14, Basic tools to carry out the task

A knife, better a pocket knife, is also needed. The basic building tools such as a hammer, tape, pliers, level, stapler, trisquare and a hand saw have to be bought to build pens and sheds. I'm not too keen to recommend a chain saw, but it may have some good use when building post and beam structures. A note of caution: do not use the chain saw's sawdust in your garden. It is full of oil transferred from the chain while sawing. These tools are the basic requirements. To produce fine potting soil, a Riddle Upright Sieve is useful. This sieve can also be used to produce sand, as mentioned in the section about the outside root cellar. It can be made by using ½" (12.5 mm) wire mesh, mounted onto a 2"x4" (4 cm x 9 cm) frame measuring about 53" high x 36" wide (135 cm x 91 cm) on the outside. A potato fork (7 tines with rounded tips) may be useful. Accessories such as a whetstone (hone), pruning paste etc. will add to the existing items around and will become necessary.

Summary of activities:

– Consider new structures, tools, animals, pens, fences.

– Monitor temperatures.

– Observe, build a connection to nature.

3

February, a Month of Ease

Planting, pruning, bees and pollination

1. Planting & pruning

There **are three basic reasons** for pruning trees: first, to **remove damaged, diseased and awkwardly placed branches**; second, to **shape the tree for convenience of cultivation**; and third, to **increase the crop and improve its quality**. Pruning is something that has to be learned as you go. It is difficult to do as every tree grows differently. But some rules apply to most of them. The basics are given here for apple trees. Care for other trees or bushes, if different from this, is explained later in this chapter. Of course, the location of the tree is important too. Do not plant in areas where frost sets in, such as bottoms of small valleys, or on the foot of a hill. Try to use a south sloping exposure. To plant a tree dig a hole large enough for the root system. Make sure that the roots are below soil level and that the grafting part (a widening of the stem just above the root) is just above soil level. The hole has to be large enough to accommodate the roots without bending them. Roots that have been exposed to the air for some time may need to have their tips cut off on most of the root hairs, including the small ones. Dig the hole and fill it half full of water and soil. Whenever possible well-rotted manure should be mixed with the soil (stinging nettle liquid manure can be substituted. See chapter 8 about how to prepare it). The mixture should be brought to a muddy consistency. Now set the tree on that mud and fill in soil around. Don't press the soil firm with your foot, as you may damage the roots. Take more water and wet the soil all around. Fill in soil until the surface is level, which then should come just below the grafting spot. In a dry area you may set the tree a little deeper down, to form a small depression around the stem that enables the water to stay. Trees like to have lots of water but don't like static water at the roots (the water table needs to be lower than the tree's roots). Try to use some easy-to-maintain varieties such as spartans or macs to start with. When you buy fruit trees, ask about the spacing required between them. As a guide, space semi-dwarf and standard root stock fruit trees between 15 to 18 ft. (5 to 6 m) apart, dwarf root stock as close as 10 ft. (3 m). When planting closer, make sure that the spot has good air circulation and has sun exposure. Healthy trees like to have plenty of room.

When planting a young tree, you may follow an old tradition. Take a spade full of top soil from around an old tree to mix in with the soil for the young tree.

1.1. Caretaking

Take good care of the trees and berries. Talk to them while walking around them, touch them and look at the foliage. Pick off some of the caterpillars that eat the leaves, specially on young trees in the spring. You will not be able to remove all the harmful insects but the tree will see that you care for it. And when you take this kind of care the tree is strengthened. In general young plants are like children, with lots of loving care they will show tremendous growth spurts.

To make it hard for the mice to eat off the bark on the bottom of the stem during the winter months, cover it up to a height of about 1 ft. (30 cm) with aluminum wraps made from printing press sheets or small mesh wire netting. The aluminum sheets can usually be picked up at no cost from printers. It may be advisable to support young trees with a stick especially in windy areas.

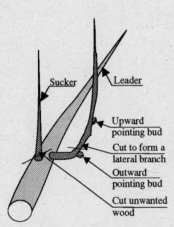

Figure 3-1, Different shoots

It is important to understand that branches going up vertically will grow well, but will generate **few fruit twigs**. Branches growing laterally (horizontally) will grow very slowly and will produce **many fruit twigs**. It is this that helps control the growth of the tree. Should we let the tree grow naturally it would grow many shoots first. These shoots would eventually bend down and produce many small fruits. The main aim of the tree is to produce more seeds. By controlling the natural growth pattern we create stress for the tree and must treat it with tender loving care.

We clean the stem and branches with a wire brush (in the winter) to remove fungi and other growth. Many larvae of harmful insects and mites overwinter on the tree, especially at the joints of branches. Cleaning the tree with the wire brush will prevent much damage from these pests. Large cuts or damaged parts have to be immediately covered with pruning paste.

Several sprays of stinging nettle liquid manure will help the development of the foliage and keep the aphids in balance. Helpful predators such as the earwig, the green lacewing and the ladybug need to be cared for with nests. For example the Canada thistle and the stinging nettle are very good hosts to the ladybug. The Canada thistle is also a very good nectar source in the months of June and July. Flower pots or similar containers filled with crumpled up newspaper and hung upside down on the lateral branches of the tree will attract lots of earwigs which feed on aphids.

1.2. Pruning unwanted wood

In the first case, the general principles are to cut out any dead or unhealthy branches, and any which are overcrowded. You should also cut out any branches which point in toward the middle of the tree, and all suckers - the long, straight, vigorous shoots which will take a long time to bear fruit (see fig. 3-1). If this is not done the shoots will crowd the centre of the tree and may take away light from the branches below. This heavy pruning should be done in late winter though never while the temperature remains below $20^{\circ}F$ ($-7^{\circ}C$). Make sure you cut out branches in the proper place, at the joints, about ¼" (7 mm) away from the other wood, so as not to interfere with the flow of the sap in the leftover wood. Wounds larger than 1" (2.5 cm) in diameter should be treated with one of the proprietary tree paints.

1.3. Pruning for shape

Pruning and training for shape should, for the most part, also be done in the late winter, and it is important to establish the general shape, or "scaffold", when the tree is still young. The scaffold is formed by the leaders, or main branches which spring from the trunk. Sub branches which grow from the leaders are called the laterals, from which the small fruit twigs and buds grow as shown in fig. 3-2. It's best to keep the number of leaders which form the scaffold to a minimum (5 or less). How you prune will depend on the general shape you want. For example, if you want a branch to spread from the middle of the tree, cut it down to an outward-pointing bud as shown in fig. 3-1. If you want to prevent the tree from spreading, cut it down to an upward-pointing bud and try to gather the tree together. In each case, it's important to leave at least ¼" (7 mm) above the bud. Two forms of shapes have become a standard (see fig. 3-3): the open-centered cup or goblet scaffold, where the spreading branches allow light to get to the middle of the tree; and the basic "Christmas tree" formed scaffold, called a pyramid or spindle. The latter has the advantage of carrying a great weight of fruit, or snow and ice in the winter. Other shapes may be useful for trees grown along a wall and pruning will be similar to the methods described above.

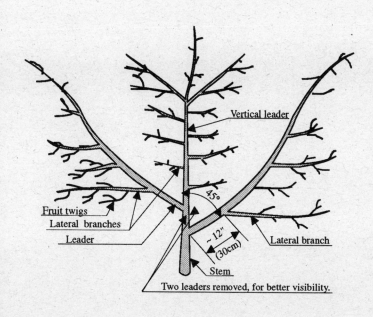

Figure 3-2, Parts of the tree

1.4. Pruning to encourage fruiting

Summer pruning has the opposite effect from winter pruning: it inhibits tree growth by encouraging the fruit spurs to develop rather than the lateral branches. Trimming back the new season's growth helps the tree to fruit more heavily and earlier. If the fruit spurs are overcrowded, you should thin them out to allow the fruits to flourish. With summer pruning, **never cut into old wood**, and remember not to cut back closer than ¼" (7 mm) above the bud. Certain varieties of apple and pear trees fruit at the tips of their branches. Prune these very little; just cut out surplus branches. If you tip the leaders and the laterals the tree will cease

Pyramid   Goblet

Figure 3-3, Tree shapes

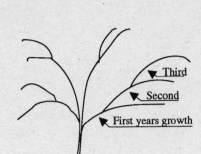

Figure 3-4, Apricot tree growth

to bear fruit altogether. I myself do not do any summer pruning, and beginners should do this with careful consideration.

Cherry and apricot trees (and some other fruits with a pit) bear fruit only on two-year-old growth or older. So don't cut all the new growth off or you will never get any fruit. On the apricot tree, the new branches always grow in a bow above old branches (fig. 3-4).

1.5. Grapes

Some hardy varieties such as the Himrod or the Concord vines will grow in climates where you can grow apple trees. Select a south facing wall of your house to get extra heat. Commercial growing may not be easy within this area as the house wall is only so big. The Guyot method is a sound way to prune. Let the plant grow for 3 years, then cut all branches but two. In the following fall cut the weaker off and tie the other to a horizontal (lateral) wire. This branch will send out fruiting branches and new shoots will appear from the base. Again, select the best two. The following winter, just before spring, cut off the old horizontal branch and replace it with one of the two new ones (the stronger one of the two). Treated in this manner the vine will stay small, as seen in vineyards, but may not be quite what you want.

To grow it along a building wall a slightly different approach is needed. Instead of cutting the vine right back each year, let it establish a framework of old wood and then allow horizontal branches to develop as if the top of the old wood were at ground level. For a high wall plant two vines or more; let the permanent wood grow tall on some and keep it short on others. Vines fruit at their extremities so, if you try to make one vine cover the whole wall, you will only get fruit at the top. Spray vines (and berry bushes) with horsetail tea or soap water to keep mildew under control. The blue concord (nowadays available seedless) is a good and resistant variety. The smaller grapes like the himrod are well suited for wine making but more susceptible to mildew.

1.6. Currants, gooseberries and jostaberries

These plants should have from 8 to 12 good stalks (shoots). Generally speaking you should treat red and white currants in exactly the same way as black currants and jostaberries but there is one important difference. (Jostaberries are a cross between the black currant and the gooseberry). The fruit on red and white currant bushes is borne on not one year old but two-or three-year old wood. This means that you prune for the first time when the bush is two years old by cutting out all the wood except 7 or 8 good shoots. Each year after that cut all new shoots, except for three or four which suit your plan for the shape of the bush and will bring the total of stalks up to a maximum of 12. Side branches going off the main stalks may be cut to allow air and light into the bush. To accomplish this you could remove the old growth and leave the fresh growth as shown in fig. 3-5. In the third year and every year after that, cut the oldest shoots right back to the ground. The main aim is to have a few one-year-old, a few two- year- old and a few three-year-old shoots on every bush, with plenty of short fruiting spurs on each branch. Gooseberries go into the same category as the red currants. Try to trim down 4 year and older growth and have the bush receive light into the center to avoid mildew. Because these berries are easy to propagate they are a wonderful survival food.

To propagate currants or gooseberries you cut, in the early spring fresh grown (one year old) 1 ft. (30 cm) long sticks off the existing bushes (if possible just before the buds open). Push them into the soil where you want a new bush until only 2 buds are above ground. Keep them well watered for the whole season. You can thus renew or expand your collection of bushes. If the soil is too hard you may use a spade to provide an opening in the soil by pushing the spade in and then moving it back and forth a couple of times. Of course you can plant the cuttings into pots as well and then set them out in the fall. Another method is to cut the sticks in the fall (November) and bury them in a trench in the ground. In spring, before the dandelions flower, you plant them as described above. This second method may produce better results in very cold regions. The distance between plants should be about 6 ft. (2 m). Jostaberries will make shoots with their roots which you dig out and transplant to a new location in the early spring.

1.7. Raspberries, blackcaps and loganberries

These berries are easy to prune. They bear fruit in the second year of growth. Young shoots will come out of the ground during the spring and early summer to develop into the new fruit-bearing canes ready for the next season. The new cane will be nice and green and easily distinguished from the old cane which is brown in colour. Right after the crop is over you can cut the old canes out. The heavy and straight canes of the thorn-less raspberries can be cut into about 4 ft. (120 cm) sticks and used to tie up tomatoes. You can easily push these canes into the ground and then tie 4 together on the top to form the shape of a pyramid. This structure will hold 4 tomato plants tied up to it quite well. The rest of the canes are chopped up into short pieces and left around the roots of the plant. Later mulch will

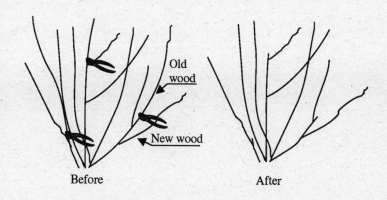

Figure 3-5,Pruning currant bushes

cover them and decomposition will take place. The new fruit-bearing canes are tied up to a wire or other structure for support.

When planting new plants in the spring you must cut the canes down to about 6" (15 cm) above the roots. Space them about 2 ft. (60 cm) apart. Plants which are allowed to bear fruit in the first year may die off. Take care not to break off the delicate new buds formed between the roots and base of the stem. Planting can be done the same way as the trees. Mulching, 6" (15 cm) or better, is a very good technique for the raspberries to keep the ground moist and to provide the fine roots that grow into it with lots of organic matter. Blackcaps and loganberries can be nicely tied along a fence or wire, and will form a beautiful looking hedge. To propagate berries such as blackcaps and loganberries you let the end of the cane touch the ground. The tip of the cane will now form a root.

Use the old thorn-less raspberry canes to tie up tomato plants.

1.8. Herbs

Some herbs are perennial in nature but need no pruning. The commercially grown sage may be pruned to activate growth. In the fall half of it can be cut down and used. The other half will go into seed in the next season and the seeds can be used to grow new plants. The trimmed down portion will grow vigorously.

The lovage plant, if not cut before going into seed, will spread lots of seeds that will germinate in the next season. This may be a reason to cut them just after flowering.

Bees	493	75.9%
Bumble bees	49	7.5%
Flies	24	3.7%
Ants	23	3.5%
Bugs	22	3.4%
Wild bees	16	2.5%
Wasps	3	0.5%
Other insects	13	3.0%

Table 3-1, Insect visits for a given time

2. Pollination considerations

It is logical to harmonize your operation as well as possible and, at the same time, be rewarded with some delicious honey. Of course not everybody can make friends with bees, but after you get stung a few times, your body adjusts to the pain (poison). For me, a mosquito bite itches more than a bee sting. Bee poison is reputed to be a cure for arthritis. Nature has, of course, other insects to pollinate your trees and berries, but we can certainly enhance the outcome in terms of well-shaped fruits by sufficient pollination. A survey done by HOOPER (1913), England, as shown in Table 3-1 gives some information about the effectiveness of the bee. With warm spring weather, $64^{o}F$ ($18^{o}C$) or more, a strong bee hive should have about 75 bees entering the hive per minute carrying in pollen.

Ask the person who sells you the plants about the need for other plants in order to get proper pollination.

Pollination is simply the transfer of pollen from the anthers to the stigma of the plant's flower. Self-pollination takes place with the transfer of pollen within the same plant, sometimes within the same flower. In cross-pollination, two plants are involved. Self-sterile plants require cross-pollination, but other plants may be self-pollinating and self-fertile. Still others require no pollination at all. Pollination is the first step in the sexual reproduction of plants which eventually gives rise to seeds, fruits, and the next generation of plant life. Modern agriculture now favours large fields, intensive mechanization and, with this, the use of chemicals for pest control. All of the

Pollination is the first step in the sexual reproduction of plants.

above are detrimental to natural pollinators. Although agricultural productivity is now far higher than it was, native bee populations have been reduced. Domesticated bees have become the most important pollinators of crops and help to bridge the loss of natural insect life. The movement of bees from one location to the other to avoid the chemical sprays, in fruit orchards in particular, puts the bees under stress. Bees can be artificially manipulated by feeding pollen and sugar very early in the spring to strengthen the colony before the natural cycle really starts but this puts the colony under more stress. Stress situations like these can weaken the bee's health and should be avoided.

Small fruits, such as raspberries and strawberries, depend on insects for cross-pollination. Honey bees are excellent pollinators of raspberries and strawberries although some varieties are self-fertile. It is particularly important to know if a tree or a berry bush needs other bushes for pollination. For example, a filbert hazelnut tree needs another variety of hazelnut in close proximity, to get pollinated. The old variety Barcelona is commonly used as a pollinator. Ask the merchant about this before buying. The information in table 3-2 has been received from The Summerland Research Station, British Columbia (see Appendix A) and compiled to represent the most common and a few new varieties. It shows the days of **full bloom** in relation to each other. For the best pollination, trees should bloom at the same or close to the same time. Table 3-2 should be used as a guide. Blooming periods vary between different varieties and weather conditions will also influence the duration of blooming. It is therefore difficult to give more specific information. It will benefit the reader to observe the fruit trees in her/his own region in order to get an idea at what time of the year the blossoms start to open. For example in our region the MacIntosh variety starts blooming about mid May.

There are some varieties, such as the Jonagold listed in table 3-2, which can not be used to pollinate other trees. Crab apple trees can be used to successfully pollinate and are sometime used in commercial orchards. Crab apples should bloom about two days ahead of the main variety to provide the best pollination. New apple varieties have been developed that are 100% scab free, such as Liberty, Jonafree, Florina and Redfree. There are a number of very new ones on the market that you could experiment with. Belle the Booskoop is a

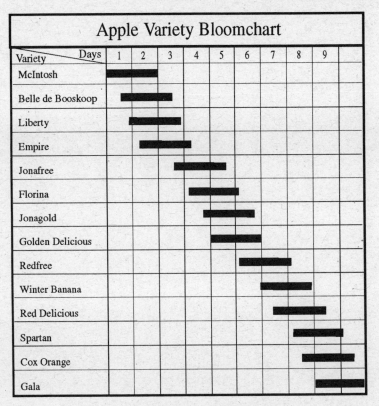

Apple Variety Bloomchart									
Variety \ Days	1	2	3	4	5	6	7	8	9
McIntosh	▬	▬							
Belle de Booskoop		▬	▬						
Liberty			▬	▬					
Empire				▬	▬				
Jonafree					▬	▬			
Florina					▬	▬			
Jonagold						▬	▬		
Golden Delicious						▬	▬		
Redfree							▬	▬	
Winter Banana								▬	▬
Red Delicious								▬	▬
Spartan									▬
Cox Orange								▬	▬
Gala									▬

Table 3-2, Relative blossom periods

very good cooking apple but rather sour to be eaten as is.

3. Beehive construction

Manufacturing your own bee hives with wood will require some good tools such as a table or radial arm saw, cutting blades and common hand tools.

For hive boxes the standard Langstroth super is the most common one used. Around 1851 Reverend L. L. Langstroth of Philadelphia was the person to come forward with the findings that the minimum space the bees like to pass through is 5/16" (8 mm) also called "bee space". With this in mind the design was born. Pine or cedar will be the wood to chose with the exception of the inner cover, top cover and bottom board where plywood can be used. Try to use dried wood or allow for shrinkage. All parts are nailed and glued, using non-toxic glue, except the frames which are nailed only.

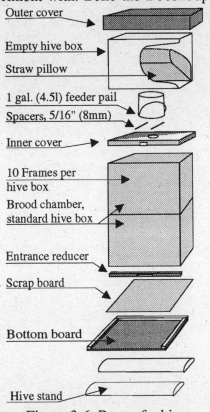

Outer cover

Empty hive box
Straw pillow

1 gal. (4.5l) feeder pail
Spacers, 5/16" (8mm)

Inner cover

10 Frames per hive box
Brood chamber, standard hive box

Entrance reducer

Scrap board

Bottom board

Hive stand

Figure 3-6, Parts of a hive

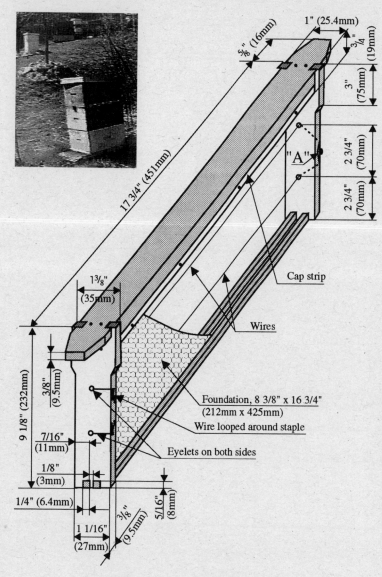

1" (25.4mm)
5/8" (16mm)
3/4" (19mm)
17 3/4" (451mm)
3" (75mm)
"A"
2 3/4" (70mm)
2 3/4" (70mm)
Cap strip
1 3/8" (35mm)
Wires
9 1/8" (232mm)
3/8" (9.5mm)
Foundation, 8 3/8" x 16 3/4" (212mm x 425mm)
Wire looped around staple
7/16" (11mm)
1/8" (3mm)
Eyelets on both sides
1/4" (6.4mm)
3/8" (9.5mm)
5/16" (8mm)
1 1/16" (27mm)

Figure 3-7, Hoffman frame

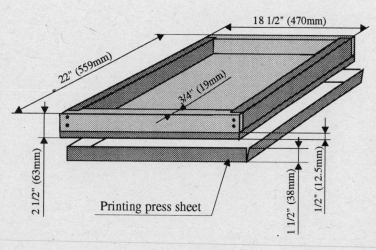

18 1/2" (470mm)
22" (559mm)
3/4" (19mm)
2 1/2" (63mm)
1 1/2" (38mm)
1/2" (12.5mm)
Printing press sheet

Figure 3-8, Hive cover

Fig. 3-6 shows a hive with the necessary components to house the bees. The hive stand can be anything that keeps the bottom board above ground and does not allow mice or ants to dwell underneath. A 6" to 8" (15 to 20 cm) diameter cedar pole, split in half, will do just fine. The bottom board will rest on it and, in a very good year, up to about 150 lb. (68 kg) of honey and bees as well. The entrance reducer (as shown in fig 3-10) is used to protect the bees from intruders such as wasps, robbing bees or mice. It can be placed to provide either a ½" (1 cm) or a 3" wide (7 cm) entrance. Each of the hive boxes holds 10 frames. The outer cover (as shown in fig. 3-8) is protected with a printing press sheet, stapled and folded around the corner, using a technique similar to the process of wrapping a present. The cover is rested on the front rim of the top box, the one providing the space for the feeder pail or the pillow. With the outer cover now slanted to the back slightly, air traveling through the hole in the inner cover (see fig. 3-10) can escape and reduce the chance of condensation inside the hive. Instead of a feeder pail a canning jar will work as well provided the lid is punctured with about 10 holes having a diameter of about 3/32" (2 mm) each.

Frames are rather difficult to cut and it is strongly recommended that frames be purchased from a beekeeping equipment supplier. Pieces must be cut absolutely accurate to the given dimensions. The exact measurements for a Hoffman frame are shown in fig. 3-7. Once the frame is assembled, place eyelets in all holes and wire it fairly tightly with a #28 gauge (0.3 mm) wire and secure the wire ends with staples (as shown in fig. 3-7). The nail, "A" in fig. 3-7 which is set on the other side bar, is then used to lift the wire over it in order to get the wire nice and tight. Place the foundation into the frame now and nail the cap strip (fig. 3-7) with 3 to 4 nails to the top bar. For embedding the wax sheet (called

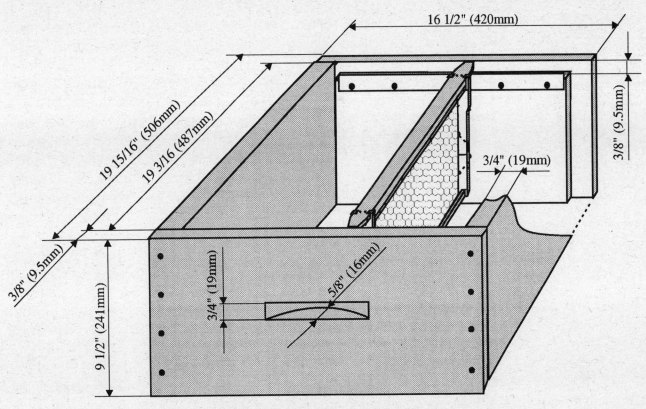

Figure 3-9, Standard Langstroth super

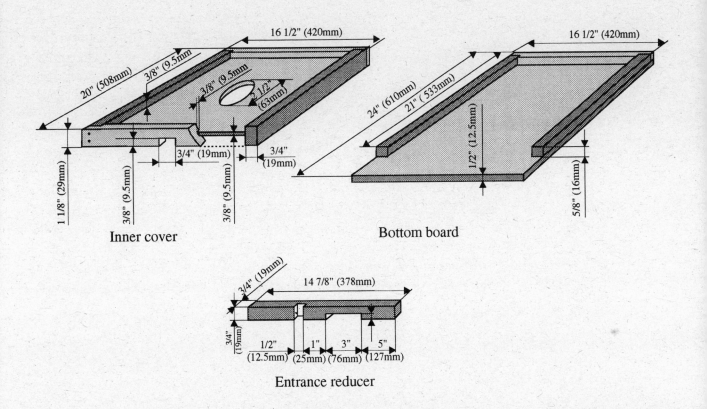

Inner cover

Bottom board

Entrance reducer

Fig. 3-10, Bottom board, entrance reducer, inner cover

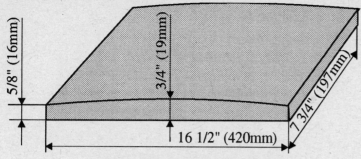

Figure 3-11, Embedding board

foundation) use a slightly beveled wood board, the embedding board (as shown in fig. 3-11). The frame should be placed on the embedding board with the foundation beneath the wire. You will require an embedding tool. This is a transformer with two probes supplying about 12 V. It is commercially available from beekeeping equipment suppliers (see Appendix A). Apply the probes to the ends of the wire until they get hot and sink into the wax. You may have to press the frame gently downwards in the process. Do not heat excessively or you may cut right through the foundation. Use a vertically wired foundation with two wires across on the frame or put 4 wires into the frame. When using the heavier, stronger foundation (5 oz. (150 g) or more) that you will get when manufacturing it yourself you can use just two wires in the frame.

Fig. 3-9 and fig. 3-10 show the dimensions of the different components used. The outside of the hive should be protected with paint, oil or some non-toxic preservative. Use linseed oil or a non-toxic product and apply two coats if possible. Do not use anything for the inside of the hive. Pine boxes painted with linseed oil may need to be repainted after 4 years, but some of our boxes just turned dark and have resisted the weather quite well for over 10 years. When building hive boxes, check to make sure that they are square. They may tend to warp if not glued and nailed properly, especially if the wood grain is from the center wood of the tree. Handles can be cut on all four sides. I have, however, never used the handles across the smaller distance of the box. Metal rests are produced from #26 gauge (0.5 mm) sheet metal or ordered from a beekeeping equipment supplier. Building the hive box so that the frames are flush on the top will ease the removing of the frames. This however requires the use of the inner cover in order to provide space for the bees in the top box. The inner cover, in conjunction with the empty hive box, has the advantage of placing the feeder pail in a position where other bees cannot rob the food. It will also provide a space for the pillow during the winter months. The scrap board, as shown in fig. 3-6 consists of a ¼" (6 mm) plywood, good one side, with the dimensions of 14½" by 23" (368 by 584 mm).

4. Examining a bee hive

Many books will tell you much about keeping bees. I don't want to distract the reader with information overflow. For this reason I only mention the necessary actions in regards to the seasons which will be the basics for a beginner to keep bees. I encourage you to visit the library which has many books about bees, their anatomy, their life cycle, etc. A listing of some literature is given in Appendix A. During the whole book I try not to mention concrete dates about when to do what. Instead I direct the reader to observe the plants or animals in his area in order to find signs that trigger these actions.

Up to this time of the year the bee keeping activities have been minimal. Of course frames with new foundations can be made ready to be put into the hives for the spring management. You may also want to build some new equipment, as described in this chapter, find some used equipment or repair old boxes, etc. After the bees have been fed in the fall (about the end of September of the previous year) no other action is needed until the first warm days in the new season. The best experience with bees is to watch them and take action according to their behavior. During this time of the year it is important to check the entrance of every hive to make sure that there is an opening in the hive for the bees to fly out on their cleansing flights. Bees have to empty the waste built up from digesting honey during the cold winter. If not given such a chance the waste will be deposited inside the hive creating the possibility for infections that lead to dysentery. All this can turn into nosema and nosema sometimes causes the introduction of dysentery. Brown watery splashes, formed like small drops, fallen onto the surface all around the hive point towards the existence of nosema but could be just dysentery. A better diagnosis can be achieved by pulling apart the abdomen of a fresh bee, to reveal the intestines, called midgut and rectum. In normal circumstances the colour of these parts would be light-brown to red-brown but, with infections of nosema they become white or milky coloured to dirty brown. To provide 100% evidence, a lab test is necessary. The few signs given should act as a guideline. Such hives should not be used for further rearing!

Normal excretions in the spring have a brown to dark-brown colour and a firm shape. They form stripes on the hives, or small squiggle lines (as shown in fig. 3-12).

Such signs are most welcome. Many bees will fly out at the first opportunity, to empty their waste, but never return. You will notice dead bees on the snow up to a radius of 30 feet around the hive, usually in the direction towards the sun at the time of flight. Brown spots will be visible in the snow as well. Many dead bees will accumulate at the entrance during the winter. These are all normal signs.

Fig.3-12,Squiggle lines around top entrance

The first warm sunny days in early spring will encourage the bees to empty their waste. Temperatures will be about 55 to 60°F (10 to 15°C).

The reusable scrap board (fig. 3-6) can be easily pulled out in the early spring. When "scrap boards" are used, they can be diagnosed for many signs in the early spring. To incorporate a scrap board, it becomes necessary to change the design of the bottom board of a bee hive. The height of the rim, which is normally ½" (12.5 mm) needs to be increased to ⁵/₈" (16 mm) as shown in fig. 3-10 or a thinner scrap board has to be used. The scrap boards and pillows are usually removed on a nice sunny day and when the pussy willows, one of the **natural pointers** in relation to timing, just open up. Do this on a fruit day as outlined in chapter four when working with the calendar. At the same time the top entrance can be closed. Most of the time there will be no problems encountered, but it is good to know what to look for (see fig. 3-13). In normal circumstances the aged

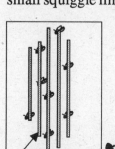

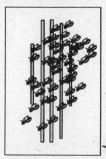

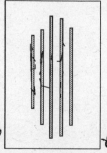

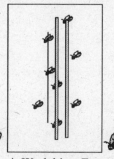

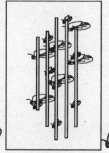

1. Few dead bees, normal use of food, brood in center. Colony is o.k.

2. Many dead bees, legs spread, dead brood. Bees starved, had no access to food.

3. Sugar crystals on the board. Fed too late in fall. Need to be fed immediately.

4. Weak hive. Few bees. Need to be requeened or bees united with other hive

5. Many dead drones. Laying worker. If weak, like #4 then resolve hive. Else unite with other hive.

Figure 3-13, Scrap board analysis

bees have an opportunity to fly out of the hive so dead bees on the scrap board should not be numerous. The uncappings, the caps of the honey cells that have been chewed off by the bees during the winter, now rest on the scrap board as small wax crumbles. If the hive tends to lean backwards, moisture will collect on the bottom board, and all the scrap will be moist, mouldy and, in extreme cases, covered with fungi. Such a hive has to be repositioned. You may look for a dead queen on the board as well. If one is found the hive should be united with another one immediately. Instructions for uniting hives will be described in detail in chapter 5. By removing the scrap board you provide the bees with a clean entrance with minimum impact on the colony. Some gray hair and wax particles will indicate that a mouse is nesting in the hive. You would have to open the hive to release the mouse. Usually mice enter the hive in the fall while young and can't leave later on when they are larger.

The beginner should not worry too much about diseases. Observe the bees, do not put them under stress, breed with strong stock and maintain a clean yard.

More serious problems are caused by diseases such as the American foulbrood (AFB). Identification of AFB is done by examining brood combs for scale. Without proper light it is easy to overlook a dark-coloured scale in a dark-coloured comb. Hold the frame by the top bar, at a slight angle, so that all of the low sides of the cells can be seen clearly. It is possible to do this now in the leisure time. Later during the year, larva can be probed with a toothpick. Look for larva with signs of discolouring. If the larva has died of AFB, a toothpick will sink into such a larva without resistance. If the larval remains are stirred and the toothpick is withdrawn slowly, the remains have a glue-like consistency and will string out when the toothpick is withdrawn slowly from the larva. A foul smell can be detected.

New diseases have found their way into Canada, such as acarapis woodi (tra-cheal mite; sometimes called acarine mite) and, as recently as 1992, the Varroa jacobsoni (Varroa mite). All these diseases have been spread not by the bees but by human beings. The Varroa mite was transported from Japan to South America in 1970 and to the USA in 1987. To learn more about these diseases I suggest that you get the publication called Honey Bee Diseases & Pests from the Canadian Association of Professional Apiculturists (see Appendix A). For a beginner it may not be necessary to bother too much about all of this. When you think a problem is arising, the first thing to do is to ask another bee keeper or the bee inspector for advice. The important things to do are, **to observe the hive**, not to put the bees under stress, to breed with strong stock and to maintain a clean yard. Do not leave honey or beekeeping equipment lying around outside!

Summary of activities:

- February Pruning and maintenance.
- Brush off stems and branches on fruit trees.
- Observe colonies.
- Repair/build beekeeping equipment, prepare new frames.
- Check old frames for AFB.
- Order seed catalogues.

4

Early March, Plan the Actions

Planning the seeding of crops

1. General

Good planning is the art of not setting a goal but to establish a framework of activities, a map towards the goal. Goals which appear realistic at first may become unrealistic along the journey and with it may destroy the pleasure of traveling. To explain this I use an example, the monkey trap. The monkey trap is a box (full of food) having a hole big enough for the monkey to put his hand in. The monkey sets his goal to get the food in that box. However, as soon as he holds the food in his fist he can not retrieve it. While insisting to reach his set goal he will not go anywhere and his journey may end in misery. As with any other undertaking planning gives you, if not anything else, an understanding of how complex or easy a task is going to be; in this instance the planning of crops. If it gets too complex the problem has to be laid out into smaller groups of topics and then the links established between them. This is done to the point where it reveals a solution and you will see fairly quickly that compromise is the path most often traveled.

Let's plan for harmony with a few basic things in mind:

– Plants must start out healthy.

– Nurture the soil with organic matter, the soil's natural food.

– Have the soil covered with organic material such as green manure, crops, snow or weeds.

– Allow excess water to drain and sun light to touch the plants for 6 hours or more per day.

– Take care of the soil, step onto it with the knowledge that you walk on many small communities formed by living organisms.

– Keep the soil clean of contamination.

– Shapes and forms are reflections of life. Such life feeds from the soil and will go back to it, to build other shapes and forms.

The soil forms you and you form the soil.

– The more varied the composition of a shape or form is, the more it appears to us to be alive.

A few hundred years ago Jean Van Helmont, a Belgian chemist and physician, planted a small willow tree of about five pounds (2.3 kg) in 200 lb. (91 kg) of dry earth. For the next five years nothing was added, except rainwater. The tree grew un-

Let us plan for harmony.

til it weighed 169 lb. (77 kg). The soil was dried and re-weighed and was found to have lost only two ounces (57g). While the tree got about 33 times heavier, the soil almost maintained its weight. Another impressive piece of research was done by A.F. Herzeele from Germany in the 1940's in regards to seed quality. Organically (exactly bio-dynamic) grown "cress-seeds", grown in distilled water inside a sealed glass tube had gained some weight by the time of sprouting (first day). This was not the case with regular cress-seeds however. We have to ask ourselves where the additional substance came from and why. Herzeele attributes this to the healthy plant's capability to transform cosmic substance into plant substance, which in turn results in more weight in the first day of growth. His theory concludes that (translated from German) such substance is of its origin, changing through imponderable existence into natural material life" (Rudolf Hauschka, Heilmittellehre, see Appendix A). He also concludes that the plant life is as old as the minerals found; not that the soil has generated the plant but the plant the soil. This may sound like the chicken and egg situation but, as long as we don't have a clear vision of such matters, we have to appreciate the **plant life as a basic building block for harmony**. It is this building block that improves the soil, supports bacterial, insect and animal life, nourishes us, heals us and makes us enjoy its beauty. The above example also tells us that the **cosmic forces can be transformed to help the plant, granted the seeds are healthy**. We will talk more about these cosmic influences later in this chapter. Plants are generally divided into three groups: annuals, biennials and perennials. Annuals are plants that grow from seed and reproduce seed in the first year of growth (e.g. tomatoes, corn, potato roots, beans, peas). Biennials are plants that store up food in the root or head in the first season and then send up seed stalks to produce seed in the following season (e.g. carrots, beets, cabbage, onions). Perennials do not usually produce seeds until the third year, and thereafter will produce seed every year (e.g. rhubarb, asparagus). Once in a blue moon, one plant will take on the characteristics of another group. "Bolters" are one example in the biennial group. They produce seed already in the first year but the roots do not develop very well. This plant is called a mutant. Using such seeds will not lead to a healthy plant but will produce more mutants. There are also the hybrid plants. To develop a hybrid the scientist must shelter the pistil or female part of the flower to pollinate it with the introduction of pollen from a specially selected plant that reflects the characteristics required by the scientist or better by the market place (e.g. big, shiny, more colourful, rounder, pesticide resistant, to mention a few). With over-tender care for these seeds and no exposure to the harsh environment of nature, which selects the fittest, these seeds will not inherit nature's harmony. The difference between the mutant and the hybrid is that a hybrid (man-made mutant) can become a very good producer for one generation of life but its seeds are degraded (usually due to breeding with too close a family member). After this exploration and some more to come, we will be prepared to put these principles to work during this season. Lots of **motivation and enthusiasm** is required to change the old ways of chemically destructive agriculture. You must recognize that it may take longer than one season of sanity to correct soil imbalances and to restore the natural cycles to the land. However the excitement, the conscious experimenting and the new knowledge you gain during the season will counter-balance and make each step toward **Harmonic Farming** so much more satisfying. It is best to plan the new season in the calm of winter.

2. Site requirements

Learn from neighbours in your area how crops, and which ones, are growing well. If they mention this or that spray, then ask for what problem it was applied, so you can prepare yourself for such infestation. Hopefully you can persuade your neighbour to spray on days of no wind and that water seepage from such adjoining properties can be eliminated by digging drainage ditches to carry the water away. You are fortunate if you find an isolated area or neighbours who can share similar ideas.

All is not lost with a garden site that faces due north. Heat-loving crops such as corn, tomatoes or squash may not be able to grow but hardier crops such as carrots, beans, peas, cabbage, potatoes or lettuce will grow just fine. Newly broken soil or soil not cultivated for one season and used to grow green manure crops such as rye, which is seeded in the fall and turned into the soil in spring, clover or just a grass mix, seeded in the spring, will rebuild the soils bacterial life very efficiently.

3. Crop rotation

Try to divide your garden area into 4 different plots, each seeded with crops with different soil requirements. With this you will avoid the same crop being grown in the same place for the next 3 years. If your garden is small and therefore cannot be split into 4 plots, you have to keep track of where you have what seeded at what time, to avoid the same spot being seeded with the same plant again. This is especially important for cabbage and potatoes. They do not grow well in the same spot and if not rotated will cause imbalance to the soil.

Adding a fifth plot will help to improve the soil more rapidly and usually calls for a rototiller or similar cultivator. For larger fields a tractor might be required.

Seed this section with a green manure crop that is then worked into the soil in the fall. If more animal manure is available than what could be applied to the fruit trees, pastures and hay fields, berries and shrubs you could apply it to that section. Horse lovers, who bring in hay for the horses and in return get plenty of the best, wonderful horse manure must use it. This manure applied in late fall, on top of the green manure and worked in, would greatly improve that plot. In the olden days farmers left one field unused each season for that reason. Of course you can always apply well rotted manure to your garden. There is no need to apply manure to the section that had legumes grown during the season as this may cause an over-achievement in terms of nitrogen in the soil. Who wants to do more then is needed anyway? Nevertheless it is nice to experience that without using much animal manure our garden has produced good crops for more than 12 years now and I only see it getting better. One reason for this may well be the mulch that we have applied every year with loving care for the plants.

Note that raspberries prefer mulching over animal manure.

You have to incorporate one leguminous crop that is capable of binding nitrogen with its root system (e.g. beans, peas, clover, alfalfa). These **roots need to remain** in the soil when the crop is harvested. It's best to have a heavy feeder crop to follow a legume crop. With such practice, crop rotation, you create a vast variety of bacterial life and fungi, established by the plants' life and later root decay, which will constantly work to keep a balance in the soil. If this happens, the disease to plants within the top soil and to some extent in the sub-soil will be kept to a minimum. At the same time we work towards polyculture (the opposite of monoculture) which will enhance the diversity of beneficial insect life above the soil. We also have to look at rotating the crops in regards to the needs and requirements of the plants. Further-

Crop rotation and crop sequence will enhance bacterial and insect life in the soil.

Polyculture will diversify the bacterial and insect life and will provide the structure of small cities and towns.

more there are a few plants that do not like to be rotated onto a spot where another plant has been previously grown, e.g. radishes not after cabbage or spinach not after beets.

3.1. Crop sequence

Plants have different requirements in regards to the soil and to grow healthily. To make planning easier table 4-1 includes a column that mentions to what group of feeders a particular plant belongs.

Soil cover will enhance bacterial and insect life **on the surface of the soil.**

3.1.a. Plants with a high requirement, heavy feeders

Plants such as cauliflower, corn, cabbage, tomato, zucchini, cucumber, pumpkin, celery and leek all require a rich soil. Soil that had a legume such as peas or beans grown the previous year will be excellent. Also a cover with mulch, the previous year, will improve the soil for these plants. To make them grow very strong, a stinging nettle liquid manure (see chapter 8 about how to prepare it) can be given every 2 to 3 weeks during the growing season.

3.1.b. Plants with an average requirement, average feeders

Plants such as spinach, lettuce, beets, fennel, carrots, onions, garlic and potatoes will grow in average soil. Of course it is an advantage to spread a light cover of animal manure in the fall and to cover the seed rows with mulch at this time but you will get by with just leaving the field as is and doing the mulching in spring as outlined later in chapter 5.

3.1.c. Plants with little requirement, light feeders

Legumes provide one of the best soil improvements in regards to nitrogen fixing (beans, peas, clover, many herbs). They need very little manure if the soil is healthy, rich in bacteria, fungi and other living soil organisms. If you change from chemical fertilizers to an organic method of gardening you may need to add lots of manure, due to the fact that these living soil organisms are not present. Pole beans, as an exception, may require some extra manure but once your soil is established as outlined in this book this will not be essential. Most herbs are light feeders but may not have the capacity to fix nitrogen.

4. Soil cover

We can further improve the insect life, specifically just above the soil, by using the mulching technique. Mulch will provide housing for the bacteria right at the top of the soil and will also keep the soil moist. In a region, with about 600 mm (24") or less of average annual rain fall, additional watering is required. You may want to install a trickle irrigation. More about mulching, the soil and water will be given in chapter 5. Many soil covers will do well but mulching with straw or hay from spoiled bales will be the easiest.

Green manure acts as a soil cover as well. For example rye can be seeded in the fall. It may grow 2" (5 cm) in the fall. Two weeks before preparing the seed bed, it is worked into the soil. The organic material now in the soil will be welcome and will improve the soil. Orach (spinach) may be seeded early in the spring.

Another commonly used soil cover is black plastic. I do not recommend this. Plastic is derived from a non-renewable source, can not be produced by yourself, does not enhance but hinders the bacteria's natural growth on the surface and if not removed in the fall in time will remain in the soil and become a nuisance.

5. Companion planting

Tables 4-2 to 4-7 show companion plants and their tendency to like (attract) or dislike each other. With companion planting you are one step closer to eliminating monoculture. Many plants like to grow within the aura, smell or root system of another. This becomes evident when you see the amazing results produced by growing onions and carrots side by side or beets and garlic. Similar mechanisms apply between plants and the insect life, sometimes also referred to as allies. These become evident by certain plants showing a tendency to attract or repel insects. Many experiments have shown such positive influences between growing plants and many useful recommendations have been made. When following these recommendations a lot of new and exciting experiences can be gained. Other literature may contradict with our experimental findings. Capital letters in Tables 4-2 to 4-7 reflect valuable experience over the 12 years at the Gooly Mooly Art Farm. Small letters reflect recommendations from other sources, as long as they did not contradict with our findings. It's up to the reader to explore these recommendations for companion planting.

You will find the plant hemp listed in the tables. I like to make the reader aware, that in some countries, it is illegal to grow hemp. In the United States hemp was the major fiber producing plant to be used in the manufacturing of paper until 1937. Influenced by the new industry that started to produce paper from wood, hemp was portrayed as dangerous mainly due to its "magic power". To remove hemp from the industrial scene has become more and more questionable, especially since 1990, when French researchers developed a strain of hemp that has so little THC (tetrahydrocannabinol, the mood altering ingredient), that it is useless as "grass" but still possesses all the other many virtues of the plant. Several countries have now legalized hemp, e.g. France, England, Belgium and Spain. Seed catalogues may list it under the name agrimony.

Companion planting will enhance bacterial and insect life **above the soil**

6. Beneficial plants and insects

Table 4-8 shows relations of predators, and in some cases the plant life, if they act as a host or a repellent and the influence of their action. It also refers to emulsions (tea), sprays and smoke treatments. In recognition of insects for their qualities as a predator or not, the Ministry of Agriculture and Fisheries has produced an excellent colour printed booklet called "Field Guide to Harmful and Beneficial Insects and Mites of Tree Fruits" (see Appendix A, for more details).

Because insects of different species can have either a positive or negative influence in the garden it is important to encourage not only plants which provide hosts for beneficial insects (predators) but also plants which act as a repellent to harmful insects. In many instances because beneficial insects are attracted by a host plant they in turn will help another plant to succeed. For example, the Canada Thistle will act as a host attracting the ladybug, a beneficial insect to the fruit tree. Conversely, some plants act as a repellent to keep unwanted insects away e.g. marigold which is said to keep the soft bodied insects away. Yet another mechanism is to lure away the unwanted insects. This is to be said for anise hyssop which attracts the white cabbage butterfly. We are experimenting with hyssop to see if this is the case. Table 4-8 will assist in the selection of the beneficial plant or insect that needs to be enhanced or supported.

*Products based on pyrethrum will kill all insects, predators or not.
Using Bt (bacillus thuringiensis) brings with it the dependence on an outside source.*

While gardening, some crops will become survival crops. As you keep the seeds for regeneration, they will become climatized and bring forth successive healthy crops.

Chrysanthemum leaves dried and pulverized can be used as an insecticide. The leaves contain pyrethrum which is used in many commercial pesticides. The strong poison will fight many insects, including predators, therefore I do **not recommend** the use of it. The available product Bt (Bacillus thuringiensis), discovered in 1901 kills a variety of caterpillars, especially on cabbage plants, not harming other insects or birds, and would be a better alternative. Unfortunately certain moths have shown resistance to it. You are, however, again dependent on an outside source which is not a desired alternative. We have had some success with catching the white butterflies that lay 200 to 300 of these yellow eggs per day on cabbage plants. Our children have done most of the catching with a net used to scoop up small fish. With a little incentive of 5 cents a butterfly the kids became very enthusiastic. In the following season we burned the butterflies, mixed with straw, and spread the ash at the time the first butterflies appeared. Sometimes we had not enough butterflies to catch anymore and a new cycle started. Other possibilities are to use stockings to cover the heads. Some suggest sprinkling the damp leaves with rye flour. The worms eat it and will bloat, then die. While understanding the concept of harmony it will become evident that the enforced killing of intruders will not contribute to a natural balance. Eventually harmony will be established by having enough natural predators such as blue birds, chickadees and others to keep the cabbage moth in balance.

7. What to seed

With all the above information, we can put the puzzle together. This section describes a way to lay out the vegetable garden, keeping in mind the **requirements** of the plants in regards to the **soil**, the **crop rotation**, **polyculture** and the **companion planting**. These criteria depend on each other. The timing of such a garden will be discussed later in this chapter. It is often a temptation for the learning gardener to choose the new, different or unusual plants that are so attractively advertised in many seed catalogues. But it is wiser to postpone such experiments until you have enough experience to assess such special requirements. A great number of these seeds are hybrids and are only a few generations away from the experimental stage. It takes time to determine if they are able to grow in a Harmonic Farming environment. New breeds will usually depend on chemical fertilizers. Many new varieties of plants may not be useful to the harmonic farming environment due to the seed producer responding to the commercial growers, their prime customers.

We call certain vegetables the survival crops, due to the fact that we maintain our own seed stock for these, most dating back to 1981. They are:

– Carrot, garlic, potato

– Pole and bush bean, corn, pea, tomato, pumpkin

– Cress, spinach (green and red orach), rhubarb, comfrey

Comfrey, once planted will re-grow very easily, can be propagated via roots and does not need to be seeded again. It can grow in a separate spot away from the vegetable garden, requires very little tending and is shade tolerant. In conjunction with all the berries, fruits, herbs, animal products, filbert nuts and some flowers, a balanced range of nourishment can be enjoyed. And this is not meant physically only but spiritually as well, keeping in mind what has been said in chapter one.

Fig. 4-1 shows a layout of four garden plots (a to d) and the rotation to follow. I'm sure that other layouts will be as useful if not better. It is for the advanced farmer to try out such things. It takes into account all the criteria discussed previously. It is important to ensure that the plot with **beans and peas** is **ahead of the cabbage** plot, in order to enhance the soil with nitrogen. Also remember that because garlic is seeded in the fall you must make sure that the spot on the next plot will be vacant in the fall. Corn and tomatoes will only stand until the first frost at which time the seed bed can be cleaned and garlic planted. Potatoes also can be removed early, but for storage you may leave them a bit longer in the soil as they can take a light frost. They seem to keep longer if handled thus. These plots do not need to be side by side, but can be, if so desired. They can also be arranged in a circular manner. With a circular arrangement boarders may become mandatory in order to separate crops like cabbage and potatoes. Border crops could also be seeded within the plots and eventually they will re-seed themselves; this approach is suitable for coriander, sunflower, dill, parsley, borage for the bees and lovage, a rich herb. Hyssop (anise hyssop) need not

Herbs don't need to be separated into an herb garden, but given a chance to interact with all other plants.

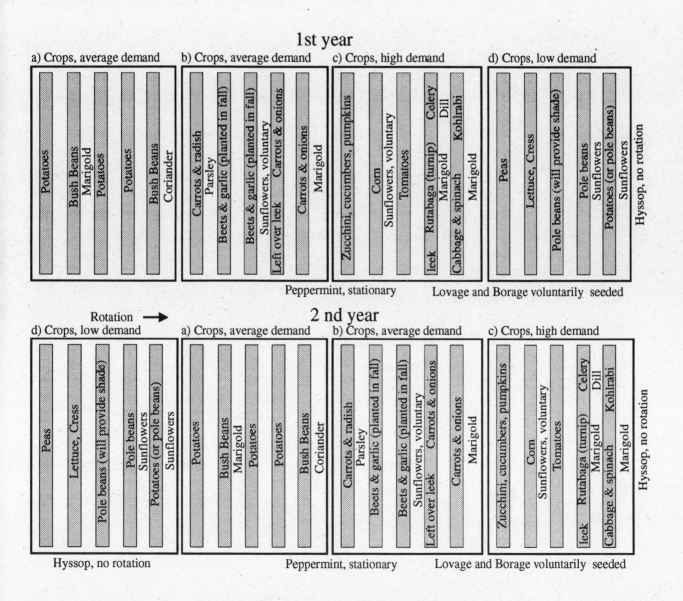

Figure 4-1, How and what to seed: a sample

be re-seeded on the same spot as it is a perennial, but carried along one year ahead of the cabbage crop.

The sunflowers can be seeded within crops, except for potatoes, where the sunflowers do not grow as nicely. The tables 4-4 and 4-6 show a small "d". After many years of observations we found that about 2 ft. (60 cm) in diameter around the sunflower plant, there is little else growing. We attribute this to the large roots they form and with it take away all the moisture. We therefore consider them as being neutral. They do, however, produce a lot of food for the goats and rabbits and harmonize with the rest of the garden. They may be seeded in such a way as to provide shade to the lettuce and peas, which do not like the intense sun in the more southern regions during the summer. However, the most beneficial part of the sunflower is the seeds it provides for the birds as well as the pollen for the bees in late fall. With lots of birds around a garden will be well protected. Despite some advice to the contrary we have planted sunflowers near pole beans with positive results. So long as they are planted about 1 ft. (30 cm) from the roots of the beans, and grow about the same height or higher at the same time there should be no problem. Pole bean crops have been plentiful and the sunflowers grew very well too.

Because the sunflower orients itself towards the sun and is neutral in regards to companion plantings, we are experimenting extensively with this plant to provide a certain shade cover and protection from ultraviolet rays for the vegetable crops below (ultra violet rays penetrating the now depleted ozone layer have been found to cause skin cancer). Sunflowers spread 4 ft. (120 cm) apart, planted along the seed beds will not affect most vegetable crops growing below. The bottom leaves should be

For us, the sunflower has become a symbol of harmony: for us to share the beauty, for the animals to feed from and to protect the garden.

broken off frequently to achieve such a cover. The leaves can be fed to the animals. With this the sunflowers will grow fairly tall to allow enough light to the plants below, but with less direct sunlight. Eventually the still green stalks can be fed to the goats. In our research we take advantage of the sunflower as a major contributor in terms of shade and protection, beauty, soil improvement, bird and insect attraction and animal feed. More studies have to be done in this regard and, specifically, the impact of ultraviolet rays measured; something we are not able to do at this point.

Coriander and marigolds can also be seeded within the crops, especially with potatoes, cabbage and peppers (the latter is not incorporated in fig. 4-1). Coriander repels aphids while being immune to them itself and bees are attracted to the blossom. Coriander is also a healing plant and the smell it distributes throughout the area always reminds me of the large open air markets in India with all the other herbs, some that don't grow in our region, mixed in. Marigolds control nematodes and should be planted with the potatoes. Peppermint (mint) helps the tomatoes and the cabbages to repel the white cabbage butterfly, aphids and white flies. You can take fresh cuttings of mint every few days and lay them between or on top of the cabbage. Once planted, peppermint is very hard to remove from that spot, so use caution when planting it. Hyssop has the advantage that it attracts the bees, as it is a very good nectar source and at the same time is said to lure away the white cabbage butterfly. Borage is a good plant for providing nectar for the bees. Its green leaves can be used as animal feed late in the fall as it withstands light frosts. Dill will benefit the cabbage plant and improve its health and growth. Contradictory to advice from other sources our tomatoes have produced well beside corn. This may be due to the fact that we don't have the corn earworm which is identical to the tomato fruitworm.

Tomatoes, not incorporated as shown in fig. 4-1, can be grown in one and the same spot for many years if well-rotted manure is applied every year in late fall. Tomatoes support gooseberry bushes in their growth. Witloof, which is not shown in fig. 4-1, would fit in with carrots and with the possibility to store the roots in the sand over winter you could enjoy eating the tasty white cones starting to poke through the sand around the end of February or once the temperature in the root cellar is above 45°F (7°C).

The length of any row of the same plant should be kept within 150 ft. (50 m) to further limit the possibility of a disease spreading over a large area.

As you can see, the bees, birds and insects need to be taken into the layout to achieve harmony. Fruit trees and berry bushes can easily be planted alongside the vegetable garden in such a manner so as not to take away the sun-light. Alternatively you can plant them within close proximity as in an orchard. Garlic around the stem of fruit trees is used to repel certain insects and to support the tree's growth. In the young stages of the fruit trees, the vegetable garden can be with the fruit trees. Later on the shadow of the mature trees and its lush leaves, will reduce the vigorous growth of many vegetables beneath and pruning of the trees would have to be done with a compromise for both.

8. Planetary influences

For us, the universe has always been something mysterious in terms of what it may be and where its limit is. Planets, a little more familiar to us, have been studied for many thousands of years, scientifically and otherwise. As much as it may sound mysterious the planets do have an influence on the plant life as well as the animals. The most profound experience I have may be the experience with the bees and their stinging behavior. Another is the influence of the moon not just on the plants but on our moods and behaviour as well. If we now understand and know the existence and the influence of cycles as described in chapter 1, (fig. 1-1), then we can also understand that the planetary cycles influence us with positive as well as negative reactions.

As modern humans our lives are not really bound to any of these cycles, it seems. In winter we may swim in a heated pool, equip ourselves to survive in the coldest weather or take a plane to the south. We are not forced to take note of the moon, and with electricity everywhere we can ignore the earth cycle (seasons and with this days and nights of different duration). The animal life is tied much closer to such influence and plants are bound quite directly. If we would take into consideration all the factors that contribute to the health of the plant life (as explained earlier a fundamental building block for harmony), we would have to introduce the rhythms of the cosmos into our daily work. And as we travel along this new ground we may find ourselves more and more happy to integrate our lives with these cycles.

Maria Thun and other people have experimented with large plantings to study these influences as originally brought forward by Rudolf Steiner (Geisteswissenschaftliche Grundlagen zum Gedeihen der Landwirtschaft. The title of the English edition is Agriculture, see Appendix A). One of the results of this is the publishing of two calendars: a calendar published every year in the German language by M. Thun-Verlag(see appendix A) as well as a cal-

Planetary cycles influence us with positive as well as negative reactions.

endar based on the first one, published every year in the English language by the Bio-Dynamic Farming and Gardening Association (see appendix A).

Ancient cultures knew of these connections and performed their agricultural tasks in concert with cosmic events. Our modern consciousness no longer "knows" the meaning of these events with instinctive wisdom and is left only with proverbial tradition or skepticism. It is in our interest to acknowledge such experience and to gain further knowledge with the task of healing the earth. We can only hope to halt the degeneration which is prevalent in nature all over the earth by renewing our relation to these cycles. This work with the planets is one aspect of a whole approach to agriculture which is also known as Bio-Dynamics. It is based on the insights of Rudolf Steiner (1861-1925) whose inspiration has proved helpful and has given new directions to many other areas of striving where the influence of materialistic thinking had begun to show its negative impacts. The nature of Rudolf Steiner's teaching is in values of **human freedom** above all and the activity of conscious, **unbiased thinking**.

8.1. A brief outline of basic astronomy

We know that the sun rises in the east and sets in the west. During its travel over the year it moves through 12 of the 88 known constellations. Constellations refer to stars that together form a particular figure that has been given a name by our ancestors, e.g. Orion, Aquarius. In the olden days the earth was taken as the reference. This geocentric (earth centred) theory was devised by the Greek astronomer, Ptolemy, around 100 A.D. In 1543 Copernicus revealed his heliocentric (sun centred) theory which claims that the sun is the centre of the planetary system. It should be noted that positions for planets and stars still today are given in relation to the earth. In astronomy we call the equator "celestial" equator and a position of another star is given in declination and right ascension. It is the celestial sphere that is taken as a measure in order to determine positions of planets. This allows us to calculate the time it takes for a planet to make one complete circuit around the celestial sphere, called the **SIDEREAL PERIOD** (Sun 1 year, Moon 27 1/3 days, Mercury 88 days, Venus 225 days, Mars 1.9 years, Jupiter 11.9 years, Saturn 29.7 years, Uranus 83.7 years, Neptune 166 years and Pluto 247.7 years).

Another period is observed when the planet returns to the same relationship it had with the Sun. The cycle can easily be observed with the full moon-to-full moon cycle. This is called the **SYNODIC PERIOD**. It is well known that the synodic moon cycle also has its effect on the life on earth. In this case we deal with the moon's influence itself. Now it is important to be aware that the moon can work on earth only through the element of water. Water must be present as a carrier to bring the force into action. How water acts in plants and soil can be compared to how blood acts in our body. The complete synodic period for the moon is 29½ days, showing the pattern of waxing and waning. I have observed the weather pattern around a full moon, and learned that, for example, a run-off (water from melted snow in the spring) usually continues to run until full moon and then disappears with the moon waning (getting smaller again). Also changes in weather are imminent, e.g. it is more likely to rain right after a full moon if clouds are present. Further evidence of influence by the moon is the movement of the sea, having ebb and flood, the cycle of the tide. This short astronomy description in a condensed form is necessary to understand the rudimentary workings of the stars and planets and how these relate to your work with plants. To fully use the knowledge and experience of these actions, it is best to use a calendar mentioned above, in order to benefit from this knowledge.

8.2. Planetary influences and their characteristics

With many experiments and the valuable information from Rudolf Steiner, Maria Thun has come up with four main cycles that influence the plant life. They follow a pattern and are listed in sequence as follows: Root days, Flower days, Leaf days, Fruit days. Table 4-1 shows the days for the particular plants and the actions recommended. Below is a summary about what plant belongs to what cycle. Working with these cycles gives you a good tool to plan your garden activities.

- **Root days**: Radish, turnip, rutabaga, beet, celeriac, parsnip, potato, carrot, onion, etc.

- **Flower days**: Any flowers, sunflower, canola (rape-seed), flax, borage, broccoli, herbs from which the flowers are used. Flowers for drying. Fresh flowers will keep the scent longer, as well as oil produced from flowers.

- **Leaf days**: cabbage, kohlrabi, lettuce, spinach, celery, parsley, herbs from which the leaves are used, animal feed e.g. forage and hay, asparagus. Leaf plants can be harvested on leaf days but for storage flower or fruit days are preferred. Table 4-1 reflects this, as vegetables and herbs for storage are marked for such days.

- **Fruit days**: All plants of which the fruit is part of the seed. Bean, pea, lentil, soy-bean, corn, tomato, cucumber, pumpkin, wheat. All fruit plants are best picked on fruit days, and in addition, for fruits to put into storage, you wait for an uprising moon, not to be confused with the waxing moon, the synodic period (see above about the difference).

With this in mind we are now ready to start the planning of the timing for our crops. Even if you do not use the calendar mentioned above plants will still grow fine but you lose one cycle of harmony that brings a lot of pleasure and excitement to the task. Many other sources have descriptions of influences to plants by planets, particularly the moon. Important to all this is that we are no longer just preserving or restoring nature, but transforming it, through our effort, into something new. We will become creative forces in nature and society, as opposed to being destructive influences. And ultimately such life is a melody, harmony. Such a new vibration is invisible to the material form of life but it exists now.

On a more philosophical note, to look up at the stars is like looking into the soil which reveals millions of bacterial and insect lives in just a pinch of it. I wonder how many millions of lives these bacteria see in their soil and so on. Our sun is just one more star, small in comparison to others and to the many more in the milky way and in other galaxies. With such a view it may become easier to understand that there is no distance. What small or large means is a comparison to the material things around us. We are not able to grasp the vastness around us, like an ant on the ground knows little about our world. I like to speculate that we are just a fraction of a form, plant or a person? As long as we don't know, it may be of foremost importance to keep this fraction unharmed or someone may one day

Figure 4-2, Sample pattern of a garden layout.

not like it anymore, grab it and throw it away.

9.When to seed

This topic may be easily documented, but the timing for planting in your region may vary slightly. You may be able to take advantage of a location with more moderate weather and less chance of frost. The best thing to do is to observe and write down weather patterns. With this in mind, table 4-9 will guide you in your achievement. Most seeds purchased in stores or from seed houses will come with instructions on how and when to seed. If not sure take the more conservative route or, if possible, ask an experienced neighbour. Of course, if the calendar or the seed catalogue tells you to seed on a particular day, and the weather is just not cooperating, you will have to plan for another day. Timing is critical because some regions have a rather short season and a quick change from spring to summer, but all is not lost. Much can be gained by tending the seedlings and plants with some extra care during their growth. At this point you should be able to lay out your garden and fig. 4-2 may serve as a pattern. To calculate the size of the garden, row spacing needs to be addressed as discussed in chapter five.

KEY: H Harvest, store / T Tend, care / S Seed, plant
KEY: A Heavy feeder / B Average feeder / C Light feeder

Cosmic influence

Plants	ROOT	FLOWER	LEAF	FRUIT	Soil demand
Alfalfa, hay		H	TS	H	C
Aloe Vera		H	TS	H	
Amaranth		H	TS	H	C
Anglica					
Anise					
Apple tree				HTS	
Apricot tree				HTS	
Asparagus			HTS		A
Azalea		HTS			
Basil		H	TS	H	C
Bean, green				HTS	C
Bean, Bush				HTS	C
Bean, Lima				HTS	C
Bean, Pole				HTS	C
Bean, Soya				HTS	C
Beet	HTS				B
Blackberry, Blackcaps				HTS	
Borage		H	TS	H	B
Broccoli		HTS			A
Brussels sprout		H	TS	H	A
Buttercup's family		HTS			
Cabbage family		H	TS	H	A
Camomile		HTS			C
Caraway					C
Carrot	HTS				B
Cauliflower		H	TS	H	A
Celeriac	HTS				A
Celery		H	TS	H	A
Charlock					
Chive		H	TS	H	C
Clover, hay		H	TS	H	C
Coriander		H	TS	H	C
Corn				HTS	A
Cress		H	TS	H	C
Cucumber				HTS	A
Cypress Spurge					
Dandelion		HTS			C
Dill		H	TS	H	C
Dry cayenne pepper				HTS	AB
Eggplant				HTS	A
Endive			HTS		B
Fennel		H	TS	H	C
Fruit trees				HTS	
Garlic	HTS				B
Geranium		HTS			
Geranium, white		HTS			
Ginseng	HTS				
Gooseberry				HTS	
Grape				HTS	
Hemp (illegal in Canada)		H	TS	H	
Henbane					
Horseradish	HTS				
Hyssop		HTS			
Jerusalem artichoke	HTS				B
Kale			HTS		A
Kohlrabi		H	TS	H	A
Lamb's Quarter		H	TS	H	
Leek			HTS		A

Plants	ROOT	FLOWER	LEAF	FRUIT	Soil demand
Lettuce			HTS		B
Locust tree (poisonous)					
Loganberry			HTS		
Marigold		HTS			
Marjoram		H	TS	H	C
Melon				HTS	A
Mint		H	TS	H	C
Muskmelon				HTS	A
Mustard and family				HTS	C
Nasturtium		HTS			
Oak					
Oats				HTS	B
Onion	HTS				B
Oregano		H	TS	H	C
Pansy, wild					
Parsnip	HTS				B
Parsley		H	TS	H	A
Pea				HTS	C
Peach tree				HTS	
Peony					
Peppermint		H	TS	H	C
Potato	HTS				B
Pumpkin				HTS	A
Radish	HTS				B
Raspberry				HTS	
Rhododendron		HTS			
Rhubarb			HTS		B
Rose		HTS			
Rosemary		H	TS	H	C
Rye				HTS	B
Sage		H	TS	H	C
Salsify	HTS				B
Savory, summer		H	TS	H	
Shallot			HTS		B
Southernwood		H	TS	H	
Sow Thistle		HTS			
Spinach			HTS		AB
Squash				HTS	A
Stinging Nettle		H	TS	H	
Strawberry				HTS	
Sunflower		HTS			B
Swiss Chard, Mangold			HTS		B
Thyme		H	TS	H	C
Tomato				HTS	A
Tree, pruning paste					
Turnip, Rutabaga	HTS				B
Valerian		HTS			
Walnut, black				HTS	
Watermelon				HTS	A
Witloof			HTS		B
Wormwood		H	TS	H	
Zinnia		HTS			
Zucchini				HTS	A

Table 4-1, Cosmic properties and plant's requirements

COMPANION PLANTS	Alfalfa	Aloe Vera	Amaranth	Anglica	Anise	Apple tree	Apricot tree	Asparagus	Azalea	Basil	Bean, green	Bean, bush	Bean, lima	Bean, pole	Bean, Soya	Beet	Blackberry, Blackcaps	Borage	Broccoli	Brussels sprout	Buttercup's family	Cabbage family	Camomile	Caraway	Carrot	Cauliflower	Celeriac, Celery	Charlock	Chive	Clover	Coriander	Corn	Cress	Cucumber	Cypress Spurge	Dandelion	Dill	Dry cayenne pepper	Eggplant	Endive	Fennel	Fruit trees
Alfalfa																																				a						
Aloe Vera																																										
Amaranth																																a										
Anglica																																										
Anise																															a											
Apple tree																																										
Apricot tree																																										
Asparagus										a																													A			
Azalea																																										
Basil								a																																		
Bean, green																										d						a		A						a		
Bean, Bush													A						A	A		A			A	A			d			a	a	A							D	
Bean, Lima																													d			a	a									
Bean, Pole																d			A	A		A			A	A			d			a	A	A						A	D	
Bean, Soya																													d			a										
Beet											A			d									a	a		a	A		a		d	D		A		A						
Blackberry, Blackcaps																																										
Borage																																										
Broccoli											A		A			a							a				A							A		a				A		
Brussels sprout											A		A			a							a				A							A		a				A		
Buttercup's family																														d												
Cabbage family											A		A			a							D				A							A		a				A		
Camomile																			a	a		a				a																
Caraway																																									d	
Carrot																A													a							A						
Cauliflower											A		A			a							a				A									a						
Celeriac, Celery											A		A						A	A		A				A						D		A								
Charlock																d																										
Chive											d	d	d	d	d												a														a	a
Clover																					d																				a	a
Coriander			a																																						d	
Corn		a									a	a	a	a	a	D											D							a								
Cress																A																										A
Cucumber											A	A	A	A		A			A	A		A					A					a				A					A	
Cypress Spurge																																										
Dandelion	a																																									
Dill						A													A				a	a		a	A		a					A								
Dry cayenne pepper																																							a			
Eggplant										a																																
Endive												A							A	A		A																		A		
Fennel												D		D										d							d			A						A		
Fruit trees																													a	a		A										
Garlic												d	D	d	D	d	A		D	D		D			A	D								A								A
Geranium																			a	a		a				a						a										
Geranium, white																																										
Ginseng																																										
Gooseberry																																										
Grape																											a									d						
Hemp (illegal in Canada)																			a	a		a				a																
Henbane																														d												
Horseradish																																										A
Hyssop																			a	a		a				a																
Jerusalem artichoke																																a										
Kale												A		A		a										a								A		a				A		
Kohlrabi								A			A	A	A													A								a		a					d	
Lamb's Quarter																																a		a								
Leek											D	D		D		D			A	A		A			A	A	A														A	
Lettuce								A			A	A		A		a			A	A		A				a	A	D						A		A				A		A

Code: A = Attracts; D = Dislikes

Table 4-2, Companion plants (1 of 6)

COMPANION PLANTS	Alfalfa	Aloe Vera	Amaranth	Anglica	Anise	Apple tree	Apricot tree	Asparagus	Azalea	Basil	Bean, green	Bean, bush	Bean, lima	Bean, pole	Bean, Soya	Beet	Blackberry, Blackcaps	Borage	Broccoli	Brussels sprout	Buttercup's family	Cabbage family	Camomile	Caraway	Carrot	Cauliflower	Celeriac, Celery	Charlock	Chive	Clover	Coriander	Corn	Cress	Cucumber	Cypress Spurge	Dandelion	Dill	Dry cayenne pepper	Eggplant	Endive	Fennel	Fruit trees
Locust tree (poisonous)													a																													
Loganberry																																										
Marigold											a	a	a	a																	a											
Marjoram																																										
Melon																															a											
Mint																			a	a		a				a																
Muskmelon																																										
Mustard and family																	d																									a
Nasturtium								a											a	a		a				a								a								a
Oak																																										
Oats																																										
Onion		a									D	D	d	D	D	d	A		D	D		D	A		A	D								A					A			a
Oregano																																										
Pansy, wild																																										
Parsnip																																										
Parsley						a																			a																	
Pea											D	D		D					A	A		A		a	A	A	a					a		a				A			A	
Peach tree																																										
Peony																														d												
Peppermint																			a	a		a			a	a																
Potato		a			d						a	a	a			D			D	D		D			D	D						a			d				a			
Pumpkin																																a										
Radish												A		A		a			A	A		A			A									A	D							
Raspberry																	d																									
Rhododendron									a																																	
Rhubarb												A							A	A		A			A																	
Rose																													a													
Rosemary																			a	a		a			a	a																
Rye																																										
Sage																			a	a		a			a	a									d						A	
Salsify																									a																	
Savory, summer											a	a	a	a																												
Shallot											d	d	d	d																												
Southernwood																			a	a		a			a																	
Sow Thistle																																			a							
Spinach																A			A	A		A			A																	
Squash																																a										a
Stinging Nettle			a																																							
Strawberry												a						a	A	A		A			A																	
Sunflower														A																		a	a									
Swiss Chard, Mangold														A					A	A		A			A	A																
Thyme																																										
Tomato						d	a		a		A	a							A	A		A			A	A	A		a			A		D							D	
Tree, pruning paste		a																																								
Turnip, Rutabaga												A		A																							A					
Valerian																																										
Walnut, black								d									d																									
Watermelon																																										
Witloof														A																											A	
Wormwood																			a	a		a			a	a															d	
Zinnia																																										
Zucchini														A																												

Code: A = Attracts; D = Dislikes

Table 4-3, Companion plants (2 of 6)

COMPANION PLANTS	Garlic	Geranium	Geranium, white	Ginseng	Gooseberry	Grape	Hemp (illegal in Canada)	Henbane	Horseradish	Hyssop	Jerusalem artichoke	Kale	Kohlrabi	Lamb's quarter	Leek	Lettuce	Locust tree	Loganberry	Marigold	Marjoram	Melon	Mint	Muskmelon	Mustard and family	Nasturtium	Oak	Oat	Onion	Oregano	Pansy, wild	Parsnip	Parsley	Pea	Peach tree	Peony	peppermint	Potato	Pumpkin	Radish	Raspberry	Rhododendron	Rhubarb
Alfalfa																																										
Aloe Vera																																										
Amaranth																												a									a					
Anglica																																										
Anise																																										
Apple tree																									a												d					
Apricot tree																																										
Asparagus												A				A																a										
Azalea																																									a	
Basil																																										
Bean, green	d														D	A			a									D				D										
Bean, Bush	D											A	A		D	A			a									D				D					a		A			A
Bean, Lima	d														D	A	a		a									d									a					
Bean, Pole	D											A	A		D	A			a									D				D					a		A			
Bean, Soya	d																											d														
Beet	A												a	A	D	a							d					A									D		a			
Blackberry, Blackcaps																																								d		
Borage																																										
Broccoli	D	a			a					a					A	A				a					a			D				A				a	D		A			A
Brussels sprout	D	a			a					a					A	A				a					a			D				A				a	D		A			A
Buttercup's family																																										
Cabbage family	D	a			a					a					A	A				a					a			D				A				a	D		A			A
Camomile										a																		A														
Caraway																																a										
Carrot	A														A	a												A			a	A				a			A			
Cauliflower	D	a			a					a					A	A				a					a			D				A				a	D					A
Celeriac, Celery												A	A		A	D																a					D					
Charlock																																										
Chive																																										
Clover				a	d																															d						
Coriander																																										
Corn		a								a				a	A				a		a							a											a	a		
Cress																																							A			
Cucumber	A											A	a	a		A									a			A				a							d	D		
Cypress Spurge				d																																						
Dandelion																																										
Dill										a						A												A				A										
Dry cayenne pepper																																										
Eggplant																																				a						
Endive												A			A																											
Fennel													d			A																A										
Fruit trees	A								A															a	a			a														
Garlic												D																									D	a				
Geranium				a								a																														
Geranium, white																																										
Ginseng																																										
Gooseberry																																										
Grape		a								a																																
Hemp (illegal in Canada)										a																											a					
Henbane																																										
Horseradish																																							A			
Hyssop				a						a																													d			
Jerusalem artichoke																																										
Kale	D	a			a					a					A	A				a					a			D				A				a	D		A			A
Kohlrabi															A	A								a				A											A	A		
Lamb's Quarter																			a			a									a					a	a	a	a			
Leek												A	A			A												a									D					
Lettuce												A	A	A														A		D		A							A			A

Code: A = Attracts; D = Dislikes

Table 4-4, Companion plants (3 of 6)

COMPANION PLANTS	Garlic	Geranium	Geranium, white	Ginseng	Gooseberry	Grape	Hemp (illegal in Canada)	Henbane	Horseradish	Hyssop	Jerusalem artichoke	Kale	Kohlrabi	Lamb's quarter	Leek	Lettuce	Locust tree	Loganberry	Marigold	Marjoram	Melon	Mint	Muskmelon	Mustard and family	Nasturtium	Oak	Oat	Onion	Oregano	Pansy, wild	Parsnip	Parsley	Pea	Peach tree	Peony	peppermint	Potato	Pumpkin	Radish	Raspberry	Rhododendron	Rhubarb
Locust tree (poisonous)																																										
Loganberry																																									d	
Marigold														a																							a					
Marjoram																																										
Melon																																					d		a			
Mint												a																														
Muskmelon														a																												
Mustard and family													a																													
Nasturtium												a																									a		a			
Oak																																										
Oats																																										
Onion												D	a		a	A													a	a	d						d					
Oregano																																										
Pansy, wild														a																												
Parsnip																																a							a			
Parsley															D																a								A			
Pea	D											A	A		D	A																d					D		A			
Peach tree	a																																									
Peony														a																												
Peppermint												a				A																				A						
Potato				a		A						D	A	a						a	d			a				d						D		A	A	d	d	d	
Pumpkin														a																							d					
Radish										d		A	A			A				a				a						a	A	A					d					
Raspberry																		d																			d					
Rhododendron																																										
Rhubarb												A				A																										
Rose	a																											a						a								
Rosemary												a																														
Rye																												a		a							a					
Sage												a																														
Salsify													A		A	A																										
Savory, summer																												a														
Shallot																																										
Southernwood												a																														
Sow Thistle																											a												a			
Spinach												A	A																										A	A		A
Squash																								a													d		a			
Stinging Nettle																	a					a					a										a					
Strawberry	A											A	d		A	A				a								A											A			
Sunflower																								a													d					
Swiss Chard, Mangold												A				a																							A			
Thyme																																										
Tomato	A			a								A	A		A	A				a		a			a			a				A	D				A	D	A			
Tree, pruning paste																																										
Turnip, Rutabaga																A														A												
Valerian																																										
Walnut, black																																					d				d	
Watermelon														a																												
Witloof																A																										
Wormwood												a																														
Zinnia														a																												
Zucchini																												A														

Code: A = Attracts; D = Dislikes

Table 4-5, Companion plants (4 of 6)

COMPANION PLANTS	Rose	Rosemary	Rye	Sage	Salsify	Savory, summer	Shallot	Southernwood	Sow Thistle	Spinach	Squash	Stiging nettle	Strawberry	Sunflower	Swiss Chard, Mangold	Thyme	Tomato	Tree, pruning paste	Turnip, Rutabaga	Valerian	Walnut, black	Water melon	Witloof	Wormwood	Zinnia	Zucchini
Alfalfa																										
Aloe Vera																	a									
Amaranth																										
Anglica									a																	
Anise																										
Apple tree																										
Apricot tree																	d									
Asparagus																	a									
Azalea																					d					
Basil																	a									
Bean, green						a	d																			
Bean, bush						a	d						a	A	A		A									
Bean, lima						a	d										a									
Bean, pole						a	d			A			A		A						A	A				
Bean, Soya																										
Beet																										
Blackberry, Blackcaps																					d					
Borage													a													
Broccoli		a		a		a		A					A	A	A									a		
Brussels sprout		a		a		a		A					A	A	A									a		
Buttercup's family																										
Cabbage family		a		a		a		A					A	A	A									a		
Camomile																										
Caraway																										
Carrot		a		a	a									A			A				A	a				
Cauliflower		a		a		a		A					A	A	A									a		
Celeriac, Celery															A											
Charlock																										
Chive	a																a									
Clover																										
Coriander																										
Corn										a	a			a	A											
Cress																										
Cucumber				d				a						a			D									
Cypress Spurge																										
Dandelion																										
Dill																		A								
Dry cayenne pepper																										
Eggplant																										
Endive																										
Fennel				A													D				A	d				
Fruit trees												a														
Garlic	a												A				A									
Geranium																										
Geranium white																										
Ginseng																										
Gooseberry																	a									
Grape																										
Hemp (illegal in Canada)																										
Henbane																										
Horseradish																										
Hyssop																										
Jerusalem artichoke																										
Kale		a		a		a		A					A	A	A									a		
Kohlrabi				A				A					d		A											
Lamb's Quarter																					a		a			
Leek				A										A	A											
Lettuce				A									A	a	A		A				A					

Code: A = Attracts; D = Dislikes

Table 4-6, Companion plants (5 of 6)

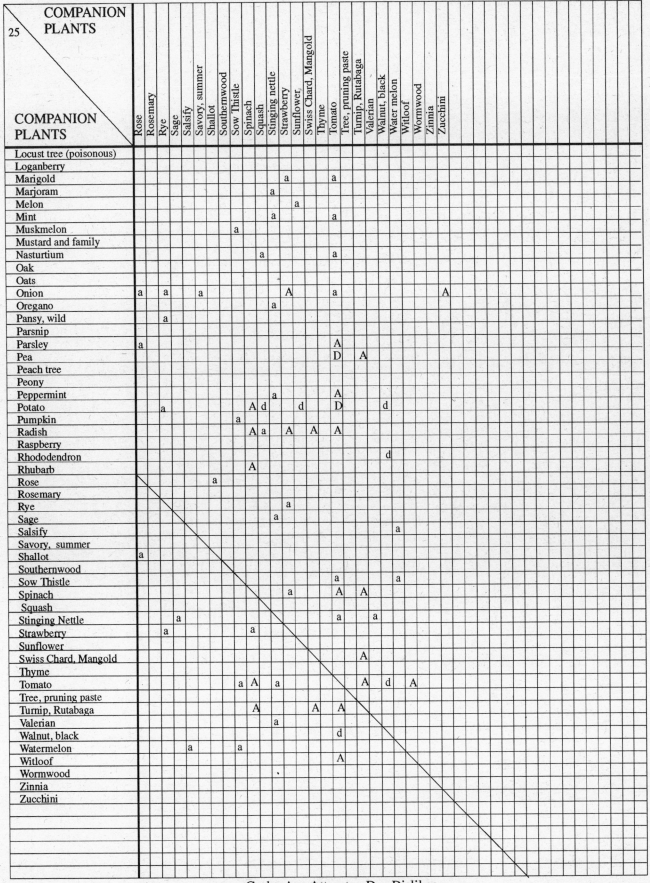

COMPANION PLANTS / 25 COMPANION PLANTS	Rose	Rosemary	Rye	Sage	Salsify	Savory, summer	Shallot	Southernwood	Sow Thistle	Spinach	Squash	Stinging nettle	Strawberry	Sunflower	Swiss Chard, Mangold	Thyme	Tomato	Tree, pruning paste	Turnip, Rutabaga	Valerian	Walnut, black	Water melon	Witloof	Wormwood	Zinnia	Zucchini
Locust tree (poisonous)																										
Loganberry																										
Marigold												a					a									
Marjoram										a																
Melon															a											
Mint												a					a									
Muskmelon									a																	
Mustard and family																										
Nasturtium												a					a									
Oak																										
Oats																										
Onion	a	a		a									A				a								A	
Oregano												a														
Pansy, wild		a																								
Parsnip																										
Parsley	a																A									
Pea																	D	A								
Peach tree																										
Peony																										
Peppermint												a					A									
Potato		a								A	d			d			D				d					
Pumpkin									a																	
Radish										A	a		A		A		A									
Raspberry																										
Rhododendron																					d					
Rhubarb										A																
Rose						a																				
Rosemary																										
Rye												a														
Sage										a																
Salsify																					a					
Savory, summer																										
Shallot	a																									
Southernwood																										
Sow Thistle																	a				a					
Spinach												a					A	A								
Squash																										
Stinging Nettle				a													a			a						
Strawberry		a							a																	
Sunflower																										
Swiss Chard, Mangold																	A									
Thyme																										
Tomato									a	A		a							A		d		A			
Tree, pruning paste																										
Turnip, Rutabaga										A					A		A									
Valerian												a														
Walnut, black																	d									
Watermelon					a				a																	
Witloof															A											
Wormwood																										
Zinnia																										
Zucchini																										

Code: A = Attracts; D = Dislikes

Table 4-7, Companion plants (6 of 6)

To affect these / Use these	Animal Intruders	Ant	Aphid	Asparagus Beetle	Bean Beetle	Black Fly	Cabbage Moth (Butterfly)	Carrot Fly	Caterpillars	Corn Earworm	Dogs	Flea Beetle	Fly	Fruit Tree Borer	Fruit Tree Mite	Insects, soft body	Japanese beetle	Ladybug	Maggots, root	Mexican Bean Beetle	Mice	Mildew	Mole	Mosquito	Mosquito, malaria	Moth, cloth	Nematode, Eelworm	Nymph	Onion Fly	Pear Psylla	Plant Lice	Potato Bug	Rust Mite	Slug	Squash Bug	Syrphid Flies	Striped Cucumber Beetle	Striped Pumpkin Beetle	Ticks	Tomato Fruitworm	Wax Moth (bees wax)	Webworm	Weevils	White Fly	Woolly Aphid
PLANTS, MATERIALS																																													
Ash, wood			R	R														R																											
Basil													R									R																							
Borage								R	R																																		R	R	
Calendula, Pot Marigold				R				R	R			R																															R	R	
Castor Bean																						R							R																
Catnip		*										*		R																															
Cauliflower with celery				R																																									
Celery												R																																	
Chive																					R																								
Elder												R									R	R																							
Flax																																	R												
Garlic			E											R	R		R				E						E													R			R		
Geranium, white							R								R																														
Hemp (illegal in Canada)							R																								R														
Horseradish																															R	R													
Horsetail																						*																							
Hot Pepper		*																																											
Hyssop				-H																																									
Lamb's Quarter																	H																												
Lavender																								R																					
Marigold									R					R			R							R																R					
Milk, sour				*																																									
Mole Plant																					R		R																						
Nasturtium			R											R																					R		R							R	R
Oak Leaves, mulch																	R																										R	S	
Parsley						R																																							
Pennyroyal, squaw mint	R																				R								R																
Peppermint		R	R			R																					R																		
Petunia												R																																	
Phacelia																																				H									
Pitch pine, Pitch wood																				R																									
Rosemary						R	R	R															R																						
Sage							R	R																																R					
Sassafras																													R																
Southernwood												R											R																						
Soybean										R																																			
Spearmint	R	R																																											
Stinging Nettle			*			*										H																													
Summer Savory					R																																								
Sunflower		R																																											
Tansy	R													R	R																					R		R							
Thistle, Canada																H																													
Thyme							R																																						
Tomato				R			R																																						
Wormwood	R						R	R				R												R								R													
INSECTS																																													
Anthocorids			P											P	P														P																
Ants			-H																																										
Birds									P					P										P																					
Campylomma			P												P															P															
Deraeocoris			P											P	P															P															
Earwig			P																										P	P															
Frog, Toad														P																															
Ladybird Beetle			P		P									P																															
Ladybug			P											P																															
Lacewings			P											P	P															P															
Parasitic Wasp			P						P																																		P	P	
Praying Mantis			P											P																															
Predaceous Mite														P																															
Predaceous Midge			P																																										
Spider														P																															
Syrphid Flies			P																																										

Code: E = Emulsion (Oil); H = Host, welcome; P = Predator; R = Repellent; * = Spray; -H = Host, not welcome; S = Smoke

Table 4-8, Beneficial plants and insects

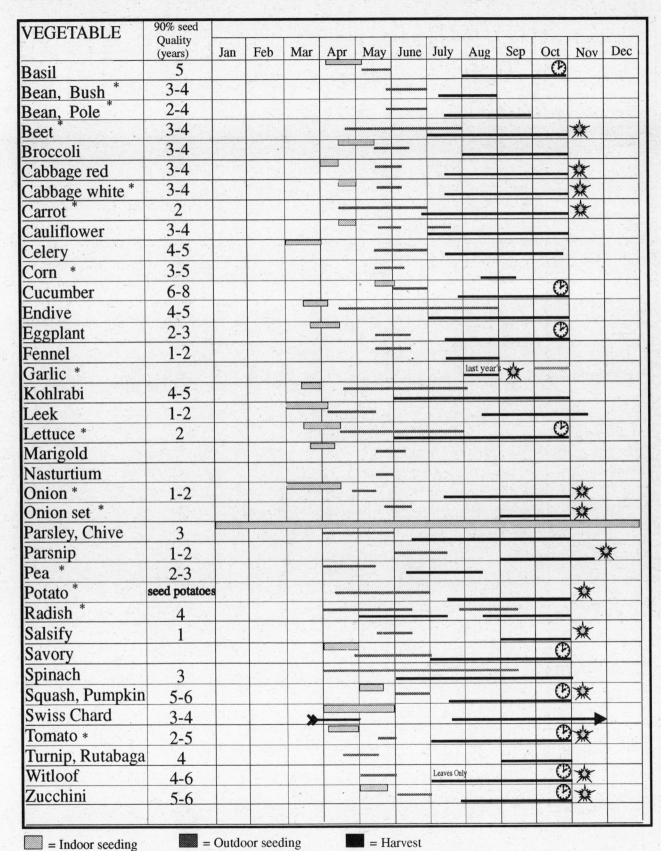

VEGETABLE	90% seed Quality (years)	Jan	Feb	Mar	Apr	May	June	July	Aug	Sep	Oct	Nov	Dec
Basil	5												
Bean, Bush *	3-4												
Bean, Pole *	2-4												
Beet *	3-4												
Broccoli	3-4												
Cabbage red	3-4												
Cabbage white *	3-4												
Carrot *	2												
Cauliflower	3-4												
Celery	4-5												
Corn *	3-5												
Cucumber	6-8												
Endive	4-5												
Eggplant	2-3												
Fennel	1-2												
Garlic *									last year's				
Kohlrabi	4-5												
Leek	1-2												
Lettuce *	2												
Marigold													
Nasturtium													
Onion *	1-2												
Onion set *													
Parsley, Chive	3												
Parsnip	1-2												
Pea *	2-3												
Potato *	seed potatoes												
Radish *	4												
Salsify	1												
Savory													
Spinach	3												
Squash, Pumpkin	5-6												
Swiss Chard	3-4												
Tomato *	2-5												
Turnip, Rutabaga	4												
Witloof	4-6								Leaves Only				
Zucchini	5-6												

= Indoor seeding = Outdoor seeding = Harvest

* = Most common crops = Harvest before 1st frost = Ready for storage

Table 4-9, Important crops and timing

Summary of activities: Early March

- After the cleansing flights have happened you can remove the scrap boards, entrance reducers and pillows (if used) at the time the buds of pussy willows open. Close the top entrance now.

- Draw the outline of the garden. The pattern shown in fig. 4-2 may be copied and used for your own purpose.

- Lay out the seed beds on a paper (rows, circles) to create 4 distinct sections. For spacing between rows see next chapter.

- Plan the desired crops in regards to the criteria mentioned in this chapter or apply the sample shown in fig. 4-1.

- If you like to plant according to the cosmic forces, order a Calendar listing the cosmic influences.

- Order the seeds.

- Seed cress, in-house, for some green salad. Use your own seeds if possible.

- Organize mulching material, preferably straw- or hay- bales.

- Once the snow is getting patchy you let the chickens roam in the garden. They may remain in there until the seeding in early April. Cover up the seed rows where the garlic and leek is placed using chicken wire. Stucco wire can be formed to a tunnel and may have to be used to protect the leek.

5

Mid March, Pussy Willows are Producing Pollen

Prepare, observe

1. Preparing the soil

1.1. Soil structure, bacteria, insects and creatures

Soil is the substance that reflects as well as assembles the cycle of life and death. Life can be divided into three general categories based on where each type lives in relation to the soil. The first is the soil organisms, such as insects, bacteria and fungi, most of which are microscopic and live out their lives in the soil only. The second category is the plant life, which lives partly in the soil and partly outside of it. The last category is animal life, which lives almost entirely above the soil. These life forms each represent cycles and are dependent on each other in complex connections not yet understood. We can understand that each natural cycle is somehow dependent on other cycles as mentioned earlier but we do not know these relations as a whole. As explained earlier, forms or shapes are made up of many other life forms and I tend to say that we are part of yet a larger form or shape. With this understanding spirit is present in all forms or shapes. But even without this understanding, one must have reverence for all

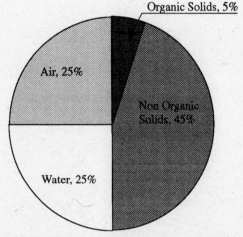

Figure 5-1, Typical soil structure

forms of life from the lowest to the highest; diligent attention and deep respect has to be given to the soil. Decaying material (bacteria, fungi, insects, decaying plant material, etc.) enriches the content of organic matter in the soil which, in turn, provides a start for the new seed or plant to grow. Typical soil is composed of the factors shown in fig. 5-1. Non organic solids are distinguished by texture, something you can feel. The smallest particles contributing to the texture are **clay**, having particles smaller than 0.00008" (0.002 mm). This is followed by **silt**, with particles larger than those of clay but smaller than 0.002" (0.05 mm). Anything from 0.002" (0.05 mm) to 0.08" (2 mm) is called **sand**. By feeling the soil, you can determine the texture of the soil. Sandy soil will feel gritty, similar to sand paper. Clay soil will be very smooth and sticky, similar to chewing gum. Incorporating organic solids, air and water with the texture assembles the soil's structure. We are able to change the soil's structure, not the texture. A fine soil offers more outside surfaces and more inter-spaces for foraging roots than does coarse soil. These inter-spaces function as capillary tubes through which free moisture from the subsoil naturally travels up to the roots of the growing plants. When rain falls, water gradually fills the spaces between the particles of soil. As gravity pulls the water down to lower levels, air returns to fill up the spaces again, thus circulating air through the soil. Not all the water is removed by gravity, however. Some water is held back by capillary, molecular and electrical forces. This is the important component of rainwater, for it is this water the plants can use. This water-holding capacity is increased by adding organic material that holds many times its own weight in water. The free water in the soil will travel and eventually enter rivers and finally the ocean, as part of the weather cycle mentioned in chapter 1, fig. 1-1. However, if this water can't be released by the soil, the passage for air to reach the bacteria and with it the root system is blocked and the plant will suffocate. If you dig a hole, remove the soil and then replace that same soil, you will notice that there is not enough soil to fill it up again. By the process of disturbing the soil, these air channels have been removed and bacterial life is required to build this up again. These billions of organisms are our voluntary work force, producing food for the roots, providing conditions for roots to grow and with their dead enriching the soil. For the soil to be able to support food producing plants or any plant for that matter, an organic matter content of at least 2% is recommended, though the average is at 5%. Every location will have its own soil texture, created over

Clay, silt and sand all are part of the soil texture.

No matter what the soil texture, organic matter can improve the structure.

thousands of years while streams and earth movements took place and still take place, maybe to a lesser degree nowadays. Many remains of glacier movements through the valleys remind us of tremendous forces that contributed to the texture of our soil. Three main groups have been found to classify the soil.

- – Loam = sand, silt, clay all equally represented
- – Silty loam = more silt
- – Sandy loam = more sand

Sand will act as a drainage but has good aeration. Clay will hold too much water in lots of small pores.

All three types of soil can be used to produce crops, while changing the structure. Organic matter acts to help bind soil particles together. To improve the soil structure, organic matter needs to be improved. Deep rooted plantings of legumes or plants with high root density will improve organic matter in the soil (e.g. rye, wheat, oats, phacelia, borage). Also tilling and mulching will improve the soil.

1.2. Potting soil

Why would potting soil be different? Such soil is usually used to bring plants to germination and to support the first growth of small roots. For this a well nourished fine soil is required. Therefore the content of **organic matter** in potting soil should be at least 25% but up to 75%. Air should be present at around 15 to 20% with silt or clay not to exceed 10%. Other materials can be added, e.g. sand (some commercial outfits use vermiculite to reduce shipping weight).

1.3. Limits to plant growth

Studies of the effect of different nutrients on plants have revealed some of the causes of limited plant growth. Soils exhibit a varying ability to supply the mineral nutrients needed by the plants and can be classified according to their fertility. Because of unbalanced structure fertility can vary from a deficiency to a sufficiency, or even toxicity (over fertilizing), of one or more of the nutrients. A serious deficiency of only one essential nutrient can still greatly reduce crop yields. For example, a soil considered fertile in all other ways could have levels of available nitrogen too low for optimum plant growth. Control of crop growth by the deficient nutrient is known as Liebig's law of the minimum. This law states that the plant growth rate is controlled by that mineral nutrient present in the most limiting quantity in the soil. These nutrients are important and all elements needed to support life are tightly related with the **nutrient cycle**. Bacteria are the microorganism most involved in keeping nutrient cycles functioning and with it providing harmony.

With current farm practices (1994), chemical fertilizers are applied to the soil to reduce or eliminate nutrient deficiency and ensure that such **created fertility** does not limit a soil's potential to produce crops. Fed with synthetic fertilizers which interfere with the existing bacterial life the soil will lack the natural process to provide the nutrients. Fertilizers disturb the bacterial life and, as explained later in this chapter, also affect the supply of minerals. Although fertilizers have dramatically changed the soil's potential and with it allowed us tremendous plant growth to produce quantities of crops, these crops are of questionable quality and at a great cost to the environment. For example DDT and PCB are present worldwide, having been found in ocean sediments and polar ice. The problem of tracing these and a thousand others is immense and environmental health researchers have just researched the tip of the iceberg.

Other variables that influence crop production are crop variety, diseases and insects. The Elements of the climate such as insufficient water, temperature extremes, and natural disasters such as wind and hail storms can all lower crop fertility.

1.4. Plants as soil indicators and soil improving agents

Some plants are true soil indicators, and their presence will often reveal the nature of the soil. This is not a complete listing of plants in this regard, but some of the most common ones are mentioned. In an old garden, one knows from experience which plants (weeds) to expect and where to look for them; yet every spring some new and perhaps completely different species may arrive, and any such change could tell us something we ought to know about the state of our land.

– Common Plantain (plantago major) will grow and prefer compressed, packed soil. You will see it grow on exposed soil used for walk ways.
– Dandelions grow in soil rich in nitrogen and in not too wet a soil. Farmers seem to dislike them in their pasture as they take over the other grasses. Usually the reason is due to over fertilizing by the animals grazing on the field.
– Canada thistle does not grow well in dry light soil.
– Stinging nettle points out nitrogen rich soil and plenty of iron. It could also be a sign of too much manure in the soil.
– Horsetail will point to a water-logged and poorly ventilated soil
– Chickweed and speedwell are infallible indicators of soil with a very high humus and nutrient content, and in particular a high content of nitrogen, so it is not

surprising that they tend to spring up in the compost we spread over our seed rows. Keeping it under control with hand weeding is important. While chickweed is really a good soil cover, it tends to take over large areas fast. Such an area can be re-claimed by seeding orchard grass seeds and using it as such for the next 2 to 3 years to provide hay.

All green manure crops are soil improving plants, for one or the other reason. Phacelia can be seeded early in spring and during the year. It makes deep roots, a fine cover, collects dew, and covers the top soil with its fine feathered leaves. Borage has soil penetrating roots to loosen up soil. As mentioned in chapter 4, legumes will bind nitrogen in the soil. Spinach will provide a superb soil cover but is an average to heavy feeder. Rye is well known to make a large root system very fast. All these factors contribute to a healthy soil.

1.5. Mulching

One efficient method to **add** organic matter to the soil is by way of mulching, particularly in sandy soil. Baled hay or straw which will separate into flats, about 3" to 4" (7 cm to 10 cm) thick, will decay within one full season. Fourteen regular hay bales will cover an area of about 1000 sq. ft. (90 m^2), leaving uncovered soil for seed rows as laid out in fig. 5-2 and shown in fig. 5-3. Using bales with less than 19 flats per bale will of course require more bales. Such mulch applied every spring will hardly be visible the following spring.

Spacing of seed rows is fixed with this method. It will make sense for vegetables such as carrots or onions to seed two rows of crops into one seed row. For cabbage the whole width of the seed row is required. When in doubt it is better to plant too far apart or else you won't be able to harvest without damaging the crop. This is particularly important with strawberries, which should be in rows at least 40" (1 m) apart. Two hay flats side by side will provide a walkway of 30" in width, which will then leave 10" for the strawberry plants. Strawberries grow very well on a patch of their own. Some garlic and onions are planted within the rows to enhance the growth of strawberries. As the name may suggest, strawberries do like to be mulched with lots of straw.

Organic matter has the greatest input to soil and crop productivity and combined with green manure (e.g. legumes, rye,

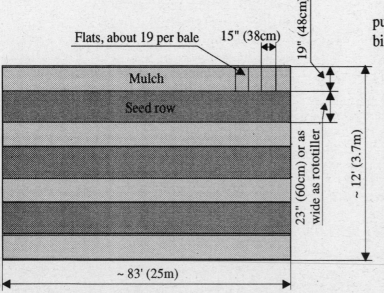

Figure 5-2, Mulching 1000 sq. ft. (90 square meter)

Figure 5-3, Mulching

spinach) will generate a healthy soil. Organic matter is formed from the break down and decay of plant materials by soil organisms, especially microorganisms like bacteria, fungi and algae. Organisms that need oxygen are called **aerobes**, the ones that can't live with oxygen are called **anaerobes**. Most soil organisms are aerobic (anaerobic approx. 15% of total bacterial life). With this knowledge it makes sense to prepare the structure of the soil to provide oxygen within. This is achieved by applying organic matter. Mulching has other advantages too. Walking on the mulch will lessen the impact on bacterial life as the force of each foot step is evenly distributed and therefore the impact lessened. Mulch covers the top soil and maintains the moisture in that region of the soil. Weeding becomes less of a problem, as weeds hardly grow through heavy applications of mulch. Weeding will be necessary along the seed rows only, more often at the early stages of plant growth, and can usually be done by lying down on the mulch between the seed rows as shown in fig. 5-4. Eventually the crop itself will cover up that soil and weeding will become minimal. For plants such as garlic and cabbage some of the mulch from the walkways can be pulled into the seed bed once the plants are more mature. The supply of air to the organisms on the surface of the soil will also be enhanced. Plants' roots will tend to grow under such mulch. Ample evidence will be revealed by the careful examination of a straw or hay mulch. Other types of mulch can also be applied, such as leaves, fir or hemlock sawdust as long as the wood is not cut with a chain saw. As mentioned earlier, the oil applied to the chain while cutting will stick to the sawdust. Leaves of oak trees and walnut trees may take a long time to decay and should be on a compost of its own. Below is a summary of advantages gained by mulching:

– provides optimal soil cover
– maintains moisture
– adds organic matter
– minimizes soil compression
– cuts down on weeding
– facilitates weeding
– enhances soil bacteria and fungi
– moderates soil temperature
– Quickly dries out weeds placed on it

Advantages of mulching are many.

1.6. To till or not to till

Before we take the step of disturbing the soil, we have to look at its condition. It would not make sense to seed in a coarse surface or an overgrown one. Tilling land that has been sitting for a while, usually with a sod-type surface, may be the **only** alternative in order to prepare a seed bed. If no equipment is available it will take some time to prepare the soil. You can cover the ground with 4" of mulch for the first year, mulch and grow potatoes in the second year and mulch again in the third year. This will generate loose top soil. Tilling of sandy soil should be done once the top of the soil starts to dry. Clay soil should not be worked while wet or it will compact to small blocks. You need to delay working clay soil until it changes to a dry soil. Once baked the clay will become solid and unworkable as well. Observing clay soil is important in order to create a good seed bed. About three days before seeding, the seed bed's surface gets raked to keep germinating weeds back so they do not grow taller than your cultivation. This is critical in the beginning of growth, specially for carrots. Soil once worked, can be kept free of weeds and compacting, if managed with mulching and early raking. Do not try to pull large weeds with the rake. Soil with a low organic matter content may have to be worked with a rototiller for several years

Figure 5-4, Weeding with ease (bush beans)

before it becomes workable by the rake only. A rototiller, adjusted to work the top 3" (8 cm), will do a good job in uprooting weeds and preparing a smooth soil to seed into. If no rototiller is available a hoe or four-tined fork and a rake can be used. Try not to turn the soil but to loosen it up and then pick the weeds. When weeds are placed on the mulched walkways they will dry out quickly and have no chance to re-grow. Evidence of one earthworm per shovel of soil is enough to ensure the continuation of a rich, loose soil. If you look carefully at the soil, you may observe the little piles of worm casts. Such soil is five times richer in nitrogen, seven times richer in phosphoric acid and eleven times richer in potash than the surrounding soil, which has not been touched by the earthworm.

Summing up, tilling will be useful to control weeds, to prepare a fine seed bed with little bodily force, to reduce soil compacting and to break up sod. With an established soil, which has received mulching over 3 to 4 years, rototilling may become unnecessary.

1.7. Minerals

Earthworms are valuable in improving the soil.

A moderate earthworm population will produce annually about 10 tons of castings, rich in prepared minerals, such as calcium, phosphorus, iodine, iron and magnesium, deposited on the surface of each acre of fertile soil (about 26 t per ha). Mineral nutrients also become available to plants through the outside surfaces of the soil particles and by way of activities within the soil. Minerals present in the rock from which soil is formed are not available to plants, since they are not water soluble. Nature provides a number of ways for the plants to access these minerals. One way is through the activities of the earthworm as described earlier. Another way is via microorganisms expelling their air (carbon dioxide, CO_2). This air dissolves in the moisture surrounding the soil particles and produces carbonic acid which in turn can react with the minerals. Now dissolved, the plants' roots can feed on it. The excreta of soil inhabitants and the waste substances of the roots themselves also help change minerals into substances which plants can feed on. The plants' roots feverishly look for these trace minerals that are so important for their optimum development and with it the well being of ourselves. These natural mechanisms will not function properly if disturbed with applications of synthetic fertilizers and insect controls.

2. Water system

Planning the crops in relation to water requirements would complicate the layout as described in the previous chapter. We feel that it is not detrimental to our crops to apply roughly the same amount of water to all crops. Crops can adjust to a sudden down pour in the natural environment as well. Most of the irrigation is supplied to the mulched (covered) soil directly and can therefore be supplied throughout the day. With other systems you may want to water in the early hours of the day or in the evening, once the shadow reaches the crops, in order to save water from loss by evaporation. Plants do not like to be shocked with cold water in the midst of a sunny day.

The best harmony with water is achieved with a stream going past your farm or garden fields or a spring, from which to draw the water by gravity, or better yet, a climate and soil management that needs no irrigation at all. However, with rainfalls of about 24" per year (600 mm per year), this latter alternative will not work. Precipitation needs to be approximately 40" per year (1000 mm/year) to achieve such a possibility. In other areas we have to fill the lack of water with an irrigation system or, for smaller areas, watering cans. Water is essential for the growth of the plant. No matter where the water is taken from (deep well, stream, lake), it has to be distributed in one way or another. If you have plenty of water maybe a sprinkler system will work fine. However spraying water into the air results in up to 50% loss by evaporation and is therefore not very economical. Most of the time water has to be applied using a limited supply from a well or similar source, e.g. 3.5 gal per min (15.8 l/min). This calls for a system that can apply the water right where it is needed and in the right amount.

Trickle irrigation is just one such system which does that. Pipes are laid out within the seed beds and emitters inserted every 1.5 ft. to 2 ft. (45 cm to 60 cm) depending on the texture of the soil. In sandy soil a distance of 1.5 ft. (45 cm) is recommended as water seeps into the soil faster and less of a lateral spreading is possible. Different products are available. The products we have used distributed by local suppliers (See Appendix A) have lasted for over 11 years now and show very little deterioration in spite of the year-round exposure to the weather.

Emitters may sometimes plug up due to accidental burying in the soil or mulch, especially when applying manure to the berry bushes. The emitters can always be easily unplugged by taking them apart. Checking them once a year in the spring will be all that's needed. There are several different emitters available, for different quantities of water over a given time, rated in litres per hour. They are marked with the number, e.g. 4 l/h, which stands for 4 litres per hour or about a gallon per hour. These are the ones used to water most of our crops. There are also emitters that regulate the pressure. If you install the line on a downward slope, the bottom emit-

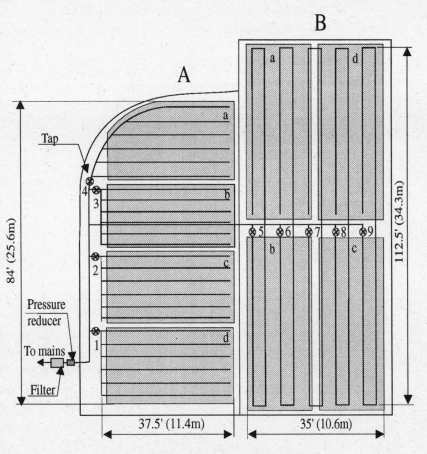

Figure 5-5, Irrigation layout

ters would get more pressure and therefore would emit more water per time unit. To avoid that pressure regulating emitters have to be used, which of course are more expensive. Some of these are used on our rather hilly place for pipes laid out perpendicularly rather then laterally. To find out how much water is drawn by the minute (which is usually the time interval specified to measure the well's capacity) you divide the number of emitters installed by 60, if they are 1 gal/h emitters. For example 180 emitters will use 180:60=3 gal/min. In this case your well would have to produce 3 gal/min. If you need more then 180 emitters and your well is limited to the 3 gal/min, you need to install a tap for another section using a maximum of 180 emitters. All sections will be supplied via a 12 psi (90 kPa) pressure reducing element and a filter. The filter element is removed during the winter to avoid frost damage. At that low pressure, pipes can be connected without using hose clamps (C-clamps).

Fig. 5-5 shows a layout of a garden area of just over 7000 sq. ft. (650 m^2). It is divided into two patches, marked with capital letters, "A" representing an area of about 3200 sq. ft. (290 m^2) and "B" of about 3900 sq. ft. (360 m^2). Rows are spaced at about 42" (107 cm). Each patch has its own crop rotation as marked with the letters a) to d).

We will have to decide how much water we can divert and use for this garden area. Let's say the well produces 3.5 gal/ min (15.8 l/min) but drops to 3 gal/min (13.5 l/min) in the fall. Leaving some for the house as utility water, we would be able to draw about 2.5 gallons every minute (11.3 l/min) or 150 gal/h (675 l/h). With 1 gal/ h (4.5 l/h) emitters we could have 150 emitters run at one given time which would result in 225' (69 m) of irrigation pipe. The two patches can then be irrigated as shown in fig. 5-5 using just a bit over 2000 ft. (610 m) of pipe and 1350 emitters. For the 7000 sq. ft. (650 m^2) area it would take us nine hours to water every spot for one hour, drawing no more than the 2.5 gal/min (11 l/min) from the well. The total amount of water used per day would be 1350 gallons (6075 l). This can easily be managed and will provide more than enough water for the very dry summer and fall days. Of course less water will need to be applied for other situations (like clay soil) and regions with different climates may need to water every second day only.

For a family of four, half of the above area in vegetables would be more than adequate, when supplemented with all the other food grown (e.g. berries, fruits and animals). For our family of eight, a vegetable garden the size of about 5000 sq. ft. (465 m^2) is supplying us with enough and in good years we can feed damaged or small

Money should not become the dominant factor in growing your own food.

sized crops to the animals. The limit on a well with 3 gal/h and a 16 hour day (that means 8 hours of sleep) would be reached with an area of 15'000 sq. ft. (1400 m^2), if watered for an hour every day.

2.1. Vegetables, does it pay?

It sounds questionable to think about money when priority is given to provide food with a high value. I'm sure that it won't be easy to compete with market prices and this is exactly the point. Nowadays food is cheap because it is manufactured that way. But let's think in terms of economics for this one time. You may realistically be able to generate Can$1.50 per foot in quality food, which would provide an income of Can$3000.00 per year. The investment in the irrigation system comes to Can$584.50, with the following cost as of 1994:

– Pipe, 2000 ft.	124.00
– Emitters, 1350	337.50
– Filter and pressure red.	23.00
– hose adapters, tabs, clamps and other small items	100.00
– Total	Can$ 584.50

To install such a system (time spent to install not taken into consideration) would bring a return in the first year of the installation. The irrigation system will be useful for at least 20 years, so per year you would need to set aside about $30.00 to replace it in 20 years (plus inflation and exchange rate losses if the irrigation product is from outside the country).Of course you need to have a market to sell the produce and you will have other expenses, such as electricity, seeds, plants, mulch, tools and, most important, labour.

Looking at it from a perspective to make a living will change the picture. First of all you would need an average of about one hour a day to manage such an area and this for the whole season, or about 180 days. This would result in:

- Salary for 180 hours   1800.00
- ($ 10.00 per hour of labour)
- Seed   120.00
- Equipment use, etc.   200.00
- Irrigation depreciation   30.00
- Pump depr., electricity   100.00
- (pump to be repl. after 6 years)
- Mulch, 100 x 50¢   50.00
- Misc., repair, cloth   <u>200.00</u>
- Total expense   <u>Can$ 2500.00</u>

The investment would earn you Can$ 500.00 not counting land tax or other administrative costs or more important, the marketing of the products. Finally, this calculation is made on the positive side, like having a good crop, no matter how the weather is. No investor would take such a gamble with such a low return and that may well be why the stock market is such an attractive alternative (no dirty hands).

On the other hand, if you do spend an extra hour a day and enjoy what you are doing, you have Can$ 2300.00 in your pocket, once the products have been sold. It would be economical for a farm family to use the produce to reduce transportation and marketing costs.

Adding animals to the picture will economically come out with a similar result. Time spent to care for a flock of 50 chickens is not as demanding at about ½ h/day (but with a lower return) and a similar time frame is valid for the upkeep of bees, with 20 hives, 3 full days/year plus an average of ¼ h/day and for the management of goats 1 h/day for 2 to 3 goats. Add to that about ½ h/day to tend the berries and fruits and another ¼ h/day for miscellaneous work, (e.g. a few rabbits) and upkeep and you will average out to about 3½ hours per day. With this you have a rounded picture, harmony. That means, with a family of

four, each will spend less than an hour per day. Children will usually participate quite well when they understand that the work is needed to feed themselves. Picking berries, cherries and apples are the most favored tasks for children but an 11 year old child can milk goats very well, while mom or dad feeds the hay and water. Feeding the rabbits, in the summer by moving the pen and giving water, and in the winter by delivering hay, water and kitchen wastes, is easy too. With younger children someone may have to check once in a while and remind the child to take responsibility. Our children respect the rabbits as being part of our food. They may still have a pet rabbit to be theirs as a companion for as long as they want and we encourage this. None of our children have shown much interest in keeping bees but they always help in the honey house, uncapping the cells. An eight year old can already take part in that task, even though, for the most part, they eat the uncappings. With all this a good team spirit can be built.

Building a team spirit is achieved by helping the children to get involved.

Getting involved in activities like this will show us again what it takes to produce rich and wholesome food. You may right now spend one hour a day in the busy stores and plugged up roads to gather your food. What you will not be able to purchase while doing that is to connect to the food and the challenge and building of a relationship with nature by doing it yourself. For me it is always overwhelming to see how much there is available in these supermarkets. When I enter the root cellar I can see the simple but very valuable food that we gathered during the year and it feels good to know that it is all right next to the kitchen.

Animals will integrate quite well with the rest of the activities.

3. A bee hive in spring

3.1. Pussy willows produce pollen

After the bees have had their cleansing flight calm may return to the colonies until

Signs of spring come with the observing of the bees and their activities to gather the first pollen.

the first signs of pollen appear. On sunny days you should watch the entrance carefully to see if you can recognize bees with pollen on their hind legs. These are, in the case of pussy willow pollen (fig. 5-6), yellow sacks packed onto their back legs. You may also find some gray-yellowish coloured pollen, which could be from the mountain alder, a species growing in many areas and also an early pollen producer (at the same time as pussy willow). These are the earliest pollen supplies in the spring in our bioregion. You have to observe the bringing in of pollen by the bees. In the first days maybe just a few bees, but within 4 to 5 days, many bees should carry in large pollen sacks, given the weather is sunny and warm, at about 59° F (15° C) or warmer. Later on you will see other colours of pollen, mainly from early flowers like snowdrops, crocus etc. But the important point about this is that bees bring in pollen now to feed the new brood in their hive. This tells us that there is a queen and that she is laying eggs. You can also tell the strength of the colony, by just watching how many bees come in with a heavy supply of pollen over a given time. Then compare the results with another colony. Building up the population will happen very quickly now and disturbing the colony now would set it back by several days. Table 5-1 will help you in verifying what kind of plant the pollen could be from. As it is very difficult to describe a colour exactly, the table should be used with caution but your

Figure 5-6, Pussy willows

observations will bring you one more step closer to your surroundings and nature. You will notice the entry for the oak tree mentions honeydew which the bees collect to produce honey. Bees do collect excretions from aphids that feed on several trees, mainly the white fir, spruce and the oak tree. As this "nectar" is not from a plant species, it is called honeydew. In some countries (for example Switzerland and Germany) the beekeeper extracts the honey in the spring separately from that in the fall. This honey, referred to as "forest honey", is usually dark coloured and preferred by some customers.

If you have some crystallized honey left over you could feed it by setting it on the inner cover by the hole. This would stimulate the population growth. But take care not to do this too early and then let them starve until the first nectar flows. Until about the end of April, when the dandelions start to flower, there is little nectar provided by nature. Don't feed any sugar water in the spring (except for splits as explained in chapter 7) or to patch up too little feeding in the fall. It will remain in the honey and such honey will be of low quality. It is best to eliminate a weak hive now. If all colonies show good activity with bees gathering pollen, which is usually the case, you sit back and continue to observe!

3.2. Early inspection

If no pollen, or very little, is brought to the hive, but lots of bees are flying in and out, mainly to gather water, something is wrong. You have some extra work to do. Usually the problem is with the queen that she could not handle the winter and the associated stress, or was too old and died. You have to open this hive on the next warm day to examine it for brood patterns. Check for diseases at this time. You may use the publication Honey Bee Diseases & Pests mentioned earlier (see Appendix A) to verify symptoms. If no brood is found and no symptoms of diseases are spotted, the bees can be united with another hive. Sometimes, due to loss of the queen, a worker bee may start laying eggs. Unfortunately she is laying drone eggs only (male) and the population will slowly de-

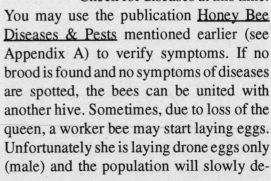

Pollen colour	Flower colour	Name	Period of flowering	Nectar
Blue	Blue	Phacelia tenacetifolia	June-August	Y+
Brown	White	Clover, white	May-September	Y
Brown	Purple, dark, with brown	Figwort	June-August	Y+
Brown, dark	Red	Clover, red	June-September	Y
Brown, greyish	Pink	Marjoram	August-October	Y
Brown, light	White	Cherry sweet, sour, wild	April-May	Y
Brown, light	Orange, red	Honeysuckle	July-August	Y+
Brown, light	White	Plums	April-May	Y
Brown, white	Blue	Cornflower (Bachelor buttons)	July-August	Y
Cream, grayish	White to pink	Bindweed, lesser (morning glory)	July	Y
Cream, brownish	Greenish, yellowish	Yew	February-March	?
Green	Purple	Loosestrife, purple	June-September	Y
Green, light	White	Crabapple	April-May	Y
Green, light	Greenish-yellow	Currant, red	April-May	Y
Green, light	Greenish-white	Gooseberry	April-May	?
Green, light	Greenish, yellow	Maple, big leaf (Oregon Maple), ash leaf	March-April	Y+
Green, yellow	Yellow catkins	Oak, white	June	HD
Grey	White	Bean, lima	June-July	Y
Grey	White	Blackberry	May-June	Y
Grey	Green	Elm	April-May	N
Grey	Purple	Thistle, Canada	July-August	Y+
Grey, light	Greenish, yellow	Ash, mountain	May-June	?
Grey, light	Blue	Borage	June-Frost	Y
Grey, light	Blue	Chicory	July-October	Y
Grey, light	Purple, blue	Knapweed	July-October	Y
Grey, light	White	Raspberries	May-June	Y
Grey, yellowish	Green catkins	Alder, mountain	March-May	N
Orange	Yellow	Asparagus	June-July	Y
Orange	Blue	Crocus	March-April	Y
Orange	Yellow	Dandelion	April-June	Y
Orange	White	Snowdrop	March-April	?
Orange, golden	Orange, yellow	Poppy, California	May-September	N
Orange, red	Yellow	Mullein	June-August	Y
Purple, dark	Red	Poppy, field	June-July	?
Red	Red, cream	Chestnut, horse	May-June	Y
Red	Purple, blue	Lupin	March-April	Y
Yellow	White, pink, red	Apple	April-May	Y
Yellow	Green catkins	Birch	Late March-April	N
Yellow	Yellow	Broccoli	August	Y
Yellow	White	Buckwheat	July-August	Y
Yellow	Yellow	Cabbage	July-August	Y+
Yellow	White	Dogwood	May-July	N
Yellow	White	Lilac	May-June	Y
Yellow	Cream	Plantain	April-August	N
Yellow	Green catkins	Poplar, trembling aspen	Late March-May	N
Yellow	Yellow, yellow-brown	Sunflower	June-September	Y
Yellow	Gray catkins	Willow, pussy	February-March	Y
Yellow, dark	Creamy, white	Elder, mountain	June-July	Y
Yellow, dark	Red, cream	Chestnut, sweet	June-July	Y
Yellow, dark	Yellow catkins	Hazelnut	February-March	N
Yellow, dark	White	Lilac, wild	April-May	Y
Yellow, dark	White	Onion	June-August	Y

Y= nectar,   N= no nectar,   HD= honeydew,   + = good source,   ?= not known or conflicting information.

Table 5-1, Plants and pollen colour

crease and eventually die off. You recognize such behaviour by looking at the brood pattern. There will be **many** cells with more then one egg placed in it. Sometimes a newly fertilized queen will show such patterns but for a few cells only, and of course not at this time of the year. Also, if the brood has advanced to the stage of a pupa, the covering of the cell will be protruding from the comb instead of being flush with it. At this stage uniting is no longer recommended. It is a fact that the laying worker bee, hard to detect, acts as a queen very strongly and the method below (with newspaper) will not work. These bees have to be eliminated.

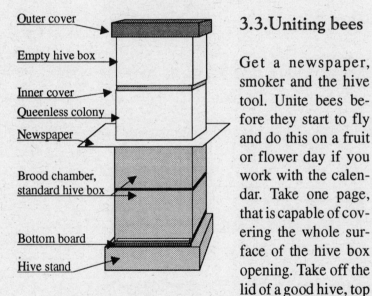

Outer cover
Empty hive box
Inner cover
Queenless colony
Newspaper
Brood chamber, standard hive box
Bottom board
Hive stand

Figure 5-7, Uniting bees

3.3.Uniting bees

Get a newspaper, smoker and the hive tool. Unite bees before they start to fly and do this on a fruit or flower day if you work with the calendar. Take one page, that is capable of covering the whole surface of the hive box opening. Take off the lid of a good hive, top box (empty) and the inner cover (use some smoke). Place the newspaper immediately so as not to disturb the bees and to keep them in their box. Now place the one box of the **queenless** hive on top of the newspaper, aligned with the lower box. Place inner cover, top box (empty) and lid back on as shown in fig. 5-7. The newspaper will act as a mediator. The bees will slowly chew through the paper and happily unite with the other bees. By not using the paper, the queenless bees will try to kill the existing queen, as they want to protect their population from an intruder and you will loose the queen of the good hive too. Now you can see why it may be of great help to have at least two hives. First of all you can compare and secondly you can rescue some of the bees if so required.

4. A bird nesting box

A very simple but effective birdhouse for blue birds is shown in fig. 5-8. The entrance has to face south to south-east and to be located in an open space on a pole 7 ft. (2.2 m) above ground. Fig. 5-9 shows unusual behaviour for a swallow, to take a nesting box for its home. This box has a hole of 1 $^3/_8$" (3.5 cm).

5. Raising chicks yourself

We have found it to be the easiest to have the chickens do it themselves. Nowadays "modern" chickens are bred to lay eggs but not to sit on them. For this reason bantam chickens, also called banty chickens or just banties, are the best hens to keep around for this purpose. You can put up to 10 eggs under a banty chicken with good success for all of them. Half of them may be roosters (male). Bantam chickens will start to lay once the weather turns warm, signaled by the flowering of the dandelions.

It is possible however to use an incubator and with that you could start as early as end of February. Of course it is up to

6 1/2" (16.5cm)

1 5/8" (4cm)
No resting board at entrance!

5"   (12.5 cm)
7"   (18cm)
All built with 3/4" (19mm) thick wood

Figure 5-8, Blue bird nesting box

Figure 5-9, Swallow nesting box

you how much earlier than the natural cycle you want to start. You will need a thermometer and a heat lamp, the latter to keep the new born chicks warm. With an egg candler you can determine the fertility of eggs in the early stages. A box with a light bulb inside and a 1" (2.5 cm) hole at the top will provide an alternative to a commercial egg candler. Make sure the design allows heat to escape from the box. You may want to check out when the last opportunity is, to buy chicks on the market and plan to have yours hatch before that time. That allows you to still buy them on the market if all else fails.

5.1. Preparations

- Set up the incubator in a room with 60° F (15° C) temperature or less and not in direct sunlight. Avoid vibration or bumping of it.
- Use eggs that are less than 10 days old and from vital 2 to max. 3 year old chickens. You will most probably experience, that after 4 years many chickens will not be able to go through winter and many need to be put to rest. To keep the size of a flock it would be best to breed every second year.
- Turn eggs daily while storing. Store them around a constant temperature of 60° F (15° C).
- Use clean eggs only, properly formed and without cracks or rough shells.
- Don't use eggs from hens being exposed to artificial light in the pen.
- Chilled eggs will not be useful.
- Keep equipment clean.

5.2. Incubating (still air incubator)

Incubation takes 21 days. Set the temperature just above the egg at 103°F (39.5°C) throughout the hatch. You may run the incubator for a couple of days with some eggs of any kind to adjust the temperature. Temperatures above 107°F (42°C) will destroy the embryo within hours. Relative humidity should be 50% from the 1st to the 18th day and increased to 65% during hatching. Moisture needs to be supplied by a water pan or similar, filled with hot water.

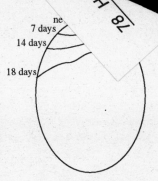

Figure 5-10, Air space

The eggs need to be turned 180° once at the 2nd day and **three times per day** thereafter until the 18th day. Put a pencil mark on the egg in order to know which ones you turned. Test and remove bad eggs by checking white shelled eggs at the 4th day, dark shelled ones at the 7th day using the egg candler described earlier. A fertile egg in that stage will reveal a picture similar to fig. 5-11. For the first 7 days the time it takes to turn the eggs will provide sufficient cooling. After that eggs should be cooled off for 10 minutes gradually increasing to 15 minutes per day, up to the end of the 18th day. Eggs may be sprinkled with warm water on the 18th day if necessary to raise the humidity. Do not disturb eggs after the 18th day until they hatch. Shells of eggs stored for a while will harden and you may want to sprinkle the cooled off eggs with hot water once each day starting at day 15. This also will raise the humidity inside the incubator. To determine the moisture, the air space in the egg has to be analyzed as shown in fig. 5-10 and action taken as required. The air space will be larger in a too dry environment.

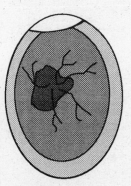

Figure 5-11, Fertile egg

If some of the eggs hatch late and you want to remove the hatched chickens already, the room should be warm so the chicks will not be chilled or the eggs cooled. Do not feed or water the chicks until they are 48 hours old. Usually the chicks will not do so anyway. Keep new born chicks under the heat lamp at a temperature of 90° F (32° C) but not higher than 95°F (35°C) for the first few days, slowly decreasing the temperature as feathers grow. For information on raising chicks see chapter 6.

Summary of activities: Mid March

- Fig. 5-12 shows a garden layout as mentioned in chapter 4. A plan similar to this should now be established in order to plant the crops in the right area of the garden.
- The planting of **cress** and **spinach** (highlighted in fig. 5-12) directly outside is possible. Cover these rows with chicken wire to protect them from the chickens. Seed the spinach along the edges of the seed bed to leave room for the succession planting of cabbage. The spinach should poke through the soil at the beginning of April. The remaining cress can be easily worked into the soil once the lettuce is ready to be transplanted. You may leave a couple of feet free to seed lettuce later on. It is a bit early for lettuce to be seeded outside and we wait until early April.
- If you have planters, inside along a window, they also could be seeded with cress and harvested after about mid April, but keep some planters free to start up your own cabbage, kohlrabi and tomato plants.
- Witloof (chicory) that you have put into the root cellar's sand bed

last fall may now have some fresh cones available.
- Order irrigation material as required.
- Observe pussy willows, other early pollen plants and the bees.
- Make sure bees carry in pollen or unite if required.
- Start a new batch of chickens using the incubator.
- Seed celery or celeriac inside.
- Pruning and propagating currants and gooseberries as described in chapter 3 can be done before buds open. Red and white currants may be a bit later than black currants and gooseberries.

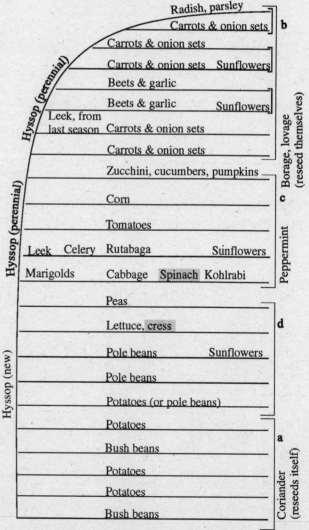

Figure 5-12, Sample layout of garden area

6

April, Animal Care and Garden Activities

Winter is over

1. Goats

1.1. General observations

With the weather now warming up, goats will soon be able to taste the first green grass emerging. The goat pen is cleaned out from the winter bedding as soon as the frost is out of the ground. Now we await the time when the first baby goats (kids) will arrive. The gestation time (from mating to giving birth) for a goat is about 5 months (145 to 155 days). Goats usually give birth to two kids. Housing the goats has been mentioned in chapter two. In wet or cold weather the goats are kept locked in the pen. Some goats do not like others to be close, specially when from the same family. This happens more often with having three goats together. The isolation pen is the best way to solve that problem. Goats are also very sensible and given the opportunity will make their rules. Once the habit is established it will not go away. Try to train new goats together with a well trained one.

1.2. Feeding and pasture

Feeding can become a major issue. For us the goats are a survival food source and we do not want to depend on fodder from the feed mill. During the winter the goats are fed hay mixed with some alfalfa. Those goats that are milked get three-quarters of a tin can of oats twice a day while milking. That amounts to about 1.5 lb. per day (700 g per day). Feeding the oats while milking will keep them occupied and no tether or other device is required. Milking should take place in a quiet surrounding away from the other goats. A milking table as shown in chapter two will make the job easy. In the beginning you may milk slower than the goat eats the oats, and you need to tie her up or feed more oats. Otherwise the goat becomes restless and hard to control. A young goat will have to get trained to jump up to the milking table and to stand still and may need to be tied up for the first few times. During the season, starting as soon as fresh grass is available, the goats are tethered to a cord out in the field. It is important not to switch over to fresh forage only, but change over from hay to grass or other fresh food gradually. A simple system to keep them from getting tangled up is shown in fig. 6-1. Our experiences with four goats have all been excellent. The kids need not be put on the line, as they stay with their mothers until about five months old. This is true for a setting away from the garden and fruit trees. Otherwise all goats need to be tied to the line. The nylon rope can swing sideways. Goats will walk along the rope, dragging along the pipes that slide on the nylon rope. The swivel bolt snap must be made out of brass. They won't rust and the wear and tear will be on the snap, but very little on the rope. Snaps last for

Milking goats needs some planning.

Goats provide us with milk and meat and are fairly simple to keep.

about three seasons, the rope for eight or more years. A hose clamp together with a ½" (12.5 mm) copper bushing made from plumbing pipe and about 1" (25 mm) long, placed inside the plastic pipe will re-enforce the ends of the hose. This will prevent the tether from splitting the plastic pipe's ends. Such a system works well in open fields, otherwise you will need to build fences as described earlier in chapter two. Tying the goats to trees and bushes in the forest, for example to clear a path, works fine, but you **need to check twice a day** to untangle the 6' long (1.8 m) tether. You also have to make sure that one goat does not reach the other goat's line and become entangled.

Supplement the goat's food with leaves and acorns.

During the winter months hay can be substituted for grass in quantities of 30 bales per goat for 8 months of no green pasture. We substitute hay with dried birch leaves raked in the fall. Some years there are more leaves than other years, depending on how often it rains in the fall. The leaves are fed together with the hay and stored on top of the hay, sometimes in bags or sacks. Of course in early spring you can start feeding branches from trees that you trimmed back or pruned. During the cold days in winter give them some extra protein in the form of acorns (about a handful per milking) or alfalfa mixed with the hay. Salt has to be provided all year round. The blue as well as the red kind are available in the feed stores. These salts are enriched with minerals such as cobalt, selenium, etc. Ask the supplier what to use. Regular salt would also do. Finally, during the fall when the carrots are put into storage, some should be cut into small pieces and fed to the goats. This is to de-worm the goat and should be fed for about a week if necessary. Twice a day the water in the pail needs to be replaced, and the pail cleaned if dirty. An average goat drinks about ½ a gallon (2.2 l) of water per day, depending on weather and the goat's condition (pregnant, kids, etc.). Just feed the average amount and increase or decrease thereafter as required. Make sure the rim of the pail is just a touch higher then the tallest goat's tail, to prevent defecation into the pail. Goats fed like this, with no dairy ration, may not produce top yields of milk, but will give a steady supply, except for about two months just before kidding. Moreover you are one step closer to independence and have the freedom to know what the goat eats and what you eventually will get. Try to milk and feed goats always at the same times and in the same intervals. We do this at 8 a.m. and 8 p.m. In some rare cases we may deviate by as much as an hour earlier or later.

If problems arise, that a goat does not eat at all, let her walk through the forest with you. She will automatically eat the plants and shrubs necessary to help her get better. This may take some patience on your side in order to attend to the goat.

Pink eye can be cured by washing the eyes with black tea 3 times daily.

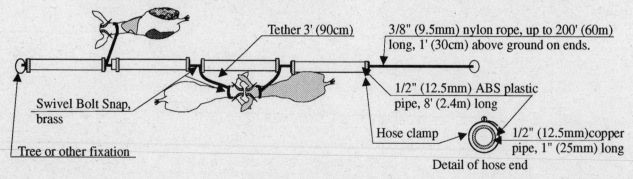

Figure 6-1, Tethering goats

Sometimes tits clot up. Let the kids suck more often and milk three times per day. Feed chamomile tea. Clots will usually work themselves out like this.

With small goats, sometimes a cold will make their kidneys not function properly. They will just lie around as if dead and you need to act fast. Try horsetail tea. **In general, use herbs as prescribed to cure humans**. If you do not know the problem a veterinarian can help. They can give a good diagnosis, sometimes over the phone if you describe the symptoms well, and of course will recommend this or the other antibiotic. At that time tell the person that you would like to try herbal treatments and the veterinarian may still have some good advice. A very good book on herbal medicine is Health through God's Pharmacy by Maria Treben (see Appendix A).

Most of the time goats are lost due to age or when just born and not cared for. In bad weather the doe sometimes will give birth outside rather than in the pen and the kid may suffer. You will have to check periodically, to rectify any problems. Poor tethering can result in goats getting mixed up in each others tethers. This is a problem to watch for as one of the goats may lose out in any resulting fight.

1.3. The cycle of milk production

During the life of a goat (about 10 to 14 years), many litres of healthy milk can be obtained. There are many ways to keep goats producing. The following description takes a most natural approach to it, with the least amount of involvement. Goats would still be able to survive in nature in regards to feeding themselves. In order to have milk however, breeding of the doe (female goat) is required. It can be done in a one-year cycle or a two-year cycle. To increase the herd, and with this the amount of meat later in the season, you use a one-

year cycle. For mainly milk production a two-year cycle will work fine. For either routine nothing changes in the way it is described below. Does are usually bred in the fall, when in heat. Goats will start coming into heat as soon as the weather gets cooler, usually in late September. Their cycle is 19 to 21 days, lasting 1 to 3 days. Signs for this are:

Breeding goats for different reasons.

- Vulva (genital opening) swollen, moist looking and pink to red.
- Restless
- Wags her tail frequently

Goats in heat and the signs.

With such signs, it's time to go to the buck. It usually will only take a few minutes for them to have it done. To keep your own buck may save you the time and monitoring of the goat(s), but you trade for some strong scent for most of the month of October, peaking in November, and December. Of course artificial insemination could also be used, if you don't mind the high tech dependency.

If everything went right you will have some baby goats five months down the road. Two months before they freshen the milk supply will decrease. You just milk until the goat is dry. A large swollen vulva will point towards an imminent (2 to 3 days) delivery. Make sure the bedding is fresh. The goat will take care of the rest, will clean the babies and eat the after birth and remains of the happening. All there is left are usually two but sometime only one little cute kid. For a week or so after freshening, the doe may have a slight vaginal discharge. Don't worry about this, it's normal. The kids need to drink the milk from the mother for the first three to four days. It is critical that newborn kids receive their first milk, containing colostrum produced by the

Prepare for the arrival of baby goats.

doe in the first days only, within a few hours of birth. Their defecation may be yellow coloured for the first few days.

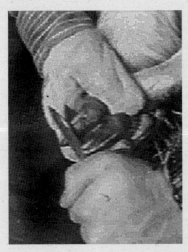

Figure 6-2, Hoof trim

After about 10 days, the strong and healthy kids can be separated overnight and with this more milk will become available. If you want the kids to become very friendly, and also very fat, you would feed some of the milk back. Use a pan, baby bottle, beer bottle with nipple (available in pet stores) or glass bowl to do so. Measure how much milk the doe produces. A kid should be fed no more than 1½ to two litres per day. If you use a pan or glass bowl the kid should be allowed to dip its nose into the milk for some time till it finds the required procedure. Feed the milk right after milking while it is still warm. You can mix some water with the milk later on. The mixture depends on the kid. Try a mixture of half-half first. Some don't like it at all. Excessive milk feeding will produce exceptionally nice looking does but they have improper stomach development and will subsequently be low milk producers. Anyway you do it, the kids will be with mom during the whole day. They will start to eat fine hay and grass. After about two months you can use all the milk for your own consumption by separating the kids during the day as well. Again, you can feed some back to fatten them for meat production or continue to have them with mom. It depends on how many goats you have and what you can live with.

Young bucks always seem to find an opportunity to climb, jump or break a fence, or rip the line to find a good looking doe.

In the fall you can breed, butcher or sell the offspring. The doe will keep supplying you with milk for approx. 20 more month (two-year cycle) to come. With feeding of above quantities, a four year old doe can supply about four litres of milk per day after the first week of freshening. The amount will increase to about five litres and then settle to about three litres in the fall, while changing over to hay feed. You may experience an increase in milk production from a doe in the spring, while another doe is freshening. It stimulates the doe and in this case the milk production will go up for that goat, even though she was not bred.

1.4. Trimming hooves

The goat's hooves grow, much as human fingernails. When they get longer they will fold over and cover the sole of the feet, eventually causing hoof rot. It is necessary to trim hooves **at least** twice a year. A pocket knife, pruning shear or a special tool called the foot rot shear can be used. It is helpful for the first time, to watch someone demonstrate the process and the illustration in fig. 6-2 may help in this regard. The white lines along the edge of the hoof show the fresh cut hoof surface. Be careful not to cut the foot itself.

1.5. Castrating buck kids

Castrating bucks becomes necessary to keep the herd together. Bucks can be fertile at as young as three to four months of age and separation would be required. Meat from castrated bucks will not have any goat taste. This part of goat husbandry however is a rather tough one. You can use elastrator bands in the first week to cut off the blood supply. This method has not worked well, as most of the time, the kids got infected and it was a rather painful process. Surgery is much more effective and therefore recommended. It can be done with a sharp pocket knife and some experience about the procedure. A demonstration may be required, in order to learn the practice, but the description below will outline the procedure.

The testes or testicles are carried in a pouch like structure called the scrotum. The scrotum is covered with a rather tough skin for protection and to control the temperature of the testicles. In farm animals, the two types of scrota are the pendulous type, common to goats, horses, cattle and sheep, or the swine-type that carries the testes adjacent to the hind quarters. Buck kids can be neutered by removing the testes or severing or crushing the cords that supply the testes. It is recommended to cut the testes when the kid is about one week old but not older than 10 days. Neutering animals at one year or older may not be easy at all and I do not recommend that.

To remove the testes the kid is kept in position while holding the animal in your lap, facing away from you, and the back legs held under your feet. Clean the pouch (scrotum) on the outside, if you can, with some alcohol mixed with propolis.

Propolis is collected from plant resins. These sticky resins, the propolis or bee glue, are collected by worker bees to block holes and cracks in the hive and to "embalm" carcasses of intruders that have been killed but are to large to transport out of the hive, such as mice. Propolis has some anti fungal and antibacterial properties. It is known to have local anesthetic qualities, similar to that of cocaine. It also finds acceptance as an ingredient in tooth paste, soaps, deodorants, shampoos, etc. Stradivari used propolis to achieve the maximum sound quality from his violins, by applying it to the surface of the instruments. It is also said to inhibit the growth of fungi such as candida albicans, aspergillus ochraceus, saccharomyces cerevisiae, kloeckera apiculatus and others.

Cut the tip of the pouch to have about a ¾" (19 mm) opening. The testes can now be gently pushed out one at a time and held to cut the cord. The wound is left open to promote natural drainage and will heal within a few days. If you do this on a nice day and provide clean bedding, a dressing (e.g. aloe vera) may not become necessary.

1.6. Disbudding the kids

I do not recommend that you do this without any pain killer or similar treatment. For this reason we do not dehorn our goats. Some kids, especially well-grown buck kids of the Swiss breeds, are already beginning to sprout horns at birth; most starting at three to eight days old. The skin on the head of the polled kid will move freely across the horn area when rubbed by a finger. The horned kid's skin will seem attached to the skull at the horn sites. Also, most horned kids have a whirlpool of hair around the horn buds. ¼" (6 mm) high horns can still be burned off. If you are thinking of dehorning, consult a veterinarian or experienced dairy goat breeder. I do not have any experience in this matter, but the description below will outline the procedure. If using a red-hot iron, about 1" (2.5 cm) in diameter, burn about 10 to 15 seconds, until the horn bud comes off. Then sear (burn to dryness) the entire area where the horn bud was, down to the skull. Be careful to keep the ears out of the way. Apply a dressing such as pine tar, once the process is finished. Then proceed to the other horn bud.

There is however nothing wrong with leaving the horns. Of course you can not go for exhibitions with such a goat, as the breeders do not have much sympathy for the wonderful shape of the horns and majesty and strength it represents for the goat. For the breeders it's a bother and constantly in the way. It is unfortunate that there are pet lovers who have a goat and are concerned about getting hurt by the horns. Our children have never had any problems and show respect for the animal. None of our does have ever hurt any children. The procedure to remove the horns is rather painful.

It seems more natural to leave the horns, if the pens are large and enough room is available for the goats to roam around. We have had no inconvenience regarding the horns, as long as all goats have them. Horns on bucks grow very large and with these horns a buck will tear down slab wood fences fairly easy. As bucks are more aggressive, they need to be tethered or it will become dangerous for children. But this is not so with does.

1.7. Glossary

- **Doe:** A female goat (Goat aficionados never use the term "nanny")
- **Buck:** A male goat (billy goat)
- **Kid :** A young goat
- **Yearling:** A one year-old goat.
- **Polled:** A naturally hornless goat.
- **Wattle:** An appendage of skin, which hangs down on some goats, frequently on the neck but potentially anywhere.
- **Udder:** The mammary gland
- **Teat:** The nipples of the udder.
- **Purebred:** A goat whose ancestors are all of the same breed, and all purebred themselves.
- **Pedigree:** A document showing a goat's ancestry.
- **Grade:** A goat of unknown ancestry, but usually not purebred.
- **Freshen:** Giving birth, and coming into milk.

Figure 6-3, Chicken fencing

- **Disbud:** To burn out the horn buds of very young goats (three to 10 days) with a disbudding iron or caustic chemical).

2. Chickens

Chickens bred to produce eggs lay considerably more eggs than those bred for meat production. Laying hens on average produce about 240 eggs during their first year of laying and then enter a molting and resting period when they generally stop laying. After a molting period of about eight weeks, the hens return to laying but will produce about 10 to 15% fewer eggs than during the first year. During the consecutive years the eggs are usually larger. Both ready-to-lay hens (pullets) and day-old chicks, for those who may wish to raise their own flock, are available commercially. Breeding stock from eggs is described in chapter five. It is a rather tricky undertaking, and should for the first time be done with the guidance of an experienced person. A natural way of raising chicks is to put fertile eggs under a bantam hen. Bantam hens still have the natural instinct to sit on eggs. This is in contrast to the laying hens who have been bred to lay eggs only. Make sure that when they hatch, no cat or other domestic pet will go after them.

2.1. Fencing

Fencing chickens is an easy task, but you may have to cut back the hens wings, if they get too ambitious to fly over the fence. It is practical to have two large pens to switch them to, with lots of land to roam about. They can be kept together with the goats without any problems. Chickens will scavenge the droppings from the goats. This has the added effect of efficient spreading of the manure by the animals themselves. But again, switch pens at least once a year. 42" (1m) high chicken wire on posts 6 ft. (1.8 m) apart will provide adequate fencing.

If slab wood is available, the top and bottoms between the posts can be connected and a 36" (90 cm) mesh stapled onto these boards as illustrated in fig. 6-3. This may give a more permanent solution. Bantam chickens will however grow their trimmed wings back fairly fast and with it will find it easy to leave the fenced area. Try to keep the wings trimmed during the spring time. Later in the year the bantam chickens will not do damage to the garden, except maybe to eat the strawberries. You may want to cover the strawberries with a nylon mesh to keep the birds out as well. I usually leave some uncovered to maintain a fair relation with the birds.

2.2. Mites and fleas

Make sure you have no fleas as they can be quite uncomfortable to you, especially when milking the goats. There is always the likelihood that fleas will be present during the spring months, April to May, especially if cats are around. These creatures spread quickly and eventually will infest humans. To keep them under control you need to spread wood ash in the chicken house and scratch pen regularly (twice a week). If no wood ash is available lime can be used. What you try to achieve is to dry out the manure so that these insects have no water for their development. Fleas and mites also do not like the etching effect of these substances and so do not develop well. Red mites, traveling with the chickens under the feathers or resting under the roost bars waiting for the host, are usually present. If in small amounts they don't cause any damage. Try to keep the chicken house as dry and clean as possible. Red mites find cover in the chicken manure and therefore you want to clean it out more often in the spring, when red mites are starting to populate. Again use ash or lime to counter the hatching of new insects that rely on the moisture in the manure. Do not use Sevin or Malathion, two very poisonous treatments, for such instances. It will kill more than you intend.

2.3. Feed

The easiest way to feed your chickens is to buy non medicated layer pellets from your local supplier. These contain everything the hens need and are fed twice a day in the amount of a handful (a closed adult fist full) per chicken. If there are leftovers in the feeding channel at the next feeding time, reduce the amount slightly until no leftovers are encountered. Of course you feed slightly more if all is eaten up. Do not change the feeding formula abruptly or the birds will stop laying, but gradually change from one system to another no matter what system you want to use. If egg shells are thin, you can crush the ones you have and feed them back or buy some oyster shells.

Kitchen scraps are always welcomed by the chickens. Make sure you separate these from other waste while going about the daily kitchen activities.

Keep the fleas and mites under control, especially in the spring.

You normally do not know from what source the ingredients in the layer pellets comes but it will be an easy way to start with chickens. Some feed mills claim not to use any protein derived from animals (e.g. fish meal) in the fodder, this is what you want to aim for. A further step to independence (but a bit more work) is to feed them as follows. In the morning you mix equal amounts of bran, soy meal (for the protein) and a handful of ground egg shells to a mush by adding water (or milk). Feed about a handful (after the first time you will of course know how much that is) of this per chicken and check for left overs. In the evening you feed a mixture of equal amounts of oats and wheat and barley or rye if you have any. This will provide enough nutrition for the laying hens. Furthermore you need to make sure that there is clean water available to them at all times. This is very important. No matter how much food you feed them, egg production will be low if dirty water is provided. The best plan would be to locate part of the pen by a creek if possible or have a tap dribble constantly.

2.4. Raising your own hens

Raise your own chicks.

After about three years, laying hens decrease their egg production rapidly. You can kill these hens or just let them continue to finish their life in the pen until their natural death. You may also check and remove chickens that suffer due to their aging. The latter option means to check often for dead chickens in the pen and chicken house and if the same amount of food is needed for less return. Try to keep a new flock of chickens in another pen. Younger chickens may not integrate easily with the older birds and you can not control the feeding as accurately as you need to for the new flock.

If you bought some meat birds or have more then one rooster (for whatever odd reason) then you can butcher these as broilers after about 8 to 9 weeks or as roasters at about 14 weeks. Meat birds can be reared separately and fed on broiler feeds. They will grow faster on these higher-protein, higher-energy rations.

To raise your own birds, you can purchase one day old chicks from a commercial hatchery. Brood the chicks under electric or gas heat, starting them at 95°F (35°C) at the level of their backs for the first week. Drop the temperature 5.4°F (3°C) each week until they are 6 to 8 weeks old, at which time the heat can usually be discontinued, depending on the surrounding temperature. Place the water close to the heat. You can use cut off plastic containers made stable by placing a rock in the water. Make them not too high as the little chicks can easily drown. Distribute chick starter in flat bowls again using cut off plastic containers. A feeder channel with a roof, and the sides barred to about 1¼" (3 cm) to allow the head to go in only, will keep the food clean

and less is wasted. Unfortunately in our region chick starter is only available as a medicated product. After six to eight weeks you can switch to non medicated chick grower until they start laying at about 20 weeks of age. At that time you feed them as described for laying hens. Make sure that chicks have dry, clean bedding with shavings.

2.5. Chickens, does it pay?

Well here we are again. Does it pay? We consider a flock of 50 birds to be a small size flock. In the cost analysis we don't take into account buildings and depreciation as they may be built fairly reasonably with slab wood and only a tin roof may have to be purchased.

Egg production:

– 1st year	240 eggs
– 2nd year	200 eggs
– 3rd year	170 eggs
– Total per hen	610 eggs

This results in an income for the whole flock of (2541 doz. at $ 2.00) a total of Can.$ 5082.00.

Expenses are layer pellets for 50 hens ($71.00 per month) at $ 2556.00 and 50 new chickens at $ 212.00 for a total of Can$ 2768.00.

The total net income over three years will result in Can. $ 2314.00

This comes to about Can$ 711.00 per year or a salary of about $ 4.30 per hour, putting in a half an hour per day to look after them. These figures are based on 1994 prices, but the bottom line usually reveals a similar result. It does not sound like much and you may see why large chicken factories need be set up to compete with other markets at the cost of quality of life for the chicken. What you really need to value on this whole deal is that you provide a wholesome product and feed yourself with healthy eggs. You also do not keep the animal in a questionable environment. And lastly the by-product, a wonderful manure, is free to be integrated in your way of Harmonic Living. If these values bring you the substance of life and you feel right with it, it's worthwhile to travel that way.

3. Rabbit meat

Rabbit meat is a white and very tasty meat. Properly prepared it can be a delicacy. Grown on green food stuff, the meat will be very tender. Rabbits have large litters and therefore it is easy to produce a large number of animals in one season (spring to fall). For the meat eating person, this is one easy survival food.

3.1. Fencing, feeding

As rabbits are kept in pens (as described in chapter two) fencing is not an issue. Try not to have rabbits run around free. They can damage fruit trees, especially young ones, easily by chewing off the bark on the bottom of the stem. Of course they also like the carrots and other goodies in your garden later on during the year. Fences do not work if not buried into the ground for about a foot. Using one of the pens as shown in chapter two will provide advantages over the commercial cages. During the summer season the rabbits are moved along the grass patches and act like a lawn mower and at the same time fertilize. The droppings from the rabbits slowly deteriorate, and are gradually worked into the soil by the weather, and are therefore not too strong for the grass. The rabbits get fat and all that is required is to move them regularly, twice a day, and to bring them water. No special food is required, but you can provide them with some extras such as dried out bread, carrots, peelings from the kitchen and the outer leaves from lettuce, etc. Towards the end of the season you try to keep just one or two does and a buck.

Come winter, it is necessary to feed the rabbit hay containing a bit of alfalfa. During the winter one male rabbit consumes about 2½ bales of 1st class hay. Some dried bread may also be obtained from a bakery and of course kitchen peelings, apple cores and other kitchen waste, will provide extra food. Clean water should be given from time to time, but rabbits also do fine with just fresh snow.

Rabbit meat, one of the survival foods.

3.2. Breeding rabbits

Rabbits usually breed throughout the year, though there may be a seasonal winter depression. The doe remains fertile for long periods and it can be assumed that a doe is fertile at all times. The gestation period, the time from mating to giving birth, is 31 to 32 days. The breeding age varies between different breeds but starts around four to five months. Try not to over feed the rabbit as breeding success diminishes with fat build up for the doe or the buck. Older bucks do not like heat, and temperatures above 84^{0}F (29^{0}C) over several days will cause infertility. With short days approaching in the fall, does are affected in the reproductive cycle and start to prepare for winter (thicker coat).

Rabbits are kept in movable pens.

Natural mating is the best method to achieve a high conception rate. Bring the doe to the pen of the buck, as does are protective about their own pen. Place the doe with her back to the buck. This way he can mount her quickly and accurately. A receptive doe will raise her hindquarters and throw up her tail to permit entry by the buck. Upon contact, the buck ejaculates almost immediately. In the act one or both animals may give off a cry. After mating, the buck usually falls over on his back or side.

At time of kindling, make the doe feel comfortable.

Kindling (giving birth) is a critical time so it is important that the doe is comfortable and prepared with proper nesting material before the delivery of her young. Most does kindle at night and they resent interference. A nest box containing hay or straw has to be placed in the doe's cage 27 to 28 days after she has been bred. The day before the doe kindles she may refuse to eat but will drink freely. Just before the young are born, she will complete the nest with a layer of hair which she pulls from her belly. The bunnies are born blind, deaf and almost furless. As soon as possible following kindling, you should quickly and quietly check for babies left outside the nest. If discovered in time, the young may be saved by warming them and placing them in the nest covered with fur. One safe method for warming a baby that is unconscious with cold is to place it under your armpit until it is revived. However, there is the possibility that the mother may not accept it anymore. During the first inspection you may take a count. Litters vary from two to nine kids, but usually there are four or five. The young rabbits remain in the nest box for about two to three weeks, during which time they rely solely upon their mother's milk for nourishment. Losses may occur at about three weeks of age when the young begin to leave the nest box and eat solid food. From 3 to 10 weeks the most common cause of death is diarrhea or rabbit dysentery, sometime attributed to too low-fiber diets. The nest box should be removed after three weeks. While stress is not a disease, it is a contributing factor to many health problems in rabbits (for that matter for bees too). Stress can come from transporting rabbits, pregnancy, kindling, lactation, changes in diet, infections, nervousness to noise, etc. Try to avoid situations of compounded stress. To elaborate on that do not transport rabbits while pregnant through down town city traffic on a sunny summer afternoon and on a bumpy road.

Animals should not be kept under stressful situations.

Figure 6-4, Handling mature rabbits

3.3. Handling rabbits

Rabbits are often frightened by loud, strange or sudden noises. You need to lift and handle your stock to examine them for disease or injury or to move them. Small rabbits may be lifted by grasping them around the loin (around the waist, between last rib and the hip). A mature rabbit may be lifted by grasping the fold of skin over its shoulders with one hand and supporting its rump with the other hand as illustrated in fig. 6-4. Tuck its head under your arm to calm it and keep it from struggling. Determining sex of young rabbits is important for breeding. You can sex a bunny as early as three days after birth, but you may run the risk of injuring the delicate organs. A good time to determine sex is at about two months of age. Hold the rabbit on its back on your lap. Carefully push the fur covering the sex organs into the rabbit's body a bit to reveal the organ. In the buck, the penis will protrude as a rounded tip (cone shaped), while in the doe a slit will be revealed.

4. Rhubarb leaf spray

Liquid leaf spray, also called rhubarb spray, is effective to fight off aphids on fruit trees. It may not be as effective as stinging nettle, but is available early in the spring, in time to fight the first parasitic aphids. To make rhubarb liquid spray do the following:

- Take a bundle of rhubarb leaves (whatever you can carry comfortably under your arm). If you have too many leaves the mixture does not get any stronger, but it will be awkward to take liquid from the mixture.
- Put the leaves in a 10 gal. (45 l) garbage can filled half way up with water.
- Stir this twice a day for about 10 days (or until it does not give any foam off anymore). The brew will give off a strong odor, a sign that it is ready. You may want to keep the lid on this mixture. Adding some rock dust may remove the smell and it may still be useful, we have however never bothered about the smell. Spray this liquid diluted by 1 part to 10 parts water over the leaves of the fruit trees every third day or after rain, whatever comes first.

Summary of activities:

5. General

- Cress and spinach, seeded in March, will come up at the latest towards the middle of this month, with spinach making its first broad leaves. Some weeding for these crops may be needed. The long-standing variety of spinach will also show first signs of coming through the soil and some varieties will reach a height of 3 ft. (1.2 m) in early summer.

- In general, seeds should not be covered with more soil than the seed's largest dimension. Very small seeds may be broadcasted, but for carrots, thinning later on may be easier if seeded in rows. If inexperienced, mix the seeds with some fine soil and then seed. Follow the instructions on the seed packages if in doubt. We usually gently pack the covered rows with the back of the rake to discourage the birds from picking the seeds out again.

5.1. Activities, early April

- The emergence of the first weeds will be the signs that the soil is warm enough to seed the first crops. Another natural pointer may be the opening of the rhubarb leaf.
- Garlic, planted the previous fall, will also poke through the soil.
- As long as grapes are not starting to show enlarged buds, you can still prune them.
- Transplant raspberries, blackcaps or loganberries (see chapter 3) or get them now from the market.
- Clean the goat pen.
- Finish mulching all garden areas including berries.
- Rake seed rows.
- Start with setting up new irrigation system.
- Build or repair chicken pen fencing. Chickens need to be locked out of the garden now.
- The outside seeding can take place as shown highlighted in fig 6-5.
- Climbing peas need a fence or similar structure to climb up as shown in fig. 6-6. Using an iron rod the holes are prepared spaced at about 7 ft. (2.1 m). The minimum 36" (90 cm) high chicken wire fence is then stapled to the posts. Posts, taken from thinned out

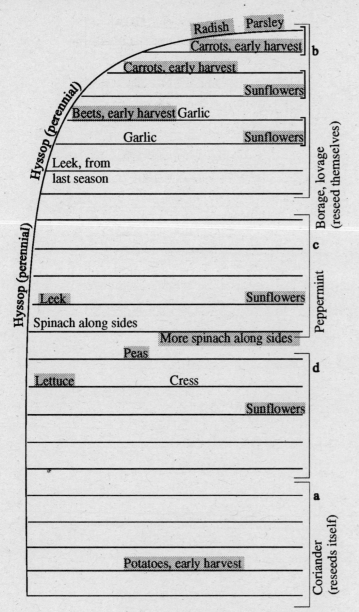

Radish   Parsley
Carrots, early harvest   **b**
Carrots, early harvest
Sunflowers
Beets, early harvest Garlic
Garlic   Sunflowers
Leek, from
last season

Hyssop (perennial)

Hyssop (perennial)

Borage, lovage
(reseed themselves)

c

Peppermint

Leek   Sunflowers
Spinach along sides
More spinach along sides
Peas   **d**
Lettuce   Cress
Sunflowers

a

Coriander
(reseeds itself)

Potatoes, early harvest

Figure 6-5, Seeding in early April

bushes, can be as thin as 2" (5 cm)
in diameter.

– Beets are seeded in the centre,
garlic running along the sides of
the seed bed. Or, for more beets
and less garlic, the garlic would be
seeded in the centre next fall.

– More spinach can be seeded along
the edge of the seed bed in such a
manner as to leave room for the
succession planting of cabbage.

– Sunflowers will re-seed themselves
every year but you have to start out
with seeding some the very first
time. Spread the sunflower seeds

over the whole garden if you have
that many. Later on you thin them
out. Transplanting them in the
early stages works but sets them
back a bit. Space them at a
distance of about 4' (1.2 m). Like
the sunflowers, coriander and
borage will re-seed themselves.
Some of the borage, voluntarily
growing, can be transplanted with
good results.

– All the seeding should take place
at the appropriate time, using the
calendar. The root crops seeded for
early harvesting may be skipped
and seeded later, given that the
root cellar can store such crops for
close to a year with little loss in
quality. Potatoes will usually start
sprouting and with it lose some of
their taste. It is always enjoyable
to taste the first fresh potatoes or
tender carrots as early on in the
summer as possible. Seed the
carrots alongside the seed bed but
leave room for the onion sets later
on.

– Chives could be added and grown
together with the carrots.

– Seed a small patch of early lettuce
in the designated row.

– Inside seeding of tomatoes, cabbage, lettuce and marigolds, (broc-

Figure 6-6, Fence for climbing peas

coli, cauliflower, eggplants, peppers and swiss chard if planned into your garden layout) can take place no later than mid April.

– Oak barrels to be used for water storage should be kept wet to prevent shrinkage.

5.2. Activities, late April

– Transplant inside seeding of tomatoes, cabbage, celery and marigolds and other crops as planned into the garden layout. We use cut off milk cartons as planters but peat pots can be purchased reasonably cheaply. Transplant when the plant is at the four leaf stage. Lettuce can be transplanted at different times but prime time is at about 2" (5 cm) of growth.

– Fig. 6-7 shows the next step in seeding.

– Peas grow well and should peak out now.

– Leeks, will take a bit longer to show up.

– The early seeding of lettuce should also show good results, with poking through the soil towards the end of April and the same goes for the radishes. Another small patch is seeded with different varieties of lettuce and later on transplanted throughout the seed bed. Regular transplanting will provide lettuce over a long period of time.

– Flakkee Long carrots, a variety of **large** carrots, store better in the sand bed and are easier to find. For us they are one of the survival foods. Seed them alongside the seed bed to leave room for the seeding of onion sets later on.

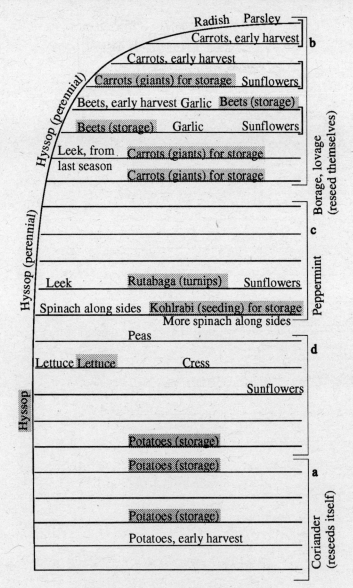

Figure 6-7, Seeding in late April

Carrots can not be transplanted so you try to seed them rather sparsely. Use some sand mixed with the seeds. However, you can always thin them out. Pick a few good shaped carrots and beets from the root cellar and plant them out for seed. Plant them in a sunny spot. They will go into seed to be picked in early October.

– Rutabaga (turnips) and beets can be thinned out and transplanted successfully once they are about 1½" (4.5 cm) tall. They will grow quite readily.

- The planting of kohlrabi will take away some space from the cabbage row. You need to decide what you like more. Kohlrabi tend to get woody and are not as ideal for storage as the cabbage. Fresh kohlrabi however have a wonderful taste.
- Peppermint, lovage and Hyssop are perennials. New hyssop can be seeded a year ahead of the cabbage patch, in order to be used to lure away the cabbage moth (butterfly).
- For a larger garden or the farm, clover can be seeded to be used as pasture and as a green manure crop.
- Most probably all rows need some weeding now. Take the weeds while they can be uprooted with a rake and place them on the mulch to wilt. Weeding at this point of time will save you from digging the soil later, once the weeds are established. For larger fields, a diamond harrow can be used.
- Tend indoor plantings.
- Trim hooves of all goats.
- Castrate young bucks.
- Pick some dandelion flowers for tea.
- Set up a system as in fig. 6-1 for goat tethering.
- Check state of fir tips. They can be collected at the stage when they just open up. This happens around mid May, but sunny south facing hillsides may be a bit ahead of that. They can be eaten raw and are a high source of vitamin C. Dried, in the shade to maintain the colour, they can be stored for a whole season and make a wonderful tea to remind you of spring while in the coldest time of winter.
- Check the state of the yarrow flower. They start flowering around this time of the year and well into June. Just the flowers, dried, make a tea to be used against headaches. The tea is said to be of help especially for women. It is however not recommended to be taken when pregnant.
- If you have access to old oak whisky barrels you may be interested in purchasing them to be used as water barrels for your garden or, cut in half, to be used as planters. They last a long time. Before you engage in these aforementioned projects, it is said that some whisky remains in the wood of these barrels and that it could be "rescued". The process is called swishing or grogging. Consult with the appropriate authority about the legality before proceeding and acquire the necessary license if so required. As of this writing, in British Columbia it is legal to do so for your own consumption. Also confirm with the supplier that by no means the inside of the barrels have been contaminated.
- The whisky is collected by soaking the inside with about one gallon of water for about three weeks, while turning the barrel twice daily, to end up with some liquid. Strained with a milk filter it will become very clear. I leave it to the reader what to do with that much whisky but if you are not drinking it you may use it as a disinfecting solution or to prepare tinctures. Chapter 9 will reveal some recipes about how to make liqueurs with whisky using the different berries then available. I'm sure that this is not a requirement to maintain harmony with nature but in the cold winter a sip from a nice tasting berry liqueur may be gratifying.

7

Early May, Bee Keeping

The dandelions, key to timing

1. General

In the real sense of the word, as a bee-keeper you get stung once in a while. It is an experience of lesser pleasure but the body does adjust to the pain rather quickly and further stings become less painful as the season progresses. The sting should be scraped off using a fingernail as soon as possible to minimize the amount of venom pumped into the wound. Start to scrape the skin with your nail about an inch away from where the sting is and continue scraping through the sting. One should never try to remove the sting by pinching it, since the pinching will release more poisonous venom into the wound. The best first treatment is immediately to chew some sage leaves and to apply that juice to the wound. Honey applied to the wound will also reduce the pain and so does baking soda. If you are allergic to bee venom it is highly recommended that you do not keep bees but direct your efforts to some other activity. Treatment for people with strong reactions is simple but will disrupt the continuous flow of handling the bees while shifting attention to cure the pain. It is however possible that one of the family members is allergic to the bee venom as is one of our sons. This person may stay inside at the time honey is removed from the colonies and wear shoes when walking close to the apiary. Bees are not likely to attack people and the danger is minimal. Locating the bees a 100 ft. (30 m) distance away from the house will provide a very low risk.

Several remedies can alleviate the pain of a bee sting.

Bees have a very sensitive system of alarms built into their colony. Every bee has its job assigned, according to age. A colony consists of about 5000 bees in the spring and up to an average of 50000 bees in the summer. The guard bees are the ones which set the colony on alert. Once the alarm has gone off the beekeeper must protect himself from bees trying to protect what is theirs by wearing a veil and gloves. Two to five colonies will constitute a reasonable size of operation for a beginner. With one hive only, you run the risk of losing all the bees in case the queen goes missing. With multiple hives the bees can be united with another hive as described in chapter five.

1.1. Location

Locate the hive away from areas of agricultural activities involving heavy use of pesticides or herbicides or other activities detrimental to the environment, such as air pollution by heavy industry, incinerators, etc. Nectar from monoculture cultivation should be avoided. Try to place the hive facing towards the south or east. It is advantageous to have some shade in the late afternoon. A natural windbreak, particularly against the cold north wind, is recommended and, if possible, the hive should be located on top of a bump or hill rather than in a gully where air is stagnant and wet. Keep the entrance of the hive so it faces away from areas frequently used by

Orientation and location of the hive is important.

Figure 7-1, Electric fencing

Most queens are imported from overseas. Find a local bee keeper from whom you can purchase colonies.

humans. To keep bears out of the apiary, electric fencing, as used for cows, is a workable solution and very effective. Install four wires, the bottom one not more than about 8" (20 cm) above the ground with posts 32" (80 cm) high and about 7 ft. (2.1 m) apart (see fig. 7-1). In some cases a light close to the hives may work as well. Our good sized, barking dog does not, however, impress a full grown bear.

In the spring bees need access to clean water. A stream or pond nearby is welcome or you can provide water by having it dribble down a wood board or something similar. To avoid drifting of bees (bees entering the adjacent hives due to the inability to orient itself, usually because of wind) and to minimize robbing, particularly at the time you take honey out, **hives should be at least 10 ft. (3 m) apart**. For just two or three hives it may not be so critical but with lots of hives it will definitely ease the process. Usually the smell of fresh honey travels quickly to any nearby hive. These bees once mobilized will then try to come and rob the hive you are working on and with it trigger the guard bees to go on high alert. You should also have a good nectar and early pollen supply nearby.

To maintain a breed with just bees from your own apiary would require a large area without influx from other queens or drones. You have to consider that queens and drones could come from sites as far apart as 10 miles (16 km). The nests of origin are however most commonly separated by 3 to 4.5 miles (5 to 7 km). Other colonies in that area will, to some degree, affect your breeding stock. To provide an abundant selection of drones, it is recom-

mended to have 20 or more hives involved in the process.

1.2. The bees

Bees can be obtained by buying package bees, which were imported from the US until about 1988, but now come primarily from New Zealand and Australia. In most cases, just the queens are imported, united with some local bees, and sold as nucs. A nucleus or nuc is a four or five frame colony with a laying queen. When moving bees make sure to check with the local regulations. Install the four or five frames in one deep (full) hive body, from now on called box, and fill the rest of the spaces with foundation or clean drawn comb. Feed, as mentioned later in this chapter, for about two to three weeks, depending on nectar sources available and provide additional room as the colony increases in size. These bees should be producing honey in the following year. Another way is to find or catch a swarm. Such bees should be isolated until proven not to have a disease. A swarm found (right after swarming) high up in a tree usually has a young, virgin queen, sometimes called a singer swarm. A swarm found low usually has an old queen. A working colony in the spring will consist of one fertile queen and about 5000 to 10000 bees. The queen lays the eggs, which are small, white elongated-oval shaped and slightly curved. The egg will at first stand up almost straight for the first day and slowly recede into the bottom of the cell on the third day.

Later in the spring (May), drones, the male bees who take 24 days to hatch, will also be present. They are quite a bit larger and rounder. They can not sting. Their sole purpose is to enjoy life and, if possible, mate after which the drone dies. All drones will live throughout the year until fall, when the worker bees ban them from entering the hive. So much for the drones.

Worker bees usually hatch after 21 days and are assigned many activities such as house cleaning, brood tending, queen tending, comb building, food handling, ventilation, guard duty and orientation flights before the nectar gathering task is finally assigned to them. During the summer peak month a bee may only live about a month in which time she may be able to collect the amount of a tablespoon of honey. During the winter month the bees have a life span of up to 7 months before they are replaced, many losing their lives to maintain the cluster.

The queen is the main impulse for the colony. She lays up to 2000 eggs per day in her peak season. If a queen is not up to snuff (aged) the bees start to produce new queens by feeding one day old female larvae with royal jelly. At the fourth day of development from the point the egg was laid the larvae is formed having the shape of a letter C. As it grows it will turn into a pupae at the time the cells get covered and eventually a new queen will emerge from the cell. There will be many queens hatching but only one is allowed to stay. Within sixteen days of the eggs being laid the old queen will suspect that she is about to be replaced. Before the first new queen hatches the old queen will leave the hive with some of the bees.

There is no clear understanding about what triggers the event but the obvious influence is the weather and internal communication factors. The swarm will usually appear between 10 a.m. and 1 p.m. According to some literature the bees swarm just after covering the queen cells. This would mean about another 7 to 8 days until a new virgin queen would hatch. My own experience, however, shows that the first swarm will leave the hive more towards the end of the development of the queen cells, sometimes just shortly before the hatching of a new virgin queen. This is based on listening for the sound that virgin queens give off to determine if other queen cells are present in the colony. Once the swarm is placed in a new hive I make sure it has the old queen with it. This is determined two days after by the appearance of a brood pattern, eggs visible in adjacent cells usually in the centre, bottom half of the comb.

Hearing a "Tuuu-tu-tu-tu-tu-tu" piping in the original hive tells the observer that a queen is about to hatch or has already hatched. Some of the other queens in the colony will actually answer the call back with a sound similar to a frog, "Quack-quack-quack-quack". These sounds can be heard as early as 2 days after the first swarm leaves and as soon as 2 days later a second swarm with a virgin queen may emerge from the colony. This may well be the reason why a second swarm is sometimes called a singer swarm (especially in some German literature).

During the swarm period of a colony it is extremely exciting to observe the hive by watching and listening.

I suggest that close attention paid to the hive at this particular time could be well rewarded. About two days after the first swarm has left the hive press your ear to the hive box and knock gently. Eventually you should hear the sounds of the queens. After the old queen has left you could cut out the extra queen cells to prevent the loss of more bees (due to swarming) and use them to start new colonies (see details under "forced swarming"). Be sure to leave one queen cell in the hive. However the preferred outcome would be not to have a swarm at all but a honey producing colony.

Swarms will usually appear on nice sunny days between 10 a.m. and 1 p.m.

Sometimes the first hatched queen will destroy all the others by stinging them before they emerge from their cells. Occasionally two queens will hatch at the same time and this could end up with a fight which only the stronger queen will survive. These are just some of the highlights of beekeeping. For further details please refer to the books listed in Appendix A.

2. What's involved

2.1. Nucs

The first nucs, a fertile queen with bees on 4 to 5 frames, will be available in late April, usually bred in warmer climates. It is however perfectly all right to breed with your own colonies in colder areas, where the dandelions will not open till late April or early May and the nucs therefore will only be ready in late May or early June. These nucs will not produce much honey in the first year but they have a distinct advantage by being locally established and adapted to the surrounding environment. They will be more disease resistant, especially if bred with that in mind. This means that the bees have not been pampered by using antibiotics or similar drugs to maintain their productivity but have been selected by the **survival of the fittest**. Try to buy from a local beekeeper who is selling some of his colonies or providing nucs.

2.2. Equipment

If you did not have the time to manufacture your own equipment as described in chapter three, you can still order it. Below is a list of materials needed for two hives. In the first year you can get by with only 40 frames, 7 lb. (3.3 kg) of wax foundation and 6 boxes. Eight more frames have been included in the listing to have adequate quantities of frames in coming seasons. Still more equipment would be needed to establish new colonies.

Item	Qty.
– Wired frames, Hoffman	88
– Foundation, 8 3/8"x 16 3/4" (212 x 425 mm)	15 lb.
– Bottom boards	2
– Entrance reducer	2
– Inner covers	2
– Outer covers	2
– Boxes, standard	10
– Frame rests, (sometimes included with box)	20
– Feeder pails	2
– Nails to put it all together	

2.3. Tools to handle bees
- Gloves
- Hive tool
- Bee brush or feather
- Hat and veil
- Smoker
- Maybe a suit

2.4. Tools to process honey
- Extractor
- Two uncapping knives
- Double sieve
- Jars, containers (glass preferred)
- A scale, if the honey is to be sold to the public

2.5. Miscellaneous tools
- Embedding tool
- One plate burner and pot to keep knifes hot

2.6. Notes

Many of the above items have been discussed in chapter three under the heading Beehive Construction. Tools may be shared with other beekeepers, but some diseases are easily spread via the honey and precautions need to be taken. The use of gloves, veil and bee suit are subject to individual preferences. If in doubt, buy the better or stronger product. At the time of harvesting, instead of using a bee brush to brush bees from the honey combs, a large bird's feather (from a swan or eagle) will do fine. As a strainer, a nylon cloth could be used, but do not sieve the honey through a mesh finer than 1/128" (0.2 mm). Using the honey as is, called comb honey, could eliminate the process of extracting and with it a lot of expense. In this case you must make sure not to have vertical wires embedded in the foundation as this would not allow you to cut the comb into reasonable sized blocks. The wires have been put in to re-enforce the foundation and to withstand the stress while extracting the honey.

3. Honey, does it pay?

That may be what your spouse will ask the next time you come back from the bee yard covered with bees. It would be well to remember that Harmonic Farming is a life style rather than a commercial venture. Paragraphs in this book dealing with monetary values will be the first to become inaccurate due to the changing values of the currencies. Money was first introduced to facilitate the trading of commodities but has since become a commodity itself. The true value of money is in the goods and services it can buy. In order to ensure that your money is not used for projects of which you do not approve it should be invested in things that you need or that you can be involved with. Such investments would be land, rental units, housing units, your own business, a small local business or a community based co-op. In the case of a co-op you would lose some of the control over your investment but could retain some control by keeping abreast of the organization's activities. These views may not help anyone to become a millionaire but an independent lifestyle coupled with humility towards nature will help you find your place in the universe.

A piece of land with a radius of 1 mile (1.6 km) will sustain, depending on the available forage, 20 to 30 colonies of bees. Compared to other farm activities a larger initial investment will be required. Coping with new diseases and a shrinking nectar source will provide a challenging future.

Equipment and bees for twenty colonies will cost about Can$ 4000.00. To this the cost of tools and processing equipment is added to come to about Can$ 5000.00. For our method of beekeeping a lower than average honey crop of 50 lb. per colony (23 kg) can be expected. Honey of this quality is valued by the consumer and can be sold at a dealer cost of about Can$ 1.80 per lb. ($4.00 per kg) due to the high demand. In order to replace the equipment within 10 years the following yearly cost analysis can be done:

- Honey sales $ 1800.00
- Cost of equipment $ 500.00
- Cost of yearly operation (mainly
  the cost of sugar) $ 300.00

Spending 120 hours to manage the operation will result in an hourly wage of about Can$ 8.30. You may generate some additional income with the sale of wax, propolis and nucs, if you follow these avenues.

4. Spring management

At the time the first dandelions are flowering -a sign of plenty of nectar- the bees need to be managed. If nothing else, at least the third box of honey frames should be put on top of the two brood chambers. This will most likely make the colony move its brood nest into that box and, sooner or later, they may swarm. I do not approve of this method except to breed new colonies. If not yet done, close the top entrance now. You could achieve this by turning the inner cover around so that the small entrance will be at the back and facing up or just simply plug it up. Before you open the hive you should check with the calendar to select a flower or fruit day. So far you have just observed the hive and, if all went right, had nothing more to do. If you want to manage the bees it will become necessary to open up the hives for the first time in the new

It is much more enjoyable to use money, rather than to simply have money.

Paradoxically, people do lots for money and with little time left do little of what they like to do.

When working according to the calendar, manage bees on a fruit or flower day.

Humbleness needs to be fostered to overcome the power of money.

season. Fig. 7-2 shows the hive before and after the management of the colony.

4.1. Management without queen breeding

I prefer pine shavings in the smoker.

When disturbing the activities of the bees, some **smoke is always needed right at the start**. Smoke the bottom entrance first and, while you pry open the inner cover, blow some through the gap. Then lift off the inner cover including the empty box and outer cover. The guard bees, triggered to guard, are now calm and no more alerts go out and no more smoke is required. **Carefully** pull out frames to find a comb with one to three day old eggs. Start with a frame on the side and then work towards the centre of the box to minimize the danger of squeezing the queen while pulling out the first frame. You could also look for the queen but this requires experience to spot her. If you find eggs in the cells the queen can usually be found close to these cells. If the brood is swimming in lots of brood food, the whitish coloured juice, the colony may be preparing to swarm. You should become alert to check for other signs of swarming. If you find eggs, which is usually the case, put all frames back and **reverse the two boxes**. Pry the boxes apart in the front, blow some smoke in the gap and then pull the top box forward an inch or so. Flip it up so it rests on its edge on the back of the bottom box as shown in fig. 7-3. Before swapping the boxes, check on the bottom of the flipped up box for queen cells or small cups, both signs of swarming. If you find eggs or brood in the cups you can be sure that swarming is in progress.

If no eggs can be found a problem exists. Most likely the queen is missing and you should unite the colony as described in chapter five. The lack of eggs may, however, indicate that swarming is in progress. Once the swarming process has started the queen lays few eggs. However, you continue with the steps outlined here. The new situation encountered will force you to manage the colony to breed queens and you need to read about the technique of forced swarming later on in this chapter. Check all the queen cells, the ones shaped

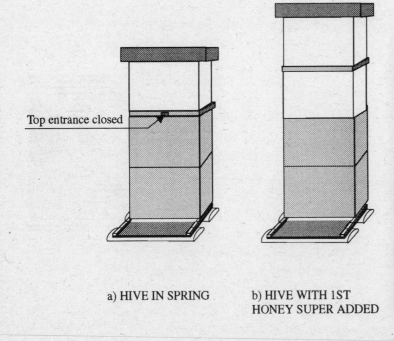

Top entrance closed

a) HIVE IN SPRING   b) HIVE WITH 1ST HONEY SUPER ADDED

Figure 7-2, Bee hive before and after spring management

Figure 7-3, Top box flipped up

to a cone, protruding from the frames (fig. 7-5). Note if they are covered or not.

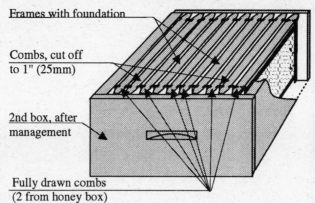
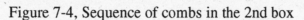

Frames with foundation

Combs, cut off to 1" (25mm)

2nd box, after management

Fully drawn combs (2 from honey box)

The top box is now placed as the first box. Set the former bottom box on top of the box just checked and take out 3 to 4 frames, which do not contain brood or pollen and are dark in colour or otherwise in poor condition. Always take out 4 frames if the hive has both boxes filled with bees.

Figure 7-4, Sequence of combs in the 2nd box

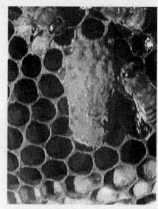

Figure 7-5, Queen cell

Cut the comb on two of the above frames down, to have just a 1" (2.5 cm) wide strip remaining below the top bar of the frame. With the use of a wired foundation this will be difficult so you will have to use pre-constructed frames.

Put these into the box as the second frames on either side, between new straight drawn combs. The rest you fill up with fresh foundation and drawn comb. Make sure that you put frames with foundation between well drawn combs (alternating) as shown in fig. 7-4. The bees will re-build the cut off frames most of the time with drone cells (fig. 7-6) which are a bit larger then the cells required for the bee brood (fig. 7-7). In two years you will manage these same frames again and cut or replace them as required.

Now add the third box, to be used to store honey, and close up the hive. To build up new combs, some of the frames in the third box need to be frames with foundations. To replace all 20 brood frames within 5 years, you would need to introduce 4 frames with foundations every year. Two frames with foundations introduced to the third box will guarantee that this will happen. In this fashion two fully drawn frames from the honey box can now be used to

replace two more old frames in the, now second, brood box. Experience shows that fresh drawn drone combs could also be used as honey frames. However not everybody wants to store honey in frames that have been used to rear brood. I leave it to the reader to make that decision. With the replacement of 4 frames per hive every year it will not be necessary to use brood frames in the honey boxes.

Figure 7-6, Drone cells (protruding caps)

Always handle the frames very carefully and try not to squeeze bees or, worse, the queen. Try holding the frames to be removed over the box, until all bees are shaken or brushed off. If the colony is not strong (only one box filled with bees), you may want to wait with the third box for another two weeks. This will help the colony to maintain the temperature more easily. On the other side of the scale, a strong colony filling two boxes with bees needs a lot of room.

Handle everything gently. Don't let yourself get irritated if stung. Do not make any fast movements.

4.2. Management with queen breeding

Some more equipment is needed to provide housing for the new colonies. Every third year the queen should be replaced by introducing a new queen. By replacing the queen, a colony will stay vital. But experience shows that older colonies will often re- queen by supersedure or swarming. Superse-

Figure 7-7, Worker bee cells (flat caps)

Queen breeding is done by establishing whole new colonies rather than just queens.

dure, the easiest way to handle reproduction, with no work involved at all, is a process where the bees themselves take the initiative to replace the queen with no swarming involved. Recognizing the signs of swarming will enable the bee keeper to apply the forced swarming technique explained later. Many ways exist to breed new queens. In most cases it is labour intensive and you need to check and manage the colony several times to achieve the goal. The methods described here will be the least labour intensive. It will avoid disruption to the colony's activities as much as possible and is therefore done at the same time as the spring management.

Two methods have been used on our farm. The first, to **split** strong colonies. This may not be the most productive solution in regards to quantities of new queens produced, but it is simple. Success rate averages at about 70% and with this method you also reduce the chance of swarming. The second method, applied to colonies showing swarm trends, is to use swarm cells derived by the technique of **forced swarming.** This is a natural way to replace old queens with, however, a loss of honey production.

4.2.a. Splitting

Open a strong colony, from now on called the original hive. Find the frames with one to three day old brood and eggs. The one day old brood is the prime target for the bees to rear queen cells. If it is a strong colony up to 8 frames can be taken out, but usually 4 to 5 frames are taken.

Assure that you take out three to four frames with brood of all ages and one frame with pollen, possibly all in sequence. this means not to use frames from different locations within that hive. Make sure the queen is not on any of these frames. If you removed the queen, the colony would rear

a new one, given you had left some one day old brood in the original hive. The honey production would be low. This action is similar to forced swarming. When you take out brood ensure that all remaining frames with brood stay together.

In the original hive replace the four or five frames with new drawn comb placed on either side of the brood nest. You may take them from the other hive box. They are usually cleaned and ready to be used as brood comb. Place the box so prepared on the bottom. The next box is replenished with two cut off frames as described earlier and frames with foundation as shown in fig. 7-4. If no frames with foundation are available drawn combs can be put in but at least the 2 cut off frames need be introduced to that box, to allow the bees to build. Should all the frames be full of brood, the frames with foundation could be introduced into the third box.

Add the third box filled with drawn comb and foundation. Now close up the original hive. You may name it in order to refer back to it. If you want to compare information later on, keep a log book.

Put the four or five frames called a split or nuc into a new hive or use a special box. A nuc consists of 4 to 5 frames of bees and a queen, usually housed in a box that can accommodate 4 or 5 frames only and is specifically used to rear queens. These boxes are therefore sometimes also called nucs. Add drawn frames to make up the box. If available, put in a frame that contains honey. For further reference we will call this colony a split.

Write down the date and mark the split so you know where it came from (just in case you took the queen away).

4.2.b. Feeding splits (nucs)

Place the split in the new location and feed it with a 1:1 mixture of sugar and water or honey for the next 30 days. Dissolve the sugar while adding it to the hot water. **Add a tea mixture of dandelion, chamomile and oak bark** prepared as follows. Add a teaspoon full of each herb for one litre (quart) of water. Bring it to a boil and then remove it from the heat source. Let it sit for about 5 minutes. Now sieve it into the feeding pails (or jars). You add about 1 dl (10 ml) of tea per 1 gallon (4.5 l) of sugar water.

This new split will now rear queen cells from the larvae available and if all goes well queens will hatch within 12 days. Due to the limited size of the colony, the first hatched queen will usually be able to locate the other queen cells and sting the queens to death by cutting small holes in the cell sides. If other queens emerge at the same time a fight will determine which will survive.

4.2.c. Forced swarming

While splitting

Observe the entrance of a new split. If lots of bees come in with pollen, you may have, quite by accident, transferred the queen as well. Open such a split after 5 days to verify. See if there are 1 to 3 day old eggs in the combs. If yes than you have **forced the original colony to think that the queen has left them with a swarm**. The fertile queen is now in the split and the original colony is busy rearing queen cells. In such a case you may, after the queen cells are covered or at the latest 11 days after the split took place, split that original colony (now it comes in handy to know which hive the split came from) into as many more splits as there are good shaped, covered, queen cells available, if you so wish or

break them all out except one. Attach those cells on the upper part of a regular comb, so as not to damage the queen cell. You may have to remove a frame to allow a bit more space between these two frames. That frame will be put back in at the next inspection, 30 days after the split took place.

Feeding the split will ensure readily available food at any given time. Make sure you feed the tea mixture.

A swarm prone colony

The forced swarming technique can be successfully applied to a colony that is showing signs of swarming. The split is taken from the original hive after the queen cells are all covered. This will provide quality queens.

The original hive of the swarm prone colony may be reduced to one box, depending on how many frames with bees have been left.

A queen cell will be without a cell cover for the first seven days. After nine more days in a covered cell, the queen will emerge. You need to look at **all** the queen cells. You can split the colony 7 days after you find eggs in the queen cells, 4 days after you find larvae in the cells. With more experience you may be able to determine more closely the age of the queen brood and may act earlier. The worst that can happen is that you will loose the old queen while swarming. With regular observation however you would still be able to catch that swarm and then start the splitting. Make sure to leave one cell in the original hive. Prepare splits ahead, one less than queen cells spotted and use frames from other hives if needed. Transfer the queen cells, except for one, and make sure not to chill them. The old queen and about four frames of bees will be housed in a new hive. Later in the year, once the sunflowers are in full bloom, the queen can be replaced. At this time remove the old queen, add the colony to a split as described in chapter five, uniting it at the site of the split and the colony may produce some honey. Do this in the early part of the day, before the bees start to fly. I have not replaced these old queens derived from such colonies for the last few years. They are all healthy, good producing colonies. I assume that they

30 days after splitting the colony is inspected for brood pattern. You can wait another 10 days if no eggs are present. If not successful, you can unite the bees with another split.

have, shortly after the split, introduced supersedure. More observation will reveal the strength and survival of these colonies but so far it has proven successful.

4.2.d. Mating

The virgin queen, once hatched (fig. 7-8),

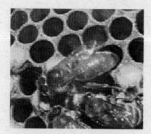

Figure 7-8, Queen

needs to fly out to get mated no matter which of the above methods have been applied. Once egg laying is observed, at the earliest 10 days after hatching, the new split will be well on its way to maintaining itself and growing until the fall. The minimum time from making the split to having a mated queen may be as little as 22 days and may go up to 40 days, with an average of 30 days. At this time you should inspect them. Earlier checking can be done, but may set a new split back or influence the development of the queen and with that her mating flight (especially in poor weather conditions, such as excessive heat or moisture).

4.3. Other considerations

The entrance of the split is kept small (½" (1 cm)) until the colony starts to increase in size. One problem with the method mentioned above is that the splits should be located about ¾ miles (1 km) away from the original hives, or too many bees may abandon the splits and fly back to the original hive. This may cause the split to become too weak to start rearing queen cells. It is therefore important to transfer lots of covered brood to maintain new bees in the split. As these new bees hatch, they will not leave the split, but take care of the house keeping tasks at hand.

The original hive will re-build the three to four frames with brood as quickly as possible and will be ready for the main honey flow. With this method some of the honey produced in the spring is used by the bees to build up new foundation which is an integral part of the operation. Old combs will produce smaller bees due to the cells not providing the maximum room for the succeeding brood, as a skin is left behind in the cell every time a bee emerges from it. Old drawn comb may also be more susceptible to disease and, when stored, the wax moth prefers them over the new ones. Renewing the combs is a necessary management technique, and in the spring it is vital for the bees to build new cells, particularly drone cells. If they are not able to do so swarming may occur.

Producing lots of drone brood in the spring may also help to control the varroa mite (varroa jacobsoni). The female mite prefers to attack the drone brood. Removing such brood will decimate the varroa mite population considerably and, over time, resistant colonies may be reared with selective breeding of mite tolerant bees. We are fortunate not to have this infestation in our apiary. This would require more time to manage and breed colonies. Below are methods to deal with the mite using natural remedies.

Bees of the kind such as Carnica and Lingustica have been found to show up to 3 times more activity in cleaning out the mites than those of the Mellifera (Otten 1991). As mentioned above, one way is to remove drone brood. Rather then cutting it completely out you could cut the cells off at about ¼" (5 to 8 mm) height and shake the infested drone brood out by tapping the frame onto a surface. With water the cells can then be cleaned further and the frames set away to dry and to be used again. The wax cut off could be stored and later processed as described in chapter 11. Such frames, one per colony, need to be replaced every 20 days or shorter (depending on infestation), starting in May and continuing throughout August. This method is quite time consuming but has the least impact on the quality of the honey and may be ideal for a small operation.

Experiments have been conducted in France using essences from plants, in particular the products thyme oil and sage oil. Using a sprayer that can produce a very fine fog frames have been treated with 1% thyme- and 0.5% sage-oil at 95°F (35°C). With above mentioned sprayer about 0.35 oz. (10 ml) of this mixture was applied to the colony, taking about one minute to do so. This treatment was done on day 0,3,7 and 10. Average success rate was over 95% and with brood free colonies 100%. This means that the treatments are more effective early in the spring or late in the fall when small amounts of brood are present. No residues have been found in the honey.

A homeopathic method may work as well, but no experience is available. You would gather the varroa and soak them in water for 3 days. Off this you would take one spoon mixed with 10 spoons of water. Shake it 100 times before you again take one spoon full and mix it with 10 spoons of water. You do this 7 times before spraying it onto the bees in the colony. No information is available at the time of this writing on how many treatments would be needed but monitoring the fallen off mites would give an indication.

Lactic acid, oxalic acid or formic acid (the last is available from beekeeping equipment suppliers, see Appendix A), can all be used to decimate the varroa population. All of these are to be handled with safety precautions. E.g. oxalic acid in its original (crystalline) form should be handled using gloves, a mouth cover and goggles. Oxalic acid has been used in Balingen (Germany) as a 3% mixture with distilled water and sprayed onto each frame in the amount of about 0.3 ounces (8 ml). It is the bees only that need to be sprayed. Two treatments after the honey crop (August,

early October) are recommended at temperatures above 46°F (8°C) and not on foggy or rainy days or after long periods of frost. No side effects have been reported and honey samples tested have shown oxalic acid contents of less then 0.0004 ounces per pound (25 mg/kg) of honey, a limit set in Germany to be acceptable. Oxalic acid is not, however, registered for use in Canada. It is naturally found in small amounts in the honey. The taste of rhubarb or spinach (0.8% in the leaf) for example is influenced by the amount of oxalic acid in them and it may be worthwhile to experiment with these plants.

5. Swarms

To catch a swarm a swarm box or a plastic garbage bag can be used. The swarm box needs to have some screened opening, a removable lid and should be build as light as possible. Calm the swarm by spraying it with water (or sugar water) and wait until it settles. Hold the swarm box below the swarm and shake the bees off the object they are clinging to. If they are close to or on the ground brush them into the swarm box (or plastic bag). Close the lid except for a small gap. As long as the queen is in the box, the rest of the bees will enter the box within the next half hour. Bees caught with the plastic bag should be emptied into a swarm box. Close the box and store the swarm for three nights in a dark cool room (root cellar). Prepare a hive box with the three centre frames removed and shake the bees in by shaking the swarm box. Gently replace the three frames and close the hive. An old queen will lay eggs after three days and you may want to unite the bees with a split as explained earlier. Swarm bees are very reluctant to sting. They have stored a large quantity of honey in their body and are therefore not able to control the abdomen as easily as usual.

Summary of activities: Early May

- Purchase hives.

- Find out when bees are available.

- Manage bees as outlined here.

- Gather dandelion flowers and dry them.

- Gather fir tips and dry them.

- Water crops seeded earlier if necessary.

- Pick the first radishes, most probably having a diameter of about 1" (25 mm) by now.

- Weed the garlic, spinach, cress and the flower beds that were seeded earlier, if necessary.

- Prepare the soil for the next seeding as outlined in chapter eight.

- Spend some time with the trees and bushes. Observe fruit trees and berry bushes and remove the insects and caterpillars you can spot but not the beneficial ones such as the ladybugs, earwigs or the green lacewings.

- Organize more mulch.

- Around this time of the year, we usually eat the last apples stored in the in-house root cellar. Red delicious and golden delicious both store quite well, but the winter banana is excellent and brings a change in flavour.

- The outside root cellar, with a temperature of about 46°F (8°C) at this time of the year, stores apples to taste almost just like picked. The cabbage and kohlrabi placed on the newspaper on the sand bed are also still fresh.

- Mulch strawberries and raspberries, if you have not already done so.

8

Mid May, Past the Last Frost

A handful of work

1. Nurturing, tending plants

Doing it is the most intensive way of learning. You will remember more readily and take in much more information by doing something yourself rather then listening to someone or seeing something, or a combination of both. By doing it, sound and movement become part of the action and you relate to an object physically, feeling and touching it as well as with a bonding to care for the object hopefully in a positive way. Such a bond may be more easily recognized when caring for children. With plants it may be more simple because there are no arguments. Such bonds to living things change in intensity but maintain a dynamic togetherness. Bonds to objects shaped by humans are very strong up to the point of ownership, usually until you buy the item, after which it can become a symbol, separate from you, but representing something for you (a car, a diploma or degree, etc.).

Less effective is learning derived by just seeing. **Try to become more aware of how you receive information that influences your travel on this planet**. You are probably aware of the fact that a blind person does not "see" as we do. Such a person's senses are more alert than normal and they can interact closely with their surroundings. We tend to rely too much on our sight to the detriment of our other senses.

Doing things, not only knowing about them, will give a better understanding.

2. Observation

Observing using the intellect

This relates to the things we acknowledge or see, as we learned in school or through other education. Relying on our knowledge of language, we instantly bypass other sensors that could bring the message across. While doing something we perceive mainly through the ears and the eyes.

2.1. Listening

Listening using knowledge

If we call our right extension on our upper body an arm, so be it. We assign sounds to objects, using the voice. This enables us to communicate with other people, using the same sounds, this is what we call language. With this tool, language, we can interact with another person and for example, can immediately tell the person how we feel. For our fast paced world this tool is very useful and different cultures have developed different languages to enable the people to most appropriately express themselves. This however eliminates the need

With plants we have no choice. Language will not help us at all to understand plants. Accepting this, we have to look for ways to improve our sensory input.

to observe a person for other signs. The knowledge of language immediately transfers the information about what state the person is in. But is the person speaking the truth? Can the words describe the exact feeling of the person? Can the person even express feelings with language or does language become an obstacle? Does the other person really understand what is being said? During the development of language expressions have formed, where for example we know exactly what a certain phrase means. But all this has silenced the other sensors we had or still have, to understand without using language. We are able to determine the meaning of many noises, such as laughing, giggling, crying and others but we can not stand next to a person and know how that person feels.

2.2. Looking

Seeing using knowledge

When looking at an object, our **knowledge of language** will immediately tell us how to name that item, and with this minimize our ability to perceive that item to be anything else. This is perfectly all right and of importance, in order to communicate with someone else, otherwise I could not share my thoughts with you. But it limits the possibility to see the object, lets say a mug as something quite different, like a holding device or a flower pot, etc. Even though two people for example look at the same mug, they almost certainly will distinguish it from another mug for a different reason. This means that the mug indeed represents something different to one person than to another but the language can not bring this to the surface, as both people call it simply a mug. We have to become conscious about our knowledge interfering with the sensory inputs. We will have to learn not to use knowledge in order to experience the sensory inputs. This does not only apply to listening and seeing but to feeling, smelling

and tasting as well. We could call it to "observe consciously". Observing things you have no clue about may help you to learn to "observe consciously". At the same time we have to become able to understand the new information so received. Once we are able to switch off our knowledge, the information may be received as outlined below. There may however be other ways to observe things that would bring such insight. I outline the technique I have come to use for my own development and therefore can easily describe.

2.3. Intensive observation

Seeing and hearing using your mind

We do use our eyes and ears but can also imagine what the properties of an object may be. Imagination is not hampered by the limitation of knowledge but can lead us to new understanding. Such vision may develop tools and equipment not yet invented. I leave it to the reader to explore and develop their own senses.

2.4. Spiritual observation

Seeing with your inner eye

Close your eyes and **try not to see with your intellect or your mind**. This may be easy to do, once the above ways of looking at things are understood. Such sensory input may be referred to as channeling and could also be via other sensors, such as hearing and talking, writing and moving (not necessary sleep walking, as in that case you are not awake). To activate or to make your sensors more sensitive to such input, meditation (see chapter 1) is one tool that can be used. This opens ourselves to our spirit to guide us, accepting the presence of our "real life" and I therefore call it spiritual observation. There is no scientific proof that this will have any change on our surroundings. However a person practising this simple way of observing can act according to the inner feelings and form a vision, which eventually will materialize within the physical limitations. You don't have to belong to any religion in order to practice this. There is no right or wrong in this matter, what is within you tells you what's right. It will however be of value to gather with other people in order to share the visions and messages that come from your "self".

3. Weeding, meditation

With a plant you can not use the knowledge of language. The plant does not understand your language. You have to look and listen to the plant differently to understand what it wants to say. Weeding a row of vegetables may result in a kind of meditation while first **using the language** that opens you up to listening, looking, consciously observing. Next, you try to see differently, without the knowledge of language, **sense** that feeling consciously, when moving your hand through the plants, touching the weeds, the plants, the insects, the drops of water on the leaves, the warmth from the soil, the texture of the soil and more. Let it become part of you. Envision what you perceive as mentioned above. Then let your mind wander, while forcing yourself to **observe spiritually**. Now you may understand what weeding is all about.

It is not by accident that weeds have an important role to play in relation to the plant's growth. They always grow when the soil or cultivated plant life needs attention, in this case, your attention. It actually forces us to go to the plant and remove the taller greens from around the freshly emerging cultivated plants. Pulling the weeds will loosen the soil around the plants, will bring you into contact with the plants and with you observing the plant as explained, your actions will become intuitive and caring.

With this you will understand what the plant needs.

The same applies when caring for the soil. Tending a seed bed before the first weeds poke through the soil will hamper the successful germination of the weeds because you disturb the soil. Because of the attention given to the soil, the life in that soil will make you act intuitively and you will provide the care necessary, in this case by raking the surface.

The more life there is in the soil, fed by organic matter, the more will your attention be gratified. Of course applying manure or mulch are all tending activities. I do not deny that the scientific factors are involved in the plant's growth, but with your **intuitive care the actions you provide will become amplified by the amount of life in the soil**. Poor or overworked soil has no life left in it, no insects, no bacteria, no fungi and with it no growth. In Harmonic Farming we depend on the life in the soil. Chemical fertilizers do show excellent plant growth but they feed the plant without the interaction of the bacterial life and problems that arise with this have been explained in chapter five.

While weeding we may try to "observe consciously".

Applying what we now learned will strengthen our skills in observing and we may be able to connect to the life forms in the soil or the plants. It actually is not important what physical activity you undertake as long as you form a vision as described and work in harmony with nature. Do not however assume that you know everything now or you will fall victim to the knowledge of the language, your intellectual body. We have to apply this kind of observation to become more intuitive. I will not be able to tell you how the microorganism in the soil will respond or what the plant will express towards you, but do interact with the plants as I described and you will be fed. Since we have worked our soil,

Nothing is by coincidence and weeds have a purpose to fulfill.

every year was a new and exiting adventure with an unknown outcome, but we always had food in abundance. Do this in good spirit and if nothing happens you have lost nothing. At this time of the year a basket full of seeds and plants, that look for a place to be, are waiting for us. With the seeding we allow the stored life in the seeds to take on new form and to provide food for ourselves, physically as well as spiritually. The crops as highlighted in fig. 8-1, the last major planting and seeding activities for the year, will fill in the yet empty rows.

4. Stinging nettle liquid manure (tea)

Stinging nettle can be used as a liquid manure, to feed plants at their roots or fruit trees via the leaves. It also helps to keep the aphid population on fruit trees down. With vigorous trees the problem may be minimal anyway. Watering plants with the tea will help the plant to stay vigorous. Use the following mixture:

Put approximately 8 lb. (3.6 kg) of green stinging nettle to 10 gal. (45 l) of water in a garbage can. Stir the mixture once each day, until it gets dark and no foam is generated anymore. It will smell rather unpleasant once the manure is ready (about 10 days later). Rock dust may cut down on the smell, but we have no experience with the manure's effectiveness afterwards. Filling the nettles into a jute bag may help keep the liquid clean from particles (useful when spraying). Do not pour over the centre leaves of lettuce. Use the manure while mixing it 20:1 with water for feeding of plants or 10:1 for the spraying of aphids on fruit trees. Repeat the spraying after rain. Heavy feeders like corn or cabbage may be watered with the 10:1 mixture.

Summary of activities:

5. General

If you aren't sure another frost is coming, wait. In our area you can seed some varieties of corn, tomatoes and beans as late as June 5. That's about 30 days after the dandelions opened. If you did not plant inside you can buy bedding plants at this time for planting. Be prepared for a bear to visit the apiary around this time of the year, especially if you live in a more remote area. It is quite impressive to know that the bear can carry away the whole box with the frames in it, not to be found anywhere nearby. Some bee-keepers have seen whole hives disappear. Bears usually appear in the early morning just at dawn (4.30 a.m.) and in the evening before dusk but they could visit at any time during the day. The encounter with a bear will put a bee-keeper into high gear, to set up some electric fencing or other devices as described in chapter seven. Crops seeded or planted at this time are highlighted and shown in fig. 8-1.

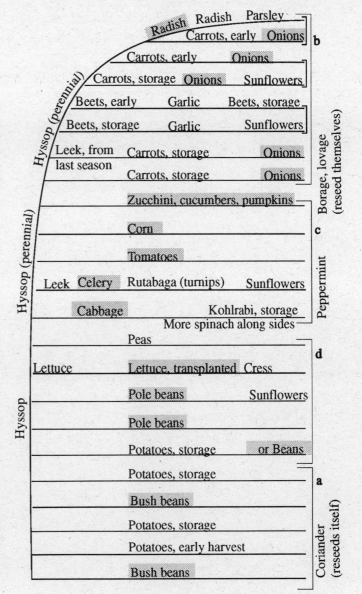

Figure 8-1, Seeding and planting after frost

5.1. Activities, after last frost

- Prepare all remaining rows three days before planting or seeding takes place.

- Set up poles for the beans and tomatoes.

- Hill the potatoes, once firmly above ground and pull the weeds. The mulch has to be temporarily pushed to the side to achieve this.

- Seed corn, bush and pole beans, onion sets, cucumbers, pumpkins and zucchinis. You can also seed some marigolds. Cucumbers could be started inside into peat pots and planted outside anytime after the last frost. Our experience has shown that planting them directly outside (after the last frost) is more effective.

- More radishes can be seeded while enjoying the earlier seeded crop.

- The seed bed may be wide enough to fit two rows of onions, next to the carrots.

– Transplant tomatoes, cabbage, celery and marigolds (and other seedlings if so planned into your garden layout). Incorporate marigolds with corn, tomatoes, cabbage and potatoes. If you have lettuce seeded inside, plant it out as well and transplant the remaining lettuce, seeded outside earlier, into the seed bed. Use a pencil to separate the small plants. Water all plants after transplanting.

– Make and use stinging nettle tea to spray fruit trees and berry bushes if infested with aphids.

– Horsetail can be harvested and dried (not in direct sunlight). You find it in the forest around springs and moist spots. We use this herb to feed the bees in the fall.

– The outside root cellar, with a temperature of about 53^{0}F (12^{0}C) at this time of the year still supplies us with apples such as red delicious. They taste good and show no signs of shrinkage. Use the last cabbages now before they start to sprout and rot.

– If all went well we will be able to pick a good crop of fresh spinach. Break out the leaves only and more pickings will be possible.

– Cress should also be available, eventually removed and the seedbed prepared to transplant more lettuce.

– The witloof, which is still growing in the outside root cellar, will provide another source of fresh lettuce.

9

June - July, Watch it Grow

Berries, vegetables and early apples

From now on, we can watch the crops grow. Most weeds have been kept out by several weeding sessions. Weeding according to the calendar will help in planning action. Use table 4-1 to determine the kind of day (e.g. a root day for carrots) and then look up the calendar. Or simply "consciously observe", as outlined in chapter eight, and take appropriate actions. The weeds are placed on top of the mulch to dry. They will add to the decomposing of the mulch. Of course weeding will take most of the time for the month of June. The important fact with weeding is not to get rid of the weeds, but to tend the plants. While raking around them, touching them and the soil, you help the plant. Your mind wanders over all the mountains and hills of thoughts gathered during the last few weeks and new ways of looking at them appear. Just try not to focus, and you will be guided toward the things that you need to think of. With this, the quiet time with the plant will help you to new growth too, in addition you achieve the task of keeping your plants above the weeds. Water is now becoming more important to keep the plants growing. On hot days, and with sandy soil the trickle irrigation system is on for one hour per day, so that every emitter will release about one gallon (4.5 l) of water. You may want to apply some stinging nettle manure for extra growth as described earlier in chapter eight.

As we slide into July, the workload changes from mostly weeding, which tapers of to a trickle now, into mostly picking berries. Starting with the strawberries, then in timely sequence cherries, red currants, raspberries, blackcaps, loganberries, black currants, white currants and some time later the jostaberries; we end the month by picking the early apples. During June the grass has been trimmed around these berries and fed to the goats. Weed eaters (these noisy machines) may work well, but I always think that they are a very aggressive tool and that the user's only intention is to get rid of the grass. Use the hand sickle. In 15 minutes I cut a heaped wheelbarrow full every morning and eve for the three milking goats, their offspring and the billy goat and they all love it. It doesn't matter if there are some thistles, wild roses or other plants with it. They love that just as much. The grass is taken from around the trees, berry bushes, steep borders and along the sides of the garden, in general wherever the rabbit pens can not be placed. You may use a glove on one hand, to protect yourself from an uncontrolled sickle movement (at least at the beginning) and the thorns of the plants you cut.

During this time of the year it is like walking through paradise, picking from all the different berries while having a stroll.

Use the rabbit pens on the easily accessible spots to mow the grass. You may experience that young rabbits escape the cage (shown in fig. 2-10) if set on uneven ground, and go off to your garden to eat the tips of the soy beans and other tender stuff or get chased by the cat for a feast. To avoid this you have to put small mesh chicken wire on the bottom stucco mesh all along the edge about 6" (15 cm) in.

The first processing of food has to be done in order to provide food during the winter. Several methods are outlined below.

1. Drying

Drying fruits will add some additional food to the table, once there is no more fresh or canned fruit available or to supplement what is coming from the root cellar. We can also dry tomatoes and beans.

1.1. Drying apples, plums and apricots

Dried food is easy to store and a wonderful supplement.

Drying apples is easy and fast. You need two things. First an apple peeler-slicing device, a contraption available in most hardware stores and one of the very useful tools. It will peal and cut the apple into a spiral all along the core. It then can be cut into rings with one vertical cut. Second, a food dryer (dehydrator). With a dryer as shown in fig. 9-1 apple rings will be dry within 24 hours. The dryer will come in handy towards the end of July, when the early varieties of apples are available. They can not be stored very long but are excellent for drying. We have also dried halves of plums and apricots which take about 2 to 3 days, depending on the size. The trays are rotated three times. Remove the bottom most three frames and move the rest of the stack down while at the same time turning the frames horizontally so that the front becomes the back. Now place the three previously removed frames at the top. Eleven trays will fit the dryer providing a capacity of about 40 lb. (18 kg) of fresh apples. Once dry, you will be left with about 4 lb. (1.8 kg). The same set up can also be used to dry beans and tomatoes. Instead of using a mosquito net and a blanket or goat skin to close off the top, a solid 3/8" (9.5 mm) piece of plywood with a fan mounted to remove the inside air, could be used.

1.2. Drying beans

Use young tender string beans. If they are too big and too thick they may not dry well. Blanch beans first (as described later in this chapter), then put them on the tray in the dryer. It will take approximately two days. Twelve pounds (5.5 kg) of fresh string beans will produce one pound (0.45 kg) dried ones. One of the many ways to use dried beans is given here:

– Soak a ¼ lb. (120 g) dried beans in plenty of water for about 4 hours, then drain water and keep 1½ cups (300 ml).
– Heat 1 tbsp. margarine in a pot, add 2 onions and 2 cloves of garlic, chopped.
– After 2 minutes add drained beans and the drained water kept from above.
– Cook for 30 minutes on low heat, then add 1 lb. (500 g) potatoes, cut into pieces. Cook on low heat until potatoes are done. Salt as desired.

1.3. Drying tomatoes

Slice tomatoes into about ¼" (6 mm) slices or thinner if possible. Use tomatoes that have lots of flesh as the juicy type of tomatoes may make a mess of the tray.

2. Canning, freezing

2.1. Canning berries and fruits

Wash jars well with soap and hot water. Boil lids for about 5 minutes. Fill jars with fresh berries leaving about 1" (2.5 cm) head space. Pour hot honey syrup in the quantities as described below over berries, until they are just covered. Wipe rim off with a clean damp cloth and attach hot lid with screw band. Place the jars in the canner and add water until ½" (1 cm) below the top of the jars. Heat up until boiling point is reached and maintain temperature for:

- Berries 20 min.
- Pears, apricots, peaches 30 min.
- Cherries, sour or sweet 25 min.
- Rhubarb 10 min.

Rhubarb is canned using its own juice. Slice the rhubarb and mix every four cups (1000 ml) with ½ a cup (125 ml) of sugar in a bowl. Let it sit over night. Do not even heat it. The following morning fill it into jars using the juice and proceed with canning.

2.1.a. Honey syrup

For 10 cups (2.5 l) of water the following mixture is recommended.

- Sour cherries, raspberries, apricots, currants use 2½ cups (800 g) of honey.
- Peaches use 1¾ cups (600 g) of honey.
- Pears, cherries use ¾ cups (250 g) of honey.

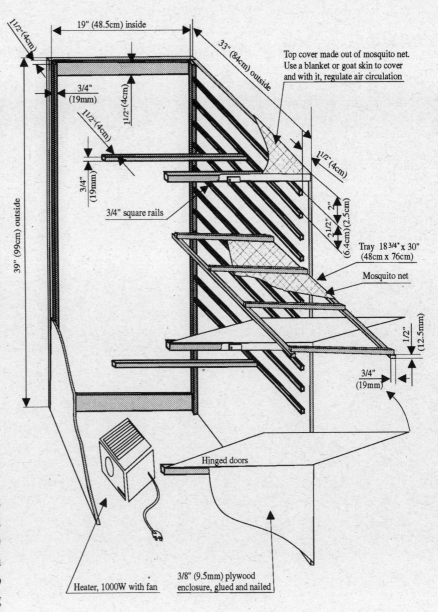

Figure 9-1, Food dryer

- Mix honey with water and use it, as mentioned above, while hot.

2.2. Canning beans

Beans can be canned raw. Wash them, trim ends and cut them into about 1" (2 to 3 cm) pieces. Pack them into washed jars. It will enhance the taste if some savory is added to the jars. Add 1 teaspoon of salt to quarts (1 litre jars) and fill them with boiling

Canning, freezing and pickling are common practice to conserve food.

water leaving 1" (2.5 cm) head space. Wipe off the jar rims. Place the hot lids and process them in the pressure canner with the weighted gauge at 10 lb. (68 kPa) for 25 min. If you are higher than 1000 ft. (300m) above sea level you have to adjust the weighted gauge to 15 lb. (102 kPa). Water bath canning is not recommended as it would take 3 hours. For other information on canning you may want to purchase the book called Bernardin Guide To Home Preserving (for details see Appendix A).

2.3. Freezing beans

Wash beans, trim ends and cut them to the desired length. Blanch them for 3 minutes. Now pack them into plastic bags or, better, freezer containers, in the amounts required for your meals.

2.3.a. Blanching

For blanching you use a large pot and bring the water to a boil. Add vegetables only about two hands full at a time and let it boil for the amount of time required (e.g. beans 3 minutes). Remove and place vegetables immediately into ice cold water and afterwards place them on a towel and let them dry off for about 10 minutes.

2.4. Canning peas

Put raw peas into jars within 1" (2.5 cm) of top rim. Do not shake or press peas down. Add ½ a teaspoon of salt to a pint (500 ml) jar. Add boiling water to cover peas. Wipe rim and fit hot lid. Process them in a pressure canner for 40 min. at 10 lb. (168 kPa) or 15 lb. (102 kPa) if processing is done above 1000 ft. (300 m).

2.5. Freezing peas

Blanch for 2 minutes. Put them onto a cookie sheet and pre-freeze them. Once hard fill them into containers.

2.6. Canning tomatoes

Cut tomatoes into small pieces. Pack them into jars, pressing gently to fill spaces. Add ½ to 1 teaspoon salt to each quart (1 litre jar). Wipe off the jar rims. Fit the hot lid and process in a boiling water bath for 45 minutes.

2.7. Freezing tomatoes

Small tomatoes can also be frozen whole. Prick the skins with a needle and freeze them. They are very nice to have for decorating stews.

3. Pickling

Cauliflower, broccoli, garlic, carrots, cucumbers, zucchinis, beets and beans can all be prepared as pickles. Hard vegetables such as carrots and beans need to be blanched first (3 minutes). Beets need to be cooked first. Cut the vegetables into desired size and prepare a mixture as follows:

For a light sour taste (e.g. cauliflower)
  – 10 cups (2250 ml) water
  – 4 cups (900 ml) vinegar
  – ½ cup (130 g) pickling salt
For beets instead of pickling salt use:
  – 1 tbsp. brown sugar
  – 2 cloves and 1 bay leaf

For a sour taste (e.g. cucumbers)
  – 12 cups (2700 ml) water
  – 7 cups (1600 ml) vinegar
  – ½ cup (130 g) pickling salt

  – Wash the canning jars in soapy water, rinse them and sterilize them in the oven at 180°F (90°C) for at least 20 minutes.
  – Mix above ingredients in a separate pot and bring to a boil.

- Add vegetables to pot, as much as is needed to fill one jar, and wait until it boils again.
- Pack vegetables into a hot jar and top off with the mixture to cover the vegetables.
- Attach a hot lid which has been sterilized in boiling water.

It is not necessary to process the jars in the water bath (canning). Let them cool off and keep everything as clean as possible. Before storing check to see if lids have sealed properly. they should have a slight inward bend.

4. Syrup (juice)

Use fully ripe berries and place them in a large pot. Crush berries and slightly cover them with water. Cook over low heat for 10 min. Pour into a damp jelly bag or a sieve lined with damp cheesecloth. A stool can be used, turned upside down, to hang up the cheesecloth by all four corners and a bowl placed underneath to catch the drippings. Fig. 9-2 shows this setup. Let it drip overnight. Squeeze slightly to remove all the juice. Measure juice and for 4 cups (1 litre) add 1.5 cups (500g) of honey. Bring to a boil and pour into the hot sterilized jars. Attach hot lid and let cool. Sterilizing jars can be achieved by putting the clean jars into the oven for a minimum of 20 min. at a temperature of close to $180^{o}F$ ($90^{o}C$).

Use this syrup by thinning it with water as desired, about 1 part juice to 4 parts of water. We found that we sometime run out of apple juice before the new crop comes in and the syrup gives us a welcome change.

5. Jam

In a wide pot mix 4.5 lb. (2 kg) of fruit with 3 to 5 cups (600 to 1000 g) of sugar. Slowly heat to boil. Simmer until desired thickness, approx. 20 to 30 minutes for black-red-white currants and blackcaps. For other berries it may take up to 60 minutes. If desired mash fruits before cooking. Put into hot sterilized jars. Attach hot lid and let it cool. Test lids for a slight bend inwards, which shows proper sealing. If this does not happen, the jam will not keep long and has to be consumed soon. However, you can heat it again and refill. In some rare cases the jar or lid may have a defect and you should check for any cracks or protruding parts.

6. Berry liqueur

We can use whisky to prepare excellent tasting liqueurs. In chapter six we briefly mentioned how to "rescue" the remaining whisky in the wooden barrels. We have used berries such as blackcaps, blackberries, raspberries, strawberries, currants, jostaberries, cherries and sour cherries. Use a large glass jar to mix the two ingredients as listed below with the

Figure 9-2, Separating berries

berries and let it sit in a warm place for about two months. We usually take just one kind of berry in order to enjoy the taste of that particular flavour.

- 4 cups (1000 ml) whisky
- 2 to 3 lb. (1 to 1.5 kg) berries

- After two months use a cheesecloth to filter the berries out (fig. 9-2) and set the liquid aside. It will be whisky with the berry taste, let's call it the "strong liquid".
- Put the berries into a pot. Add two cups (500 ml) of water and bring it to a boil. Use the filter again to end up with the "flavoured liquid".
- Mix the "flavoured liquid" with 3 to 7 cups (500 to 1500g) of sugar, depending on how sweet you like

to make it. Berries that are already sweet may use less sugar. Bring this to a boil and let it cool off.

– Pour the "flavoured liquid" into the "strong liquid", mix and fill it into bottles. No sealing is required. It will store for years or can be enjoyed now.

7. Swiss style pastry (pies)

Use a large cookie sheet 12" by 18" (30 cm by 45 cm) to prepare the pastry. Prepare a mixture for the dough as follows:

– 1¾ cups (200 g) flour.
– 2/3 of a cup (75 g) butter or margarine.
– ½ a teaspoon salt.
– Crumble the three above ingredients together.
– Add 1/3 of a cup (100 ml) water or milk and mix it to make a dough.

Let it sit in a cool place for a minimum of 30 minutes. Roll out the dough to fit the cookie sheet and lay it out. Make sure you punch some holes into the dough with a fork, to prevent the dough from rising (bubble).

Now use above to prepare pies such as spinach, swiss chard, cheese, red currant, cherry, rhubarb or apple pastry.

7.1. Spinach or swiss chard pastry

In swiss it's called "Chrutwäie" and is made as follows:

– Heat 1 tablespoon of margarine.
– Add one chopped onion and two cloves of chopped garlic.
– Take 2 lb. (1 kg) of spinach and chop it into pieces or mince it. Add this to the above.

– Steam it for 10 minutes and let it cool off.
– Mix two eggs with 1/3 (100 ml) of a cup of milk, one to two teaspoon of salt, pepper and nutmeg as desired and pour it into above.
– Spread above mixture evenly onto spread out dough in the cookie sheet. If desired you can sprinkle some small pieces (cubes of about 1/4 " (6 mm)) of bacon over the top. Bake this in the oven at 450°F (230°C) for about 30 minutes.

7.2. Cheese pastry

– Onto the spread out dough on the cookie sheet sprinkle grated cheese.
– Make a sauce to be poured on top as follows:
– Use 1½ cups (350 ml) milk, two eggs, 2 tablespoon flour and add salt, pepper and nutmeg to your taste. Mix it all together.

– Sprinkle caraway seeds, oregano, thyme, rosemary and onions over the top before baking if desired.

– Bake it at 450°F (230°C) for about 30 minutes.

7.3. Apple and other fruit pastries

The apple pastry (in swiss called Öpfelwäie) and other sweet pastries are made as follows:

– Onto the spread out dough on the cookie sheet, sprinkle about 1 cup (150 g) finely chopped hazelnuts or other nuts.
– Peel apples if desired and cut them into slices. Place slices on top of nuts. You can substitute any kind of fruit for apples.
– Make a sauce to be poured over top as follows:

– Use 1¼ cups (300 ml) milk, two eggs, two tablespoons flour, 1 tablespoon sugar (for sour fruits double this) and mix it together.

– Bake it at 450°F (230°C) for about 30 minutes. This will give an excellent tasting pastry. You can do this with other fruits such as red currants, gooseberries, cherries, plums, apricots and pears.

Summary of activities:

At the end of July the last berries will be harvested. Most of the processing has been done. Harvesting a 120 ft. (40m) row of strawberries may produce a crop of about 70 lb. (32 kg), starting to produce from mid June until the end of July. In the same period you may harvest 50 lb. (23 kg) of blackcaps from a 45 ft. (15 m) row and about 160 lb. (73 kg) of raspberries from a 120 ft. (40 m) row. Our top producing red currant bushes carry about 7 lb. (3 kg) of berries but you may only harvest half as much on average. We pick about 24 lb. (11 kg) of red currants and 8 lb. (4 kg) of gooseberries. Gooseberries are not as productive. We have been able to process most of these berries every year for our own consumption, except for some jam that we sell from the farm. A lot of fresh produce will become available now, such as zucchinis, peas, tomatoes, beets, turnips, beans, carrots, onions, potatoes, garlic, lettuce and kohlrabi (they taste great just raw at the early stage, at about 3" (7 cm) diameter). If planned into the layout of your garden, broccoli, fennel and others may be available as well. During June the rain usually keeps on coming at regular intervals and little watering is needed. We can harvest more radishes but they start to become hard and sometimes wormy.

Early June:
– Pick **spinach**.
– **Check splits** done 30 days ago to determine if a laying queen is present, else check again 10 days later. If no eggs are found, please read chapter five "Early inspection" about what to do next.
– **Remove spinach** gone to seed, except for a few strong plants for later harvesting of seeds.
– You may still seed some **corn**, depending on your growing season. Some corn needs about 120 days and in our region will still do fine if seeded no later than 30 days after the dandelions flowered.
– **Pole beans** can also be seeded. Some plants may have not come through the soil, and you can re-seed these spots.
– The spot where the radishes were growing can be seeded with **carrots**.
– **Rutabaga** (turnips), **beets** and **kohlrabi** can be transplanted now.

Mid June:
– **Weeding** of garlic, cabbage, beans, zucchinis and cucumbers may be needed.
– Be ready for some **haying**.
– A few more bowls of **spinach** may be picked from the second seeding of spinach.
– Weeding and the first **thinning of carrots** is needed. The distance between the plants should be no less then a finger wide. You can **still transplant beets** while thinning them out.

Late June:
– **Tend all plants** by loosening the soil around them and pulling some weeds.
– Pick the **first ripe strawberries**.
– Remove the **bottom leaves on** the **sunflowers** to allow more light to the plants below, such as onions,

carrots, potatoes, beets, cucumbers. The leaves can be fed to the goats and rabbits.

- The **first lettuce** can be picked and more **spinach** from the second seeding is ready.
- Be prepared to pick lots more strawberries.
- The **first sunflower heads will open into beautiful flowers**. This is the natural pointer to manage the bees. **The coming fruit or flower days will be used to increase the size of the hive by another honey box**, if needed. The box will be placed where the now full honey box is and the full one moved to the top.

Early July:
- The **first cherries and red currants** may be picked as well as **raspberries**. This activity will continue to keep you busy until the middle of July.
- **Black currants, blackcaps** and others are also ready now.
- The first seeded **beets** may now be ready to be harvested.
- **Peas are giving the first crop** and continue to do so until the end of the month. It may help to know that after the shell on peas is removed you end up with about half the weight. If you desire some more peas later in the year (they can take a light frost) you could still seed more now, provided you water them well, especially during a dry summer.
- **Pepper plants** are perennials and can be transplanted into pots in the fall. Set them outside after the last frost in spring. They will now have fresh peppers, ready to pick.
- **Tomato plants** will grow **shoots** between the leaves and the stem. They will all produce flowers and eventually tomatoes, but they will

be smaller and sometime ripen too late. We **break out these growth spurts** to leave the main stem only but sometime miss one or two. Tie the plants to the pole.
- **Carrots** may need another weeding and **thinning**. This time thin to 2 or more finger wide, depending to the variety. The thinned out carrots taste delicious. If you have too many pickle them as described in this chapter and feed the tops to the animals.
- Another weeding for pole and bush beans, corn and rutabaga (turnips). They grow well if cared for.
- Water the **corn** with some stinging nettle tea 10:1 to speed up growth.

Late July:
- **Chive** and **Sage** seeds are ready.
- The fall seeding of **rye** may be harvested. Rye is another survival crop. We use it to bake our rye bread (chapter 13). A 100 ft. by 100 ft. (30 m by 30 m) field harvested and threshed by hand will produce about 200 lb. (90 kg) of rye. To cut such a field by hand takes one person about three days. Three or four sheaves are put together to form a stook and left to dry in the field for three days, exposed to sunny conditions. This will help loosen the kernels inside the heads and hand threshing will become easier.
- Once the **raspberries** are harvested, the **old canes** can be **cut** out and the new shoots tied to the wires as described in chapter three.
- We have for the last few years **cut the tops off the strawberry plants**. The over 12 year old plants produce wonderful crops. This way we do not remove the runners and new plants grow in the rows, the not mulched area, to replace the old plants as time goes by.

10

August, Honey

Processing honey, preparing for winter

1. General

It is the bee keeper who takes all the sting out of this. Without any mystical or other feelings, one thing has always worked well for us. Just past mid August, while there is **still nectar available** is the best time to take out the honey in our experience. We usually select the next **fruit day**. When using the calendar, I prefer fruit days over the flower days, as bees seem to be even less likely to sting. These two criteria are the most important ones. It should however also be sunny with little or no wind. Once the air has warmed up and the grass has dried, we can start the work. I have not yet found any typical plant as a natural pointer, like the pussy willow, dandelion or sun flower mentioned earlier, to announce that the time has come to open up and manage the colony. This is the third and last time in this season to open the hive. Taking honey out under these conditions is a pleasure. With two people, and the honey house not too far away (100 feet, 30 meters) you can work about 20 to 25 bee hives each providing about 50 lb. (23 kg) of honey in a single day (like 10 a.m. to 5 p.m.). This does not include the extracting, which usually requires another day.

The first heavy rain storm following a hot summer will cut down the activities of the bees and consequently you will notice a reduction in available nectar. The honeydew production by the aphids feeding on the fir and spruce trees, as briefly mentioned in chapter five, may also be reduced. Logging in close proximity to our apiary has removed most of these species and with this brought a reduction in the average honey production. Experience shows that these aphids appear in large populations in a 2 year cycle and the bees usually produce a large amount of dark honey.

It is possible to forecast the possibility of a large honey crop from this source, by placing a piece of cardboard under the tree and counting the drops of honeydew fallen onto it over a period of time. This test is done during the month of June for the spruce tree and the aphid P. Hemicryphus and between July and August for the fir tree and the aphid Cinara Pectinatae. In the case of the spruce tree a method of forecasting the appearance of aphids in the coming year is to count the fallen larvae in the previous August and September. This means that you have to put some sticky material onto the cardboard to make them stay on the board.

Yet another, easier and very effective method is to shake off branches of the above mentioned trees and to count the aphids. If there are only a few, no honeydew will be coming from that source for that season. Do this test in June, for the spruce tree, in July to August for the fir tree.

When using the calendar, a fruit day will be the best time to remove honey from the colonies.

2. Preparations

Since you last opened the colony you may have spent some time to observe the bees and recognize how busy they were. When you see them flying in like large jumbo jet airplanes, with the back part of their bodies down, then you know they are bringing in some weight, usually nectar. Also an evening walk past the hive entrance or a sniff close by, can tell you if nectar has been gathered. On hot days, many bees gather at the entrance to fan their wings, blowing out the moisture accumulated in the hive. All these things are signs that honey production is under way. In June you may have checked the top box (the one we leave empty). If you find many bees in that box or see wax structures around the hole of the inner cover, you need to expand the hive as explained in chapter nine. From my experience, this is usually the case around the time of the first sunflowers blooming. If you are not sure whether to add a box or not, add one anyway at the time recommended.

A prize winning honey is not always a good honey.

In August you will see the bees bring in pollen, mainly from the sunflowers, the mullein plant and the corn, all supplying the bulk of it. Make sure you have this source to provide for the new bee population to over-winter. What they can not find now will be reflected in the coming spring with a slower development of the colony.

Tools needed to take honey out are the smoker, hive tool, pine shavings (saw dust works satisfactorily), matches, bee brush or feather of a large bird and if preferred a bee suit. I use some modified hive boxes with a hinged lid and a bottom to place honey frames into. This will reduce the chance of bees starting to rob the exposed honey and curtail the aggressive behaviour of the bees protecting their turf. A wheelbarrow will help to move these honey boxes to the shed where the processing of the honey takes place. The bee shed has to be free from dust. All items not required to process the honey should be moved out of the shed. Tools needed are two uncapping knives per person. One to stay hot in a pot of water using a hot plate, while the other one is used to uncap the honey cells. You also need some kind of an extractor to get the honey out of the cells, or you may eat comb honey. While the extractor is working, uncapped frames need to be stored temporarily in a frame or box with a tray underneath to catch drippings of honey. Eventually the honey will come out on the bottom of the extractor and go through a sieve with approximately a 1/10" (2 mm) mesh. Finally the honey is sieved through a mesh of 1/24" (1 mm) or 1/48" (0.5 mm). A finer sieve may take out particles of pollen, propolis and wax, all substantial parts of a wholesome honey. Sieving it with a larger mesh on the other hand will require a very clean environment to prevent parts of bees appearing in the honey. Not that I think this to be of any concern to me, but some people may not buy such a product. Of course for exhibitions you will need to sieve it as fine as possible. Some sheer material used for window curtains will provide a mesh of maybe 1/128" (0.2 mm) in order to be competitive. It is a paradox, though, that a prize winning honey is not necessarily a good honey. When the honey is filled into the jars, most particles and the remaining air will rise to the top of the jar. Commercial processing houses let the honey sit for a while to let it clear before filling it into containers, which makes it appear the way we are accustomed to. With this process however, and with using finer sieves, we will remove some valuable ingredients which form a cover on top of the honey jar. This part is recommended for eating if you have a cold, as it contains particles of propolis, a natural antibiotic, pollen, wax and of course the honey itself. This kind of medicine may not be present in the common honey. Honey by the way is also a good healing source for wounds and to remove puss from such wounds.

If you plan to sell your honey you might want to create a label for the jar. Use as many glass jars as you have, as plastic containers, even the food grade ones, tend to release the plastic smell into the honey. It takes about 6 months to really notice the plastic smell in the honey. I do not know about the value of such a honey. You may also need a scale to weigh the product and a place to store it. A dark cool place is the best. The emphasis should be on dark. The empty honey frames also need to be stored in a dark cool place. I store them in the root cellar which has a rather high moisture level of about 70%. This works satisfactorily if the combs are not stored for longer then two successive winters. If you keep them for too long green mold will set on the wax, due to the high moisture, and you may need to melt such combs. You may want to place some walnut leaves on top of the boxes to distract the wax moth, but frames stored in the above conditions will hardly show any damage. The moth just can't reproduce in such an environment. Mice can also damage the combs, if they still contain honey, and it is wise to store such frames somewhere else.

3. Removing honey

Wearing protective gear is great for avoiding bee stings, but you will sweat a bit under the cloth you wear, so make sure you are dressed lightly. Even without a bee suit and veil the hard work of lifting the honey boxes, which weight about 70 lb. (32 kg), may generate a bit of body heat.

The very first thing to do is to start the smoker. Start with a weaker colony first and blow some smoke into the bottom entrance. Then remove the lid, put it upside down on a flat spot on the ground and blow some smoke into the hole of the inner cover.

The next step is to pry open the inner cover for removal. Any gaps that you create are given some smoke until the inner cover is removed and with it (stuck to it sometimes) the empty box on top. Now the top honey box is revealed and the bees should not attack you. If they are coming after you, it may be better to close up the hive and rethink the date and time of your undertaking. If there are no problems, remove the top honey box and set it on the lid (as well as additional honey boxes). Now your hive should have only two boxes left as shown in fig. 10-1. Replace the inner cover now and the empty box to make the bees feel protected. Make sure the top entrance of the inner cover is to the front now and open. Go through the honey box frame by frame to see if there is still some brood remaining. If so you take the frame(s) out and place them in the top box of the remaining hive, next to the brood. This is usually the 2nd or 3rd frame in from either side. You now have to remove the inner cover again with the empty box on top, but it is better not to expose the bees to the light any more than necessary. The frames so removed can also be extracted, provided that the honey cells are covered up. Drone brood should not be put back into the hive. If a lot of brood remains in the honey boxes, you will have to put the top brood box on the bottom (swap). The bottom box of the hive usually does not have many brood combs at this

Glass containers should be preferred over plastic.

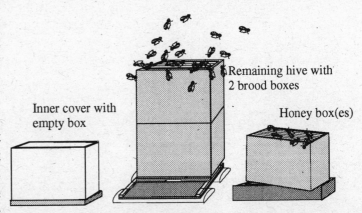

Figure 10-1, Honey box removed

Sun's ray

Inner cover and empty box in place

Top entrance to front

Figure 10-2, Brushing off bees

point of time and we can place the remaining brood frames into that box.

Bees are easily attracted by the smell of honey. Try to minimize the accessibility to honey while taking it out of the hives.

If you encounter brood in the honey boxes every year, you may think of taking the honey out later in the month especially in a warmer climate, allowing the remaining brood to hatch in the meantime. Make sure to feed them at not too late a date or the bees may not be able to put the feed into storage and the liquid may granulate

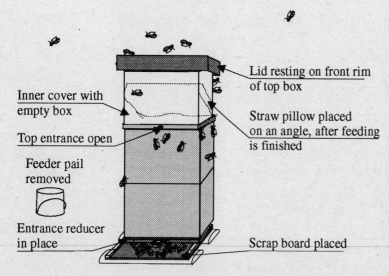

Inner cover with empty box

Top entrance open

Feeder pail removed

Entrance reducer in place

Lid resting on front rim of top box

Straw pillow placed on an angle, after feeding is finished

Scrap board placed

Figure 10-3, Hive ready for over-wintering

in the cells, rendering itself useless to the bees.

Another solution would be to reverse the two bottom boxes at the time the first sunflowers are opening, but only do this if really necessary. In this case you must replace the two bottom boxes in their original order when removing the honey. This will arrange the boxes, and with it the frames, as after the spring management.

Brushing off the bees can be done over the top empty box now, as shown in fig. 10-2. Holding the frame parallel with the sun's rays while brushing will bring the benefit that the bees become less aggressive. If aggression mounts, blow a little more smoke into the top hole as well as into the removed honey boxes. This usually cures the situation. If they still show aggressive behaviour you can also brush the bees off while holding the frame in front of the bottom entrance of the hive, taking the risk that some bees may crawl up your legs while looking for their home. Place the brushed off frames into the closed in hive boxes as described earlier, opening and closing the lid for each frame. It is important not to provide any possibility for the other bees around, to find or to rob honey from these frames, as otherwise you will end up with bees all around you. Keeping the frames free of bees will become almost impossible. It is best to remove any source of honey smell as quickly as possible, including the closed in honey boxes, as they still release some of the honey saturated air through the cracks. I wheel them to the bee shed, one or two at a time. I have also experienced that on the second day (if done over two days), the bees are already prepared to check out the surrounding area for any source of honey and work becomes more difficult. If you have many hives close together you may want to wait for a couple of days before attempting to take some more honey out. Spacing the hives further apart will also greatly help to reduce this problem.

Now that you have all the bees removed from the honey frames and have the frames safely stored in the enclosed honey boxes, you can close the hive by replacing the outer cover. Some bees may be left outside, but will quickly rearrange themselves to become part of the cluster to be formed later on.

4. Preparing for winter

4.1. Feeding bees

Once all the honey has been removed but not later then a day after removal, **immediately start feeding** the bees **continually** with **sugar** water and a **tea** mixture. Do not interrupt the feeding but check every day and replenish as required. The sugar water is mixed 3:2, 6.6 lb. (3 kg) sugar for 2 quarts (2 l) of water, until each colony has been fed **33 lb. (15 kg) of sugar**. With about 30 lb. of honey remaining in the hive, the total storage will amount to about 60 lb. This is needed in our area, close to 2000ft. (650 m) above sea level. For warmer climates, however, less is needed. The one gallon (4.5 l) feeder pails are just the right size, to hold the above-mentioned mixture and therefore I feed five pails per colony.

The tea mixture prepared in the fall is a blend of equal parts of oak bark, horsetail and valerian root. Pour water and the three herbs into a pan and let it come to a short boil. Now remove it from the heat and let it sit for 3 to 5 minutes. Pour about one cup into each pail (more does not hurt) and mix. This is it. **Make sure that during the feeding the outer cover (of the hive) is closed (not on an angle), to prevent robbing.**

4.2. Final considerations

I sometimes place a garlic on top of the inner cover, to keep away mice, ants and some insects, but I have not done that for the last 4 or so years as I have had no such problems. During the season marauding ants can be kept away by smearing garlic along the edge of the bottom board and around the entrance. Once all feeding is done and there are no more pails in the hive I place a straw pillow in the top box, for extra insulation. This procedure may get the queen to start laying earlier in the spring, as it stays a bit warmer this way. Make sure that your hive leans forward a bit, so condensed water can run out. Also have the outer cover now resting on the front rim of the top box to allow air to circulate (see fig. 10-3). Never try to make it air tight! Now put the scrap board and the entrance reducer, with the 3" (76 mm) wide opening, in place. The latter could be placed immediately following the removal of the honey to prevent mice from entering the hive.

Start feeding the bees right after the honey has been removed.

5. Processing the honey

5.1. Uncapping

Frames that have less then half the cells covered should not be used for extraction as that honey has a water content higher than 19%, and therefore would not provide good honey. The best frames are those covered from end to end (fig. 10-4). They have to be uncapped and extracted. Uncapping knifes have to be hot in order to cut just the top of the comb. The cutoff pieces, called uncappings, go into a 1/10 to 1/8" (2 to 3 mm) sieve over a pot to drip off. Eventually they can be placed into the empty top box on the hives, once the feeder pail is removed. You can, however, dump the uncappings around the feeder pail. It works, but the bees will mount the pail to the box

Figure 10-4, Uncapping

with the wax so exchanging the pail may be difficult. The bees will remove all the honey remaining in the uncappings and will form very artistic structures within that box, carrying away all the honey. Next spring you may scrape off that wax and store it with the other old wax for the melting process as described in chapter eleven. Make sure that you leave the center hole in the inner cover open at all times and only dump enough to provide room for the pillow afterwards (if you want to use a pillow).

5.2. Extracting

The uncapped honey frames are hung into a box over a drip bowl for temporary storage, waiting for their turn in the extractor. A 4-frame extractor will need equally weighted frames to be placed on opposite sides as otherwise the extractor will start to shake out of balance. You may want to consider a motor driven extractor for more than 12 hives. The frames will spin for about 3 to 5 minutes for each side, after which they are placed back into the honey box and put into storage as described earlier.

5.3. Honey preparation

There is little else we can do to make the honey taste any better than to leave it as it is.

There is nothing which makes the honey better but some people will go into the far side of preparing their honey for sale, including pasteurization, sieving to the micron, letting the honey sit to release all air bubbles before filling it into jars and so forth. I know that this will not enhance any of the honey's properties and I will not go into these applications. Simply, use the appropriate sieve and put the honey into the jars. I prefer glass jars as mentioned earlier. This is the best you can do for the product. As for a good wine, a nice label will personalize your product. Do not be shy about hand writing such a label. The clientele you will have will recognize the quality of the honey and your personal effort. Honey will

eventually crystallize, except honey from plants such as fireweed. Warming it up will liquefy the honey again. Do not heat it over 104°F (40°C) or you may as well just go and use sugar. Honey, stored in glass containers, cool and in the dark can be stored for up to five years without any loss in quality, but you may discover that you never have enough of it for even one year.

Summary of activities:

- Manage bees as described.
- Siberian tomatoes peak in production.
- Over the last 10 years we have each year gathered new seeds from the siberian tomato and every year we enjoy the wonderful crops. Seeds are removed while eating the tomato and sucking the seeds off the flesh. Place seeds on a paper towel (or toilet paper) to dry.

Early August:
- Pick beans throughout the month.
- Thin out the seeding of carrots done in early June (where the radishes were).
- Harvest garlic once the tops are dried out. Dry them first before putting them into a cool dry room for storage.

Mid August:
- Start to take out potatoes for storage.
- Remove old peas and fence. Pick remaining large peas for seeds.
- Valerian seeds can be picked.
- Second cut of hay.

Late August:
- Bee yard may be visited by the bear, so install a light or electric fencing.
- Prepare firewood.

11

September, Early October, Harvest

Vegetables, fruits, beeswax

1. The vegetables

Plants have reached maturity and a variety of food is ready to be put into storage. There is not much to mention about harvest, except the joy it brings. Some more watering may be needed during September. The season draws to the end with a first frost freezing all the remaining tender plants such as tomatoes, corn, cucumbers, beans, onions and lettuce. These have to be picked beforehand. The onions, like garlic that has been harvested earlier, can be picked once the tops start drying out. The greens on the onions can be bent down once the tips start drying out, but either way you will have good onions. Dry them in a warm room, such as the sun porch, before putting them into storage. The green tomatoes can be stored in a cool room. Our bedroom is not heated and is therefore just the right thing. You can place them underneath the bed. Spread a newspaper first, so you can easily clean up afterwards. Cover them to keep the light away and frequently check for ripe tomatoes. Some of them can be kept until Christmas. The corn can be dried and then stored in a dry room. The corn stalk can remain and be cut and fed to the goats during the month of September. It sometimes happened in the past that we went out at night to remove the remaining tomatoes from the plants just before the thermometer dropped below the freezing mark. If planned into the layout of your garden you may have some zucchinis and pumpkins remaining that can be harvested now. The plants will die off and the last fruits can be taken inside, to store in a dry cool room. We use the hallway next to the entrance door. If you seeded more peas they would also be ready now. They can take a light frost but it is better to harvest them ahead of the frost as well. Cabbage and kohlrabi do not mind a light frost, but you may as well harvest them now, they are not going to grow any bigger. Kohlrabi can be stored like the cabbage (fig. 11-1), atop the sand bed on a newspaper. Most of the string beans have been dried for winter food. When you remove the bean bushes make sure you cut off the greens above the soil, don't pull the roots out. The roots bind nitrogen in the ground and will maintain this for the next crop, usually a heavy feeder crop. The remaining pole beans and greens are a welcome feast for the goats. Witloof, (chicory) if seeded in the spring, is dug out, tops removed and put into the sand, tips down. In early spring it will grow tender white shoots also called Belgian endive.

All that is left now are the root crops, such as potatoes, rutabaga, beets and carrots. They can all be harvested before it gets too wet and cold. The carrots could actually be left out in the soil. In our region

Figure 11-1, Storing cabbage and kohlrabi

Figure 11-2, Placing carrots in the sand

however it is inconvenient to dig them out during the winter, as we have between 2 to 4 ft. (0.6 to 1.2 m) of packed snow on the ground during most of the winter and temperatures well below the freezing mark are not very inviting to go digging for food. We place them in the root cellar. The carrots and beets are covered in the sand bed as shown in fig. 11-2.

Figure 11-3, Chopper

2. Fruit and nut trees

The Italian prunes will be ready to be picked in mid September. Pears need to be harvested before the frost but ap-

ples can take light frosts without any loss of quality. The filbert bush, or tree if you pruned it, will drop its seeds. You will have to be well ahead of the squirrels and chipmunks in order to get the crop. For the first time in 12 years we have the first European style walnuts, a great triumph, as it is rather questionable to grow them at 2000 feet altitude around this part of the globe. The concord grapes do produce an excellent crop every year, as do the Himrod variety. After 10 years without problems with the Himrod we are now protecting the plants leaves from mildew using horsetail tea. It needs to be applied in the early stages of leaf growth. The funny thing with this is, that the mildew only appeared after the large fountain was placed in front of the grapes. I suspect the evaporation of the water in the fountain causes the problem. We primarily planted those grapes to cover our glassed in front porch during the summer for shade and it does that perfectly well. We eat most of the grapes fresh and some are stored in the root cellar for a limited time.

While the root cellar slowly fills to capacity, we feel more and more ready for the quiet of the winter. Some more wood has to come in and of course the apple juice has to be made.

3. Making apple juice

In order to do this in a larger quantity, you need some equipment. Some people use an

old Hoover washing machine and use the spinner part to extract the juice from the pulp. One problem with this is, that the juice is exposed to a lot of air and therefore oxidizes very fast. This is not good for the quality

Figure 11-5, Cutting blade

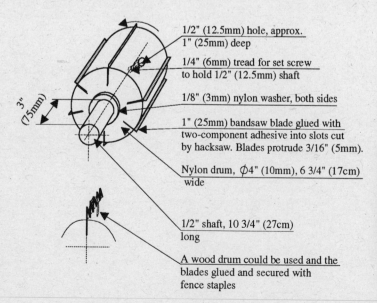

1/2" (12.5mm) hole, approx. 1" (25mm) deep

1/4" (6mm) tread for set screw to hold 1/2" (12.5mm) shaft

1/8" (3mm) nylon washer, both sides

1" (25mm) bandsaw blade glued with two-component adhesive into slots cut by hacksaw. Blades protrude 3/16" (5mm).

Nylon drum, ⌀4" (10mm), 6 3/4" (17cm) wide

1/2" shaft, 10 3/4" (27cm) long

A wood drum could be used and the blades glued and secured with fence staples

3" (75mm)

Figure 11-4. Detail of nylon drum

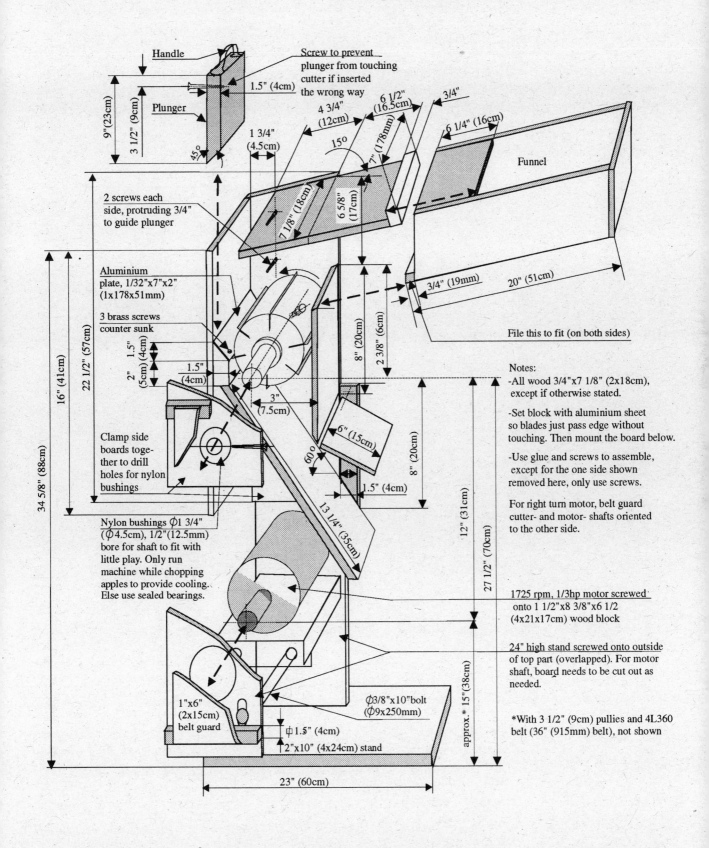

Figure 11-6, Chopper, construction details

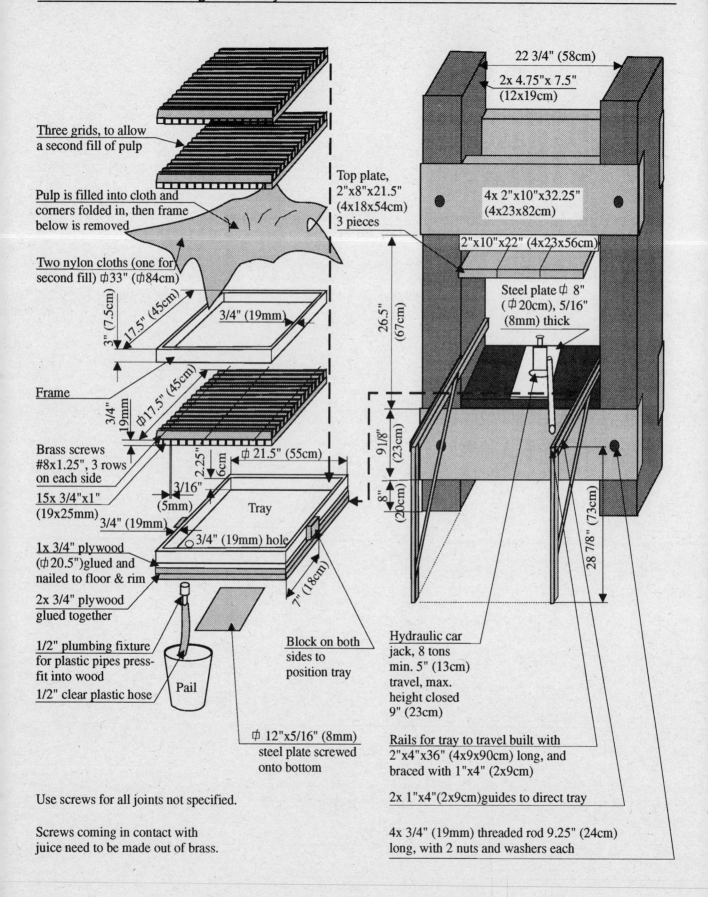

Three grids, to allow a second fill of pulp

Pulp is filled into cloth and corners folded in, then frame below is removed

Two nylon cloths (one for second fill) ⌀33" (⌀84cm)

3" (7.5cm)

17.5" (45cm)

3/4" (19mm)

Frame

3/4" 19mm

⌀17.5" (45cm)

Brass screws #8x1.25", 3 rows on each side

15x 3/4"x1" (19x25mm)

3/4" (19mm)

2.25" 6cm

3/16" (5mm)

⌀ 21.5" (55cm)

Tray

1x 3/4" plywood (⌀20.5")glued and nailed to floor & rim

2x 3/4" plywood glued together

3/4" (19mm) hole

1/2" plumbing fixture for plastic pipes press-fit into wood

1/2" clear plastic hose

Pail

7" (18cm)

Block on both sides to position tray

⌀ 12"x5/16" (8mm) steel plate screwed onto bottom

Use screws for all joints not specified.

Screws coming in contact with juice need to be made out of brass.

Top plate, 2"x8"x21.5" (4x18x54cm) 3 pieces

22 3/4" (58cm)

2x 4.75"x 7.5" (12x19cm)

4x 2"x10"x32.25" (4x23x82cm)

2"x10"x22" (4x23x56cm)

Steel plate ⌀ 8" (⌀20cm), 5/16" (8mm) thick

26.5" (67cm)

9 1/8" (23cm)

8" (20cm)

28 7/8" (73cm)

Hydraulic car jack, 8 tons min. 5" (13cm) travel, max. height closed 9" (23cm)

Rails for tray to travel built with 2"x4"x36" (4x9x90cm) long, and braced with 1"x4" (2x9cm)

2x 1"x4"(2x9cm)guides to direct tray

4x 3/4" (19mm) threaded rod 9.25" (24cm) long, with 2 nuts and washers each

Figure 11-7, Apple press, construction details

of the juice. The juice should not come in contact with steel, as it makes the juice change properties. Parts that come in contact with the juice should be wood, brass, glass and, for temporary use, plastics. Figs. 11-3 through 11-9 together with the following text will explain how to build the equipment. A product like this, build properly, will last for a lifetime, so you may want to invest some time in it. The plans may look a bit like a maze at first, but it gives all the information needed to build it. I have never learned the trade of carpentry, but once you set your mind behind it you can do it or try to find another person interested in the same project.

3.1. The process

The apples are washed with a broom in a tub or container such as a wheelbarrow, then scooped out with a sieve or basket and dumped into the funnel of the chopper shown in figs. 11-3 to 11-6. The apple pulp will fall out on the bottom, where a pail is placed to catch the pulp. A two gal. (9 litre) pail will be enough to fill the frame (layer) placed on the grid of the apple press, and the apples are chopped up in about a minute to fill the pail. You will need 2 pails to operate efficiently. The motor can be made to plug into the outlet directly or you can install a regular light switch mounted in a waterproof box (available from any electrician) and mounted on the back side of the chopper. If the plunger is pushed too hard, the drum may jam up, in which case you must switch off or unplug the machine to clear the jam. This can be avoided by using a 1/2 hp motor. Its pull will be greater than the force applied with the plunger. But we have used a 1/3 hp motor now for more then 10 years (about 80,000 lb. (36.3t)) of apples and found it to be satisfactory. Our kids are able to get the feeling for it and do not jam it. If you use nylon bushings you should make sure that the machine only runs while apples are being chopped up

and do not tighten the belt too much. The juice coming out of the apples will be enough to cool the nylon bushings, otherwise they will soften up and become useless. A sealed ball bearing may be a safer thing to build it with, especially if you consider lending equipment. It is without need to mention that while the machine is running, **you do not reach inside it** any-

Figure 11-8, Ready to fill in pulp

where. It chops very well! Do not omit to cover up the belt for safety. Using a wooden drum is possible, as long as it is balanced well and the shaft is centered. Otherwise it may give too much vibration and the saw blades could come loose. Of course from time to time you check if all the fence staples (see fig. 11-4) are still secure.

Now that the pulp is ready we are able to use the press (fig. 11-7). Lower the tray to the down position (fig. 11-8). Place the first grid into the tray. Use the frame and set it onto the grid. Place the cloth diagonally over it and fill in one pail of pulp. Fold the cloth now by pulling in the corners and placing them neatly. Remove the frame. Put the next grid on top, place the frame, and proceed the same way as just described above. If the whole package gets too high to push underneath the top boards of the frame, you may just push the tray in until it touches the top plate. Then move the top grid so it tucks underneath the top plate and lean onto the opposite end. This will press out some juice and will provide enough room to push the tray into position over the jack until it hits the blocks on the sides of the tray. If the tray seems to tilt to one side, then you may want to mount the car jack differently. Also notice that the handle of the car jack points slightly to the

Figure 11-9, Tray pumped up against top plate

right, to give room for the pail below. You can now close the valve on the jack and pump it up until a solid resistance is noticed (fig. 11-9). Do not go too hard on it or the car jack will break. From time to time you may need to fill in hydraulic oil to replenish the jack. For that purpose you remove the screw used to open and close the valve while holding the jack upside down and fully opened. Then put in oil as needed. The dry pulp can be kept for about 14 days before it starts fermenting. Feed it to the goats and chickens.

Now that you have the juice, you can do several things. Drink it right away or set it aside in a cool room where it will slowly turn into apple cider and later on apple wine and eventually vinegar. It is always nice to have some of the aforementioned before it reaches the vinegar taste. Acquire the appropriate licence to do so before embarking on the above processing. The remaining juice, that you will use during the year, you must sterilize. With a family of 8, 150 gal. of sterilized juice may be enough for a year, depending how much water and syrup you want to drink as an alternative. We usually run out, so we never seem to have enough.

Sterilizing goes as follows. Select a container and fill it with juice. Heat the juice up until it reaches 169°F (76° C). You have to stir the juice before you measure. At 167°F (75°C) the juice is sterilized. If you heat more you will change the properties of the juice and may kill all the bacteria that are good for you. So with 169°F (76°C) you are on the safe side but don't heat it up any higher. Important in the process is the cleanliness when filling jars or bottles. These contain-

Figure 11-11, Container to hold the extracted wax

ers need to be washed out well with hot water and kept warm at the time of filling. A hot water bath works well. The lids and caps need to be boiled in hot water and kept in it until placed onto the jar or bottle. When the jar or bottle is closed you have to turn the jar upside down. This will heat up the top of the jar and kill any eventual undesired bacteria. Using canning lids allows you to tell if they did not close well. A vacuum will build up inside and pull in the centre of the lid. With bottles it is not possible to

Figure 11-10, Setup to melt wax

tell, but with the above method the success rate is at over 98%. We have stored juice for over 2 years in bottles and have not found any problems. Store it in a cool dark room, moisture is not important and the root cellar will be just fine.

4. Beeswax

I recommend that you do all the extracting of beeswax outside. Hot water is heated up to the boil, for example over a wood fire, using an old washing machine tub. The frames are dipped into the hot water and the wax will melt off. The frames will get clean and disinfected. After about 15 frames, you

Figure 11-12, Double boilers

Figure 11-13, Raw wax

can make a double boiler by using an old canner with a stainless steel or enamel container placed inside, resting on a wood board with several 1" (25 mm) holes drilled to provide water circulation. This allows the wax to be heated up by the water all around it and the wax does not get hotter than the boiling water. The larger pot in fig. 11-12 shows such a setup. The smaller pot is a double boiler available on the market, the one on the picture found in a second hand store. Break the larger wax blocks into smaller parts with the back of an axe (fig. 11-13). As the wax gets flexible when warm, it is best to use cold wax and break it into smaller pieces in a cold room. Any

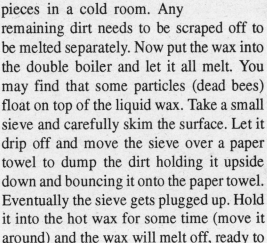

Figure 11-14, Finished wax

will notice a lot of wax and cell skins floating on top of the water. You scoop off the top (fig. 11-10) and pour it into the spinner part of an old washing machine such as a Hoover spinner-washer, with the pump removed and the hose redirected. A jute bag is made to line the inside. Close the bag after most of the wax is scooped off the surface in the tub and start the spinner. The wax and water will flow through a $^1/_{24}$" (1 mm) meshed sieve (optional) and into a container (fig. 11-11). Eventually the wax will harden, floating on top of the water. Several containers may be needed to collect the water and wax. The tub gets filled up with fresh water and the process continues. Only empty the jute bag once the next scoop is ready, in order to maintain the temperature in the spinner. Remove the jute bag and dispose of the contents, remaining skins from the hatched bees, dead wax moth and dirt. All this can be used as manure around your berry or fruit trees. Place the bag back in and scoop the next batch. Once all the wax has hardened, the remaining dirt can be scraped off on the bottom and the wax brought inside for further processing.

Inside on the wood stove or what have you, melt the wax in a double boiler. You

remaining dirt needs to be scraped off to be melted separately. Now put the wax into the double boiler and let it all melt. You may find that some particles (dead bees) float on top of the liquid wax. Take a small sieve and carefully skim the surface. Let it drip off and move the sieve over a paper towel to dump the dirt holding it upside down and bouncing it onto the paper towel. Eventually the sieve gets plugged up. Hold it into the hot wax for some time (move it around) and the wax will melt off, ready to be used again.

Let the wax harden and then remove it from the boiler. On the bottom of the wax all the dirt will have accumulated. Scrape it off and melt the wax again. This time use a soup ladle and carefully take wax off the top, trying not to disturb the bottom part where the remaining dirt has settled. Pour it into enamel or stainless steel cups, dishes or what have you and let it harden (fig. 11-14). If you happen to have another double boiler you may dump the wax into that one first and let the remaining dirt settle again before pouring it into the cups and dishes. Eventually all the wax is processed and only a small amount remains in the boiler to harden. Once hard, any remaining dirt, if at all, can be scraped off from the bottom of the last block and set away for storage as described earlier.

Summary of activities:

Early September:
- Gather firewood throughout the fall to be used for next winter. Wood dried for one year will provide better combustion and less pollution.
- Pick Onion seeds.
- Pick carrot seeds from the seed carrot planted out in the spring. For storage we use the Flakkee, a variety originating from a seed house and purchased four seasons ago. In a wet year you may have difficulty getting the seeds to ripen fully and you will need to use the seeds from the previous year. (In spring you selected a few nice large carrots from the sand bed in the root cellar). Generally, seeds are picked on a fruit day, working with the calendar. Seeds can be picked until it starts to get damp.
- Pick seeds from beets planted out as described for carrots.

Mid September:
- There is still time to cut the raspberries if you have not done so already. Make sure they are tied up onto wires or similar or the snow may bury and damage some.
- The continuing warm weather may provide a cut of clover for hay and in rare instances a third cut of other hay.
- Pick plums.
- Early varieties of apples such as Gravenstein can now be picked.

The early varieties are usually not long keepers and drying them may be an alternative.

Late September:
- Harvest hard wheat, if seeded in spring.
- Remove the onions if still out.
- You should be finished with the feeding of the bees. The scrap board and pillow can now be placed if not done so already.
- Sort out frames containing honey to be fed in spring.
- Sort out frames that have old comb in them. If you can not see through the comb any more it is time to melt it in.

Early October:
- Take old frames and melt wax.
- Put aside some beans for seeds.
- Make apple juice. With lots of apples, this can be done throughout the month of October.
- Feed excess carrots to the goats, to de-worm them, if at all needed.
- Seed garlic after first light frost. Consult your garden layout to make sure it goes into the next plot to maintain crop rotation (see chapter 4). Use good shaped cloves from the larger garlic plants you harvested in August. Place pointed end upward. Avoid using seeds from garlic that has a hard stem (bolting).
- Let chickens roam about in the garden. Cover the freshly seeded garlic rows and, if still available, the leeks.

Mid October:
- Some lettuce seeds may be picked as described in chapter 13.
- The fence set up for the second seeding of peas can be removed and stored under the roof. All poles can be removed.
- Dry apples.

12

Late October, Preparing for Winter

Cleaning up, piling manure, preparing meat

Plant growth has slowed down with the colder weather approaching. The remaining crops, such as cabbages, kohlrabi, carrots and beets have been taken into storage. In some years you may still be able to pick the last fresh pole beans in late October. This is not always the case, as the frost usually is hard enough to put a glaze onto the beans (colour changes from soft green to shiny green) which makes them less tasty. The blue concord grapes are picked throughout October, as the light frosts don't bother them along the wall of the sun porch. The red delicious apples are still on the tree and in our region can sometimes be picked as late as early November. All other apples are in storage now.

Removing tops of carrots and beets is done by twisting off the tops. Don't cut them off. By being twisted the top will break at a point which will not damage the root itself. Carrots for storage need to be handled carefully so they do not split or break. When put into the sand the smaller sized roots are stored in such a way that they can be used first. The opposite is true for onions, where the smaller ones store better. By now you should have loads of food in your root cellar, but one more thing needs to be done (if you are not a vegetarian).

1. Preparing meat

Skip this section, if you think you will never need to prepare meat. If you eat meat however, it may be good to see behind the shelves in the supermarkets, filled with almost any meat you know of. Eating meat has become something as normal as drinking milk. However neither of these foods is essential for our survival. Hunting in the olden days was a fact of survival; it has since become part of our culture due to the availability in the food markets. For our domesticated appetite meat from animals such as goats and rabbits may not be valued anymore by our society that is, by now, accustomed to beef and pork. Goats and rabbits can live on land that is marginal for gardening or farming. They harmonize with the other parts of the farm life. Goats are not picky about what they eat and, for example, love apple pulp from the apple juice produced, the greens from the vegetable crops, grass cut around the fruit trees and berry bushes and so forth. Rabbits are even less demanding, living mainly on the grass eaten while being moved around on the lawn (a perfect mower for the city person of the future) and fed with water. Of course some kitchen scraps are fed to them as well.

Skip this section if you feel uneasy with this topic.

I recommend that the person, for the first time, watch the killing and the process of preparing the animal as it may be an emotional matter. It will also help to understand the description in this chapter. A few tools are needed to butcher a goat. A sharp small kitchen knife (fillet knife), a good sized axe, a hack saw (meat saw) and a sharpening steel. A cleaver and a pair of pruning shears would be helpful but not necessary.

1.1. Skinning and removing the organs of goats and rabbits

Goats and rabbits are very similar in anatomy except for size and therefore can be handled the same way. With the need to keep animals for milk, eggs and meat comes the necessity to breed in order to maintain the stock. If you like to eat meat, part of your harmony will be to kill an animal. If you do not do that, your animal population will grow too large. Selling them or giving them away may be another solution, but who knows what the other person is going to do? Meat is a valuable source of food. For the person on the farm, who may not have (or does not want) the immense palette of foods (canned and fresh) available in the supermarkets, meat is a welcome change. It becomes more valuable to us to know what the animal was fed with and how it enjoyed its life on the farm. We can care for the animal and provide a good home. It is unbelievable how some of the meat is produced. Tens of thousands of chickens are fed for 4 months in small wire cages and then trucked off to the supermarkets and restaurants. The sheer numbers are an indication that the scale of harmony has been tipped towards disaster.

It is most important to provide animals with an environment to grow with "dignity" and that we appreciate their presence. Before killing an animal this understanding needs to come to mind and we should **thank the animal for the contribution to our growth, physically and spiritually**. Anytime I kill an animal knowingly (no matter how many times I have done this), my body vibrates at another frequency then usual. It feels similar to the body feeling you may have when involved in an accident but it has a different effect. It's not a weak feeling but builds the strength to face death. Talk appreciatively to the animal which becomes part of your development. What is alive in the animal will be set free and will continue to live. You should provide that same appreciation for the plant world, at the time you remove a plant from the soil. You discontinue their cycle in order to feed yourself.

Now we look at the practical part of the process. If an animal is killed by shooting, it is practical to shoot into the forehead. For people who can't shoot an animal (for lack of a gun or other reasons), the animal has to be knocked out.

One full day (24 hours) before butchering, the animal should not be fed any solid food. While you bring the goat to the site, talk to it in a moderate voice and be thankful for the food it provides. Set the goat up on a short leash in front of a heavy wood block. Give the goat a bit of oats to eat. While the goat eats, hit the back of the head between the horns with a heavy device, such as an axe. (Don't try to hit in the front where you usually shoot the animal. The animal would see your action and try to move away). This will stun the animal and no pain will be felt. The goat will fall to the ground. Remove the collar, place the neck on the wood block and cut off the head at the neck with two or three cuts with the axe. It is important to cut the arteries. In doing so you will observe a sudden gush of blood. You may need to cut the rest with the knife if the axe is not sharp enough and therefore not cutting the skin well. If you are not skilled enough with the axe to sever the head, another method is to use a knife. Cut the throat, jugular veins and the carotid arteries and disjoint the head from the body where the backbone joins the skull (where the goat turns the head). At this time life has left the body but reflex movements may be visible for a short time. The first method may be easier and the second two may sound brutal, but the goat will not feel any pain after it has been stunned. Wait until most of the blood is released. The blood can be fed to the chickens. Tie the goat upside down with two cords looped around the hind legs as shown in fig. 12-1 and tie them to a beam or similar structure. With a sharp knife you cut the skin as shown in fig. 12-1 along the dotted line. Be careful not to cut the fell (the shiny thin membrane separating the muscle from the hide). Now peal the top triangle upward toward the tail while using the knife between the fell and the skin in order to separate them. Make sure you separate right up to the anus and also around both legs. Now pull the skin over the back while pulling on it from the other side (tail side) with quite some strength. The whole skin will peal off. The bung (the pipe containing the digested food in pellet form) may come with it and can be left hanging outside (fig. 12-2). By now the top part of the animal should be skinned. Cut the skin along the centre line of the body all the way to the neck. Now using your fist pull off the skin all around. At the neck you will have to use the knife in order to separate the skin. Continue this down to the knees of the foreleg. Here you use the hack saw to cut the forelegs off, leaving them with the hide for now (for rabbits a pair of pruning shears can be used).

Now carefully cut the body's abdominal cavity just ahead of the pelvis (at the level where backbone and hipbones meet) upwards as far as possible as shown in fig. 12-1 as an arrow line. Do not point the knife inwards or you may puncture some of the organs. Remove the bladder taking care not to spill the contents onto the carcass. Now cut downward as far as possible (to the front end of the chest bone) while holding back the organs with one hand. The organs will tend to fall out. Try not to damage any of them. You will find the kidneys (a couple of rounded red coloured pieces, symmetrically arranged at about centre height to the left and right). You will also find on the left side a small strip of reddish coloured meat, the spleen. Remove these parts now. Reach in and up to pull down the bung, trying not to spill it. The passage to the tail should now be free. Reach down now until you feel the liver and pull it up with all the intestines, holding onto the liver until all is separated from the body. You may need to use the knife to separate it from the backbones. The whole thing will now hang outside still attached to the food pipe. Carefully separate the liver from the intestines. Cut the gall bladder out, rinse the liver, and put it into a bowl. With some experience you can grab the gall bladder at the tip and peal it off the liver. If you damage the gall bladder in this process, the liver will be spoiled and you should not use it for human consumption. Now cut the food pipe from the organs and dispose of them by burying them in the garden (except if you like to use the intestine to make sausages). Inside the body you should now see a fell covering the bottom part. Down behind is the lung and the heart, attached to the windpipe. You reach in as far down as possible, hold the wind pipe firm and pull with quite some strength to remove all the parts. You may have to lever your arm on the chest bone of the animal and use both hands. This will leave behind the carcass. Some extra fat may be removed at

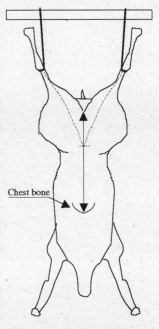

Figure 12-1, Position to remove skin

Figure 12-2, Removing skin

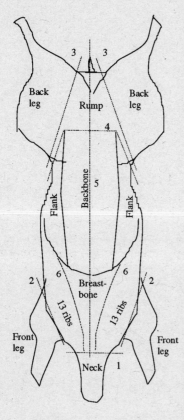

Figure 12-3, Cutting it into smaller pieces

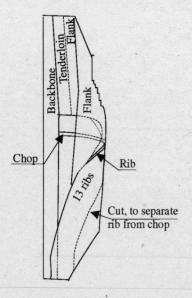

Figure 12-4, Final cutting

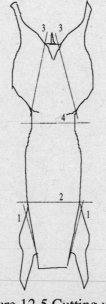

Figure 12-5, Cutting up a rabbit for stew

this stage if required. Now wash the body with cold water inside and out and then hang it in the root cellar with a temperature preferably lower or at 7°C (44°F) for 3 to 6 days to cure. This also allows the meat to harden up a bit and makes it easier to process and to remove fat.

1.2. Goats' meat

Cut the meat into pieces, in sequence of the numbers as shown in fig. 12-3. It takes some experience to find a way to remove the back legs without too much trouble. Try to find the joint by moving the leg and then cut towards the joint with the knife and eventually dislocate it. The front legs can be easily cut off with the knife. Then use the hack saw to remove the neck and rump. Cut the rest of the carcass into two halves (legs removed), starting where the rump was attached. Each half can then be cut up as

shown in fig. 12-4. With a 6 month old goat you end up with the following:

- Front legs, neck, rump and flank to be cut into small pieces for goat-burgers,   7.0 lb. (3 kg)
- Back legs,   6.0 lb. (2.8 kg)
- Chops,   2.2 lb. (1 kg)
- Ribs,   1.5 lb. (750g)
- Tenderloin,   0.7 lb. (300g).

You will also have 4.4 lb. (2 kg) of bones for the dog and 2.2 lb. (1 kg) fat and other meat for the cat, but you can also prepare it to be fed to the birds as follows. Melt the fat on the stove in a can and put a wood stick in it about 15" long. Then let it cool off. Now remove it with the stick and hang it in a tree for the birds to peck on. If you add all the weight up you will have a total of about 24 lb. (11 kg), depending on the size and type of the goat. The weight may go up to 40 lb. (14 kg) or more for a larger animal.

1.3. Smoked goat meat

Smoked goat meat is one of the best treats when put on a piece of bread or eaten with a main dish. For the people from Switzerland the closest would be called "Büntner-fleisch". The preparation is as follows:

- Brine preparation
- 14 cups (3 l) of water
- 1½ cups (400g) salt (pickling salt, which is somewhat coarser)
- 2 tbsp. (20g) brown sugar
- 1 tbsp. (5g) pepper corns
- 1" (2.5 cm) cinnamon stick
- 2 bay leaves
- 2 cloves
- 1 tsp. thyme

Heat up the ingredients to a boil and let it sit to cool off. Sieve the liquid into a container and cover the meat to let it soak. The meat should soak for about 4 days per pound (454 g) of meat. Turn the meat once a day. When the time has come to remove it, wash it off with fresh water and dry it off (let it sit outside the brine for a while) before hanging it in the smoke chamber. Smoke it for 2 to 4 days at 100^0 to 125^0F (38 to 48^0 C). After this store it in a cool but not moist area (the root cellar won't do) or put it in the freezer.

1.4. Rabbit meat

The rabbit, having a small rib cage, is not cut into two halves. Cut it into pieces as shown in fig. 12-5 and use it for a stew. There is no end to the variety of ways it may be served. It is a tasty low-fat meat.

1.5. Butchering chickens

Butchering hens is a twofold chore. If it is a laying hen she will carry a few eggs inside her body. Cleaning it out is not to everyone's taste. It is also more difficult to clean out chickens than rabbits. Chickens are not as clean, and plucking the feathers while using hot water is a smelly process.

Prepare a pot of hot water. Hold the chicken firmly by its legs. Hit the chicken over the head to stun it. Now cut the head off with the axe and immediately press the body (the back) on the ground (preferably grass) to avoid too active nerve movements and splattering of blood. Some blood will come out the neck for a short time and you should point it away from you. Wait until the body is calm before letting go. Wait a few minutes and than soak the chicken in the hot water for about 30 seconds (longer for old chickens). Move the chicken in the hot water holding its legs. Now the feathers can be pulled with ease. Cut from the anus to the breastbone, or a bit further if your hand is bigger, and remove all the organs inside. Rinse it out with cold water and store at 7^0C (44^0F).

2. Manure

Manure is a product derived by keeping animals in a small space, which happens on our farm during the winter months. This manure is then piled up in the spring for composting. It would be much more practical to leave the animals in the fields (e.g. like the movable rabbit pens) **to reduce the amount of work.** But this is not possible all year round. The goat manure will be ready as compost in the late fall. The chicken manure taken out of the scratch pen may be piled up for another year to rot further. If you have any compost, spread it to the plants now in late fall (November). You can set some aside to be used as potting soil next spring. Any compost being used as potting soil must be well rotted. Compost will not be used directly by the plant (insoluble), but will activate the soil organisms which in turn will provide plant food. Spreading in the fall has two advantages. First, you are most probably not as busy anymore doing other work while the season is coming to an end. Second, if some of the manure is not well rotted it allows the organisms to take action as early in spring as possible, usually when the soil temperature reaches about 50^0F (10^0C). We prefer not to use the chicken manure in the garden but spread it around the berries and the tomato patch (which we keep out of the crop rotation). Goat manure is used for the hay fields and the fruit trees. No compost has been applied to our garden for the last 5 years. This means fewer weeds in the garden (but don't think there are none and don't forget that weeding is part of tending the plant anyway). If you have access to manure or compost and you think you have the extra time, go ahead and get it. It will definitely help to enrich a depleted or poor soil. Make sure it comes from a farm that does not use drugs and hormone injections in their operation. Commercially available dried manure bought at garden centers and hardware stores may also contain non-organic com-

With mulching, crop rotation, green manuring using legumes in the crop rotation and companion planting, the soil reaches the optimum composition.

ponents if the manure has been taken from large scale farms as mentioned above. Such manure may be temporarily detrimental to the harmony in the soil. It is far better to apply nothing than to look for trouble. A similar problem exists with grass clippings from certain lawns, as manicured lawns need all the chemical fertilizers to make them look great.

Unproductive soil may be improved to grow vegetables within 1½ years with the following crop rotation: In the fall seed rye, followed by clover in the spring, which is cut before flowering and left on the land. The following spring, work the soil into seed beds (for large gardens or fields use a rototiller or tractor) and start planting your vegetable garden as explained earlier.

The three main components required for plant growth are nitrogen, phosphorous and potassium, commonly referred to as potash. Using **legumes** in your crop rotation will provide **nitrogen** for the heavy feeder crops that follow. **Phosphorous** is available from abundant **organic matter** and **potash** is added with mulching material like **oats, barley and rye** straw **or alfalfa, red clover** and other hay. Wood ash is another source of potash, especially if derived from hard woods. Wood ash has another effect. It will change an acid soil (PH below 7, most soils are below 7) to a more alkaline one, as does lime. If clover grows well, your PH value will be alright. Otherwise you might want to measure it and take corrective action. More important is the **availability of organisms** in the soil to transfer these nutrients into soluble foods for the plant.

Trace minerals (see also chapter 5) are another important known factor in the soil (zinc, manganese, boron, iron, sulfur, copper, magnesium, molybdenum and chlorine to mention a few). A soil high in organic material will provide the necessary trace minerals for our health. While analyzing the soil, we can say that the complexity of plant growth is not fully understood. For that reason we should look at the mechanisms in the soil and the plant life as a whole and not get lost in details. With the guidance of nature, to do what nature tells us and to remember how to consciously observe, we will be able to succeed. We may use our scientific knowledge for the satisfaction of our intellect.

Reading between the lines, you can see I'm not a big fan of composting, unless I were a city gardener. Be it as a pile or as sheet composting it generates more work. Sheet composting is the technique of laying down the mulch and then working it into the soil. The killing of weed seeds while composting is little comfort. Remember, weeds are an essential part of gardening. I'm more in favour of applying the waste products directly to the soil or feeding them to the animals. Have you ever observed in nature large piles of manure, leaves, fish scraps, dried blood, etc. piled up to rot?

Large scale livestock operations have ignored the balance achieved by Harmonic Farming. Animals are raised on huge tracts of ranch and pasture land and fattened in feed lots where their nitrogen-rich manure causes ecological imbalance instead of contributing to soil fertility. According to The Rodale Book of Composting, 1992 edition (See Appendix A) two billion tons of manure are produced annually in the US, yet very little of this vast store of nutrients is returned to the soil. Now you could argue that the need for composting is even more important, but it's a cure to a problem caused by humans in the first place, with their large feed lots used in the mass production of low quality meat. Yes, composting is forced on the farmer and more animals means more work that, in economical terms, does not pay. Each individual needs to consider this when dealing with animals. On the traditional family farm this can be achieved as part of the operation.

Applying rye as a green manure in the fall and potatoes in the spring will prevent the potatoes from getting damaged by scab. If you have scab your crop rotation may need to incorporate rye ahead of potatoes.

3. Fall seeding and soil

A seed bed for garlic or fall rye should be prepared late in September. Try not to turn or plow the soil, but use a spading fork. For large fields other than hay use diamond harrows. A hay field needs to be turned so as to generate soil for another crop. Push the spading fork in and then move it back and forth a couple of times. Remove the weeds which should now pull out easily. Afterwards, rake the top, to remove rocks, grasses, straw, etc. This will provide a wonderful seed bed. To seed rye into a large field, generate seed rows with the diamond harrows (e.g. between the stubble of the previous crop like wheat). Do not plow if possible. Seed and then harrow again. While harrowing the first time, left-over straw may plug up the harrow and this straw has to be removed from the field. It is good to do this using disks or with the help of another person.

4. Leaves

Who would think that leaves are a food source? Don't gather them for compost if you have goats. The reason becomes obvious when you watch the goats behaviour during the fall. Goats love to eat those freshly fallen, dry birch leaves. Rather than composting them, we store them on top of the stack of already gathered hay. During the winter months, this stack can be fed to the goats which in turn produce the manure. What could be easier than that? The city gardener, on the other hand has to compost them to derive humus for his planters.

5. Acorns

Acorns, unfortunately rather rare in most regions are a wonderful source of protein. In late fall acorns can be gathered from mature trees and separated from the leaves in a wheelbarrow filled with water. The leaves and acorns that have been racked together are dumped into the wheelbarrow. With a manure fork the leaves are picked out. Eventually the water is carefully dumped to reveal the acorns. Put them out to dry. The large and nicely shaped acorns are selected for planting and the rest stored for the cold winter days. Whenever the temperature drops below -20°C (-3°F) the goats are given a handful of acorns twice a day, as well as the oats and hay.

To plant acorns, fill two quart (2 l) milk cartons with soil and bury one acorn in it to the depth of its size. This is then dug flush into the soil to over-winter. In spring the trees will start emerging and will have about 10" of growth in the first year, after which (November) you plant them as is into the spot of your choice. The oak tree is not just a symbolic tree (as presented in the Olympics) or one grown in a particular culture. The tree produces a sponge-like tap root which helps to maintain the ground water table. Many oak trees together will generate an underground reservoir providing more moisture in the soil. Furthermore, the wood is an excellent hardwood used to build boats and other equipment. It is time to start planting such trees so that our future generations will have a **real** treasure, to make up for today's fast paced world of clear cuts for the profit of a few to rule the many (in the sense of "money talks"). Let's hope that many of us have the chance to plant acorns as a sign to care for nature. The oak tree might become that wonderful symbolic tree once again, a sign for a new culture, one that thinks as far ahead as an oak tree gets old. At least, it will be the first step to show our present selfish, short

"Tall oaks from little acorns grow."
David Everett
1769-1813

term thinking culture that there is another way.

Summary of activities:

You have some time now to sit down and review some of the information you might have written down during the year. The crops are all in and you can determine the total produce harvested from a garden with 1000 feet (330 m) of irrigation pipe installed. In one of our workshops in 1994, we weighed all the vegetables that had been harvested during the season. It might not have been the best year, since in August it hailed almost golf ball size stones onto the crops, something I have never seen before. There will always be some kind of a loss since nature has its own way to work things out. It is good practice to plant more than what is required. Our results were:

– Onions	36 lb. (16 kg)
– Beans	113 lb. (51 kg)
– Carrots	65 lb. (30 kg)
– Tomatoes	178 lb. (81 kg)
– Potatoes	175 lb. (79 kg)
– Beets, Kohlrabi	109 lb. (49 kg)
– Turnips	39 lb. (18 kg)
– Corn	14 doz.
– Cabbage, Broccoli	qty. 15
– Zucchini	qty. 106
– Lettuce	qty. 26

Weighing was done on the rather conservative side but it will give you an idea of what to expect. About 12 lb. (5.5 kg) peas and some cucumbers have also been harvested. Many more beans could have been picked but demand was lower than supply. No information on the amount of garlic harvested has been available. However these amounts provide more than ample basic food for a family of six (or four adults). Processed and stored properly as described earlier, it can provide vegetables for a whole year. To be able to add fruits, berries, honey, eggs, milk and meat (the latter if you are not a vegetarian) will be very gratifying and an enjoyable experience throughout the year. You will remember that it came from the land you cared for. As much as we thank the animals for being part of it, so should we thank the plants, for they are the very basic building blocks. It is the care and attention you put into this adventure throughout the year that accounts for (more than) a thank you, may I call it a "harmonic thanksgiving".

– Prepare meat for storage.
– Collect acorns.
– Breed the goats.
– Prepare some wooden trays about 5" (13 cm) high and fill them with rich soil. In the spring they can be placed along the windows or the sun porch to start your own bedding plants.
– Rake acorns before the first snow.
– Rake leaves if they are dry.
– Pick the last apples such as red delicious and winter banana, both long keepers.
– Make more apple juice.
– Still time to cut up wood.
– Take in filter(s) from the irrigation system and drain pipes (open all taps).
– Spread compost from last year.
– Clean out scratch pen and pile it into a compost row not higher than 3 feet (1 m).
– Clean out goats' pen and make a compost row not higher than 3 feet (1 m).
– Plant acorns.
– Invert oak barrels for winter storage.

13

The Peace of Winter

Slowing down

With the first snow blowing through the trees and maybe sticking to the ground for a brief moment, we know it is time to concentrate our energy on inside tasks. That feeling you get when looking back and recapturing the year's moments is something to nourish. The rewards are a full storage room and the joy of being able to depend on your own source of food during the winter; to reflect on what nature has taught you during the season; and to be happy to have time to digest and recapture all of the above.

1. Seeds

During the season, seeds have been collected and dried. It is a good time now to clean them, if necessary, by separating hulls and other particles from the seed. I made a small machine to do this as shown in fig. 13-1, but you may just use the wind to help you sort it out. The top surface of the machine is covered with a smooth surface (printing press sheets work well) to reduce friction. With this setup the tilt to the front needs to be 15°. You can always slightly change the angle, by supporting the bin on one or the other end. The same setup can be used to clean grains, such as rye or hard wheat. For larger quantities another motor from an old heater, or similar equipment, can be mounted to one side of the top guides to generate the vibration (fig. 13-2). All you need to do is

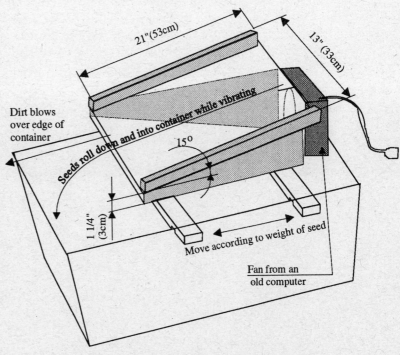

Figure 13-1, Set up to clean seeds

break off one of the fan blades to generate eccentric force. The equipment needs to be set up on a flat surface to work properly. Depending on how clean you need the seeds, several passes may be required and seeds will have to be sorted

Figure 13-2, Seed cleaner

as 1st and 2nd quality. For some very light seeds, a sieve may be more useful to separate them. Like the bachelor buttons, you dump some dry flower heads into an 8" (20 cm) diameter sieve with a 1/16" (2 mm) wide mesh. With the back of your hand, gently move the heads around, carefully

Collect and dry your own seeds as much as you can.

pushing them against the mesh until most seeds have passed through the sieve. If they are not clean enough, they can be cleaned further using the seed cleaner to remove the light dirt. You may lose some of the smaller, lighter seeds with this process. Carrots, onions and sage seeds will not pass through the sieve. They must be separated with the seed cleaner (or wind) only. Sunflower seeds separate very easily. You may have to rub the seeds to make the unwanted particles get smaller and therefore lighter. With the seed cleaner they will separate quite readily. Especially for carrot seeds, you may want to sort into a 1st and 2nd quality seed. The larger, heavier seeds in a batch (e.g. carrots), will separate more easily from the rest and become 1st quality. Parsley seeds pass through the sieve but can also be put through the seed cleaner afterwards. Valerian seeds fall out on their own and you should not rub the heads. Shake out the seeds only. They are very small and white in colour. No further separation is needed for these. Lettuce flowers such as red lettuce and oak leaf lettuce are rubbed between the palms, sieved and put through the seed cleaner. Another method of separation is to pluck the white "fins" that protrude from the flower head and with this the seeds. This may be useful if only a small amount of seed is needed. By now you should have harvested such seeds as **tomatoes, potatoes, garlic, corn, beans and peas**. They are easy to collect, need little cleaning and are part of the survival food.

2. Wax foundations

It is of utmost importance that beekeepers recycle their own wax in order to maintain a high-quality honey. Wax is the container for the bees' honey. The wax available commercially is contaminated by many drugs the beekeeping industry uses to battle diseases. Some of the poisonous agents will remain in the wax and contaminate the honey by way of diffusion. It will also be more economical to recycle wax on site. Chapter eleven described the process for recycling old wax that we can now use in this process.

To produce a foundation we need a mold with imprinted hexagons the same size as the cells the bees build naturally. Such forms are available from bee equipment suppliers (see Appendix A) and are similar to a waffle iron. It is a time consuming task to learn how to pour the wax so it does not stick to the mold. For many years I have used an aluminum mold to produce foundation. These molds are quite expensive and difficult to work with. I have come across an article written by Otto Ortner, Germany (See Appendix A) about how to make your own mold using a silicon rubber product called Elastosil M4440, made by Wacker Silicone (see Appendix A). In Canada a similar slightly softer product (M4601 manufactured by the same company) could be used.

I include the information here since it gives a possibility of producing pure wax foundation with fewer problems. The quantity of M4440 required to manufacture the mold, producing foundation for the Hoffman frame, the size of $8^{3}/_{8}$" by 16¾" (212 by 425 mm), is about 3 lb. (1.5 kg) resulting in an approximate cost of Can$ 100.00.

2.1. Producing the mold

The account below together with figs. 13-3 and 13-4 will give a shorthand description of the process.

Bottom part of mold
- Work on a clean and level surface.
- Cut a 5/64" (2 mm) thick plate made of (ply)wood, cardboard or rubber sheet to the exact size of the foundation. Of the above, the rubber sheet may work the best, as

Setup to pour bottom part of mold

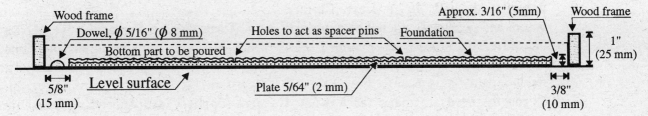

Setup to pour top part of mold

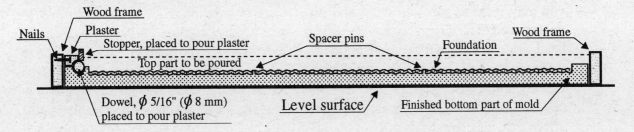

Figure 13-3, Setup to make the mold

it will lie flat on the surface. The finished mold will act as a pan to hold the liquid wax.

– Use a water soluble wood glue. Apply some around the edge of the plate to glue it lightly to the working surface and seal it off. This will hold it in position. Clean off the remaining glue.

– Drill four holes, as shown in fig. 13-4, through a purchased foundation. You can use the back of a ball point pen or similar object to punch these holes. However, the diameter should not exceed 1/8" (3 mm).

View with top mold removed

Foundation

Hinge

Spacer pins
$\emptyset$ 5/64" to 1/8"
($\emptyset$ 2 to 3mm)

3/8"
(10mm)

5/8"
(15mm)

3/8"
(10mm)

View of assembled mold

Hinge   Free space for foundation   Top part of mold

Bottom part of mold

Figure 13-4, Top and side view of finished mold

Figure 13-5,
Sealed frame

- Use a foundation that is as perfect as possible. Apply wallpaper glue to the plate about ½" (12 mm) all along the edge and place the foundation exactly flush all around.
- Use wallpaper glue to seal off the edges all around the plate and the foundation to prevent the entry of the silicon rubber between the surface and the plate or the plate and the foundation.
- Seal the bottom of the holes with a little bit of wallpaper glue to prevent ingress of silicon rubber between the foundation and the plate. These holes, once poured, act as spacer pins and avoid sagging of the top part while in use. The small holes appearing in the foundation, due to these pins, will not be of any consequence.
- Build a frame that is 1" (25 mm) high. The sides are 1" (25 mm) longer and ¾" (20 mm) wider than the foundation.
- Place that frame on the surface to have equal space on all sides except where the hinge will be. That space will be $^5/_8$" (15 mm).

- Clamp it with water soluble glue to the surface and seal the inside along the surface with the glue, wallpaper glue or vaseline to form a fillet (fig. 13-5). To apply small quantities of glue a syringe, with the needle cut off, may be useful. Forming the fillet may be done using your finger.
- The hinge is formed with a half round piece of wood, $^5/_{16}$" (8 mm) dowel cut in half (lengthwise) and fit to touch the frame on each end.
- Space it evenly between the frame and the plate and attach it with wallpaper glue.
- Prepare the silicon rubber now for the one mold according to manufacturer's instructions. You need at least 21 oz. (600 g) to end up with about a ¼" (6 mm) thick mold (for the size of a Hoffman frame). The silicon rubber is quite liquid but **should be poured slowly** to avoid air bubbles that could get trapped.

Top part of mold
- Once the silicon rubber has vulcanized, remove the wood frame and then the bottom mold together with the foundation. The plate will stay behind on the surface as it was fixed to it with the wood glue at the beginning of the process (rather than just wallpaper glue).
- The foundation and mold are put into cold water (bath tub) to remove any remaining glue using a soft brush. Take care not to damage the foundation.
- If the foundation has become detached from the newly made bottom mold place it back the same way you started out and make it fit snugly.

Figure 13-6, Pouring wax

- The other half of the hinge is set up with a $^5/_{16}$" (8 mm) dowel placed in the bottom part.
- Use some plaster to fill in the space above the hinge as shown in fig. 13-3. Place some small nails in the frame to make the plaster stick to it. Once dry, remove the frame, stopper and the dowel.
- Place the frame back and seal any gaps between the bottom mold (which shrunk by about 0.7% in the previous process while curing) and the frame with water soluble wood glue or a similar material. You may again use the syringe to apply glue.
- Apply a very thin film of vaseline to all exposed parts inside the form.
- Pour the newly prepared silicon rubber, about 27 oz. (750 g) for the Hoffman frame, into the form until you have no liquid left. Any rough edges can be trimmed with scissors. The manufacturer of M4440 recommends that you heat up the mold to the temperatures in which it is expected to operate, in our case to about 212°F (100°C).

2.2. Using the mold

The table on which the mold is placed has to be level. Cover the surface with plastic or a similar product. Wax that has aged (brown-gray colour) will not work as well. Wax at 176°F (80°C) gives best results. Use a double boiler as mentioned in chapter eleven to melt the wax. Below are the steps involved in making foundation.

Lift the top part of the mold so it still remains in the hinge. Pour in wax with a sphere-shaped spoon of about 3.5" (9 cm) diameter as shown in fig. 13-6. This will provide enough wax to pour a full sized foundation. Start at the hinge and while moving along close the top mold by rolling it gently over the wax, until the mold is closed. The remaining wax will be squeezed to the sides and can, once hardened, be put back into the wax pot. After about 10 seconds open the top part. If a corner is broken or not well formed, pour in a small quantity of hot wax and close the mold again. When hardened, remove the top as shown in fig. 13-7, turn the bottom mold around and gently peel it off the newly made foundation. Over time the mold will warm up and you might have to wait a bit longer for it to cool off. Alternatively, use two molds. Pouring water over it will also work, as long as you dry the mold before using it again.

3. Wax candles

Nothing is easier and more enjoyable than making candles. One method is to dip the wick into the wax briefly and then let it cool off in the cold winter breeze. Repeating this action will accumulate the wax around the wick and eventually you will end up with a candle. The pure beeswax candles will burn rather quickly and generate a wonderful and somehow magical ambience. Storing pure beeswax candles for about a year (aged wax) before use will double the time they burn. Candles up to 1" (2.5 cm) can be made with a wick of about $^1/_{16}$" (1.5 mm) in diameter. Making fat candles with

Figure 13-7, Opening the top of the mold

Figure 13-8, Dipping the candle

diameters of 1" or more will require wick with a larger diameter of about $^3/_{32}$" (2 mm). This will allow the candle to burn all the way out to the edge. (See Appendix A for a supplier of materials). A simple double boiler can be used as shown in fig. 13-8, made out of a tin can set into an aluminum pan.

Wax can also be poured into molds of different shapes. I have used egg cartons and filled them with wax. Punch a small hole in the bottom of the larger cups and push the wick through about 1/4 inch. Then tape it to close the hole. Support the wick with tooth picks or something similar to make it stand up more or less straight. Now pour the wax in and let it harden.

4. Baking bread

Baking for all the bread listed below is the same and is done as follows:

Place it in the pre-heated oven at 400°F (204°C) for about 45 min. As wood stoves sometimes heat more on the top than on the bottom, the sheets have to be switched around once during the baking. If you use loaf pans, remove the bread from the pans to cool off.

4.1. Rye bread
Ingredients for six loaves:
- 8 cups (1 kg) rye flour.
- 7½ cups (1 kg) whole wheat flour.
- 7 cups (1 kg) non-bleached white flour.
- 3 tbsp. salt.

- 2 tbsp. instant dry yeast.
- 9½ cups (2100 ml) warm water or milk.

Preparation
- Mix dry ingredients together in a big bowl.
- Make a well in the centre.
- Pour milk or water into the well. Mix and knead the dough until it is smooth and bubbly.
- If it sticks to your hands, spread some white flour onto your hands. To get a good dough it should take you about 15 to 20 minutes.
- Cover the bowl with a wet cloth and let it sit until the dough has risen to double its size (about 2 hours). If at that time your wood stove is not hot enough, you can push the dough down again using your fists. It will rise quite quickly again. Repeat this if needed until you are ready to bake.

- Cut the dough into 6 equal pieces and shape them to loaves. Place them on a cookie sheet or in loaf pans. With a knife slice the bread several times across the top sideways or once along the top length wise in the centre. You can also sprinkle some white flour over it, to make it look traditional.

4.2. Whole wheat bread
Ingredients for two loaves:
- 7½ cups (1 kg) whole wheat flour
- 1 tbsp. salt.
- 2/3 tbsp. instant dry yeast.
- A touch more than 3 cups (700 ml) warm water.
- Preparation is the same as for the rye bread.
- Cut the dough into 2 equal pieces and shape them to loaves.

4.3. White bread
Ingredients for two loaves:
- 7 cups (1 kg) non-bleached white flour
- 3 tsp. instant dry yeast
- 1 tbsp. salt
- A touch more than 3 cups (700 ml) warm water
- Preparation is the same as for the rye bread.
- Cut the dough into 2 similar pieces and shape them to loaves.
- Place them on a cookie sheet or in loaf pans. With a knife slice the bread several times across the top sideways or once along the top lengthwise in the centre. You can also sprinkle some white flour over it, to make it look traditional.

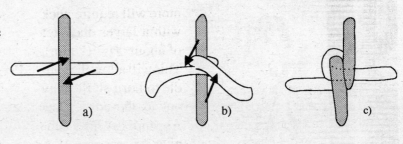

Figure 13-9, Steps to form a 4- legged braid

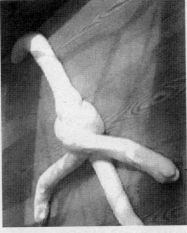

Figure 13-10, Step a done

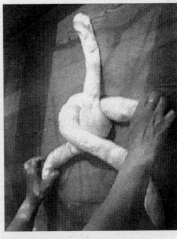

Figure 13-11, Step b done, about to repeat step a

4.4. White braided bread
Ingredients for two loaves:
- 7 cups (1 kg) unbleached white flour
- 3 tsp. instant dry yeast
- 1 tbsp. salt
- ½ cup butter or margarine
- 1 tbsp. honey
- 2 2/3 (600 ml) warm milk

Mix dry ingredients together in a big bowl.
- Make a well in the centre.
- Place the butter in the well and crumble it by mixing it together with some flour or using a pastry blender. Add the honey and then pour the **warm** milk in the well.
- Preparation is the same as for rye bread.
- Cut the dough into 2 similar pieces. Do the following to each of them. Cut it into two equal sizes and form them into 31" (80 cm) long pieces. Lay them on a flat surface as shown in fig. 13-9a. Proceed by repeating the folding as shown by the arrows in fig. 13-9a and 13-9b, 13-10 and 13-11 respectively, until finished. You will braid upwards towards you and eventually reach the ends which are then tucked underneath the tip.
- You may want to apply egg to the top of the bread with a brush (yolk thinned out with ½ a tsp. water). This makes it look great.

Figure 13-12, Ready to bake

5. Making yogurt

- Heat one litre of milk to the boiling point.
- Let it cool off to reach between $110^0 - 120^0$F ($44 - 49^0$C).
- Mix it with 2 tbsp. of yogurt.
- Incubate it (maintain the same temperature) until the yogurt has reached the desired firmness. This may take between 4 to 5 hours. If left longer the yogurt will tend to become sour.

One way to maintain the temperature for the required time is to place it in a cooler within a larger cooler. Fill the smaller one with 122^0F (50^0C) water to come just bellow the rims of the milk jars. Additional jars filled with hot water can be placed in the larger cooler.

6. Wood an abundance?

6.1. The forest

Trees purify the air; they also purify the mind. Save the trees and you save your life.

When looking out a window in rural British Columbia one can usually see trees as part of the picture. The distance between the tree and us makes us believe it is a product at our disposal. Looking across the world will confirm this thinking. In countries like India, trees are, in most areas, a scarce commodity. In Switzerland one needs a permit to cut any mature tree, be it on private land or not. At present, in the province of British Columbia, the number of trees "harvested" (called the AAC, Annual Allowable Cut) is seen by many as too high to **maintain a mature forest.** If this practice is continued, it will not provide the supply of quality timber for our future generations. This will lead to an early depletion of the resource and with it not only loss of jobs, but loss of an entire ecosystem.

The **mature** trees act as an air conditioner. During the summer months they cool the air by evaporating the water in the soil. Clear cut logging has interrupted this process. Replanting was rather a relaxed exercise of public relations for a long time. Consequently, there are few new-growth stands of mature trees available. New areas need to be incorporated and are again clear cut. Since most stands are too young, the replanted wood supply will not contribute much to the air-conditioning action for some time to come. I have experienced changes in our region. With large areas being clear-cut, the climate is affected not just in more turbulent weather patterns but also in a lower water table throughout the regions involved. Furthermore run off water in the spring is much more intense for a shorter period of time, a cycle controlled by the trees. With this soil erosion and silting of streams becomes inevitable. The detrimental effect on our fish supply is just now becoming more visible. Not even massive stock replacement programs can return the land to the abundance previously enjoyed. It is one more "paradise" lost. All there is left will be stories about the bounty once had, over time to be changed to a myth, talked about in the same way as we now refer to elves, gnomes and fairies. I mentioned earlier how the loss of certain species of trees affect the honey production. There may be many more impacts than we currently realize.

Scientists are well aware of the continued global warming due in part to the CO_2 emissions. The slowly-changing industry continues to discount as fear mongering the statement that deforestation has accounted for 20% of the increase in CO_2 over the last 10 years. In the meantime creeks and streams that once gave pleasure now look naked and dry in the barren landscapes. To enjoy nature, we will have to take a vacation trip in the few remaining parks, just to see what was once all around us. How insane can it get? Is that what we want?

With the understanding about how harmony can be maintained, it becomes obvious that we have to protect the soil from exposure and that we have to maintain the mechanisms of air conditioning by the tree. With the focus being to tend the forests, many generations will have the enjoyment we have for so long taken for granted.

My most impressive experience in life has been a visit to the old growth forest in the Walbrun (Pacific Coast on Vancouver Island) in 1991. Here for the first time I could picture the fairies and visions I had as a child about how I fit in with nature. It is beyond my horizon to think of cutting such a marvel of life, a treasure never to be regained. I will have to end this paragraph about the anomalies in our forest. Speaking of it will not change it but it needed to be said in this context for the record.

Let's start with ourselves and make a change. We know that the abundance is short-lived if not acted on. Let's plant trees wherever we can. If we cut a tree for the warmth of winter let us plant two more. There is a myth coming from the media about wood heating and the pollution it creates. A tree has, during its life cycle, contributed as much oxygen as it will use up to burn, a complete balance. We get pollution when wood is trucked in or piled into one geographical area and burned up over a short time period (like in the wood kilns to dry wood, in the case of slash burning, in big cities and industrial parks, etc.). This creates an imbalance and with it, air pollution.

6.2. Timber

Some of the most useful trees for timber are: sweet chestnut (edible chestnut), oak, birch, ash, larch, cedar, fir and spruce. Of course walnut is another valuable wood but in rather short supply. Each of them has different properties. The chestnut grows quickly, is easy to split and grows nice and straight. The oak wood, mentioned in an earlier chapter, is also easy to split and the core wood is very hard and durable. Ash is tough and supple but will rot if left in the dirt. It will grow fairly straight and is easy to split. The larch tree grows quickly and for the group of conifers its wood alters the least if dug into the soil (except maybe for cedar). Birch wood is fairly tough to split but a very good fire wood. The burning bark creates a wonderful smell. Birch bark itself can be set afire even if wet or gathered from a green tree. Cutting or removing the bark on bigger pieces may ease the force needed to split it. The bark is kept and helps to start the wood cook stove. With properly maintained birch or ash on a two acre parcel, you will yield enough fire wood to be independent. You can cut these trees when they reach a diameter of about 8" to 10" (20 cm to 25 cm). The stump will now make shoots like a bush and can be cut in about 12 years again. This can be repeated for as long as you live generating plenty of fire wood. Fir and spruce are two more important species used mainly in the building trade.

Planting trees is important even if you don't cut any trees down. I feel very joyful whenever I plant some trees. It gives me the pleasure of doing things not for my own greed or benefit but to be one with nature. Trees can make me feel centred, bringing me to the sense of caring for others. This is the greatest value I experience with trees. Rather than arguing with someone about the forest practices, I plant a tree as a symbol to care for that person.

Don't argue about trees, better plant one with ease.

Select tree species you can find locally, gather your own seeds or transplant small trees that are too close together. In the early years a distance of 6 feet (2 m) is the minimum. They will soon grow tall and will need to be thinned out for fire wood. At a later stage, you may cut the bottom branches off to achieve some clear lumber. In a yet later stage, the underbrush can be cleared by animals like the goats. But make sure that they always have enough underbrush when tied up or they will start eating off the bark of any tree except the mature birch tree. A billy goat however may eat the birch tree bark no matter how mature the tree is, and he also will damage the trunk with his horns, especially during the breeding season. So keep him away from trees you want to use as timber. If you manage a stand like that you can cut old trees which will provide top quality timber and plant two new ones for every one cut. You will yield much more lumber from the forest this way, than by clear cutting it and you will be able to set aside one area where you do not do any maintenance. It shall be for the animals and nature. The legends tell us of gnomes, elves, fairies and dwarfs which need such a place and have come to be almost extinct due to our world based knowledge of how to do things. But even if we don't accept such childlike thoughts, as long as we have no proof that they do not exist we shall give them a place where they could exist.

Summary of activities:

- Clean seeds.
- Use wax to make foundation and candles.
- Plant and transplant trees before the ground freezes.
- Enjoy the peace.

14

The Final Word

Paradise

As much as nature has gone into a dormant state so will this book draw to an end. If all went well you should have all the basic foods in storage now. Snow will soon cover the valuable soil and bring peace and quiet. Many things have been explained and problems pointed out. Many people have struggled and not enjoyed the travel within a setting described here because they tried to do everything at once. Keep the focus on what you can do in the situation in which you find yourself. Do not spread yourself too thin but start out with some ideas and expand. Even though this book will be a great help to avoid some pitfalls, you will still need to learn many new things. Build as much enthusiasm as possible and look at all things positively first. Do not waste time in fighting this or that issue or in trying to change the world but do it the way you want it yourself. Those who need to know what you have to say will come to you and listen. Give them your time and full attention, because they are ready to change.

I have learned many things by doing them. On reflection, I can say that many of the things I tried were foolish. But I had to go through the development of my "self" and this meant a lot of side steps. The faster we humans can experience making side steps without being told what is right, the sooner we can come together as an understanding people. We need to learn, and the faster the better, not just about things on earth but more so about ourselves. This may prove to be the most wonderful thing to do while traveling in this world. It is like leaving the ocean, with its many strong currents and waves that have kept us busy for so long just trying to stay above the water, to enter a pool of your own. You do see the calm water inviting you for a swim. You need not fight any waves and the movement you do make in this pool will generate ripples you can see. They will not last but will tell you what movement to do next. Nothing will last; time is not a factor, but timing is. Find your own pool and you find your "self". Know the spirit to be within you, this force that is going to support you as long as you accept its existence. Trust your "self". Gather with other people who share this common goal. Share the thoughts you have found to work for you as I have done with this writing. It will build community, will encourage others to continue on their way and will eventually bring a **paradise** in this very world that so many think of as being a struggle.

Nature belongs to those that can see.

I hope the sharing of my experience in relation to growing food and looking at nature in the context of your "self" has been clearly explained. I welcome any comments you may have in regards to this edition. As much as I tried to do a perfect job, I know I'm not perfect. I welcome any suggestions.

Appendix A

General

- Agriculture Canada
  Research Station
  Summerland, B.C.
  V0H 1Z0
  Information for bloomchart:
  David Lane, Richard MacDonald

- B.I. Chemicals (Can.) Ltd.
  Henley Chemicals Div.
  199 Cortland Ave.
  Concord, Ont.
  L4K 4T2
  Phone: 416-661-1500
  Supplier of: M4601

- Gooly Mooly Art Farm
  Box 978
  Enderby B.C.
  V0E 1V0
  Phone: 604-838-0350
  Workshops in Harmonic Farming

- O. F. Ortner
  Schronfeld 96A
  D-91054 Erlangen
  Germany
  Phone: 011-49-9131-52624
  Molds for foundations, made on order.

- Valley Waterworks & Irrigation Ltd.
  #5-368 Industrial Ave.
  Kelowna, B.C.
  V1Y 7E8
  Phone: 604-763-9107
  Materials for trickle irrigation

Beekeeping Equipment Suppliers

- Agri Supply Ltd.
  1935 East Trans Canada HWY
  Kamloops, B.C.
  V2C 4A1
  Phone: 604-372-7446

- Doug & Eileen McCutcheon
  3871-197 Street
  Langley, B.C.
  V3A 1B4
  Phone: 604-530-5428
  Mainly **beekeeping books**

- F. W. Jones & Son Ltd.
  68 Tycos dr.
  Toronto, Ont.
  M6A 1V9
  Phone: 416-783-2818
  or
  44 Dutch St.
  Bedford, Que.
  J0J 1A0
  Phone: 514-248-3323

- Hodgson Bee Supplies and
  Bee Cee Wicks & Wax
  3072 Beta Ave.
  Burnaby, B.C.
  V5G 4K4
  Phone: 604-294-1232

Books

- **Beehive Construction**
  Publication 1584/E (out of print)
  ISBN 0-662-00155-9
- **Beekeeping in Western Canada**
  Publication. 1542
  ISBN 0-662-11501-5
- **Goats and their Management**
  Publication 1820/E (out of print)
  ISBN 0-662-16808-9
  Dep. of Agriculture and Agri-Food
  930 Carling Ave., Room 118
  Ottawa, Ont. K1A 0C5

- **Bernardin Guide To Home Preserving**
  Consumer Services
  Bernardin of Canada Ltd.
  120 The East Mall
  Etobicoke, Ont. M8Z 5V5
  ISBN 0-9694719-0-4

- **Field Guide to Harmful and Beneficial Insects and Mites**
  B.C. Ministry of Agriculture,
  Crown Publications Inc.
  521 Fort St.
  Victoria, B.C. V8W 1E7
  Phone: 604-386-4636
  ISBN 0-7726-1277-3

- **Geisteswissenschaftliche Grundlagen zum Gedeihen der Landwirtschaft**, Rudolf Steiner
  Nachlassverwaltung Dornach
  Switzerland (ISBN 3-7274-3270-5)
  Agriculture (english edition)
  Bio Dynamic Farming and
  Gardening Association Inc.
  RR4, S22, C43, Kelowna, V1Y 7R3

- **Health through God's Pharmacy**
  (German version is also available)
  by Maria Treben
  Ennsthaler Verlag (Publisher)
  Stadtplatz 26
  A-4402 Steyr
  Austria, ISBN 3-85068-124-6

- **Honey Bee Diseases & Pests**
  Canadian Assoc. of Professional
  Apiculturists
  $^c/_o$ Dr. Cynthia Scott-Dupree
  Dept. of Environmental Biology
  University of Guelph
  Guelph, Ont. N1G 2W1

- **Heilmittellehre** (Medications)
  by Rudolf Hauschka
  Vittorio Klostermann
  Frankfurt am Main
  Postfach 900601
  D-60446 Frankfurt am Main
  Germany
  Phone: 011 49-6997-08160
  ISBN 3-465-02242-4

- **The Beekeepers Handbook**
  by D. Sammataro, A. Avitabile
  MacMillan Publishing
  ISBN 002-08-141-00

- **The Rodale Book of Composting**
  Deborah Martin
  Rodale Press Inc.
  33 East Minor Street
  Emmaus PA
  18098-0099
  ISBN 087-857-9907

Seed Calendars

- **Aussaattage** (German edition)
  M. Thun-Verlag
  Postfach 1446
  D-3560 Biedenkopf/Lahn
  Germany

- **Stella Natura** (English edition)
  Bio Dynamic Farming and
  Gardening Association Inc.
  Box 550
  Kimberton, PA 19442
  USA
  Phone: 1-800-516-7797
  For B.C.: RR4, S22, C43
  Kelowna   V1Y 7R3

Index